BETWEEN LUXURY AND THI

BETWEEN LUXURY AND THE EVERYDAY

DECORATIVE ARTS IN EIGHTEENTH-CENTURY FRANCE

EDITED BY

KATIE SCOTT
AND
DEBORAH CHERRY

Blackwell Publishing

First published as Volume 28, issue 2 of Art History, with the exception of Démoris' article which was first published in Volume 28, Issue 4.

BLACKWELL PUBLISHING
350 Main Street, Malden, MA 02148-5020, USA
9600 Garsington Road, Oxford OX4, 2DQ, UK
550 Swanston Street, Carlton, Victoria 3053, Australia

First published 2005 by Blackwell Publishing Ltd

Library of Congress Cataloging-in-Publication Data has been applied for

ISBN 1-4051-3168-3

A catalogue record for this title is available from the British Library.

Set in India
by Macmillan India Ltd., Bangalore, India
Printed and bound in the United Kingdom
by TJ International, Padstow, Cornwall

The publisher's policy is to use permanent paper from mills that operate a sustainable forestry policy, and which has been manufactured from pulp processed using acid-free and elementary chlorine-free practices. Furthermore, the publisher ensures that the text paper and cover board used have met acceptable environmental accreditation standards.

For further information on
Blackwell Publishing, visit our website:
www.blackwellpublishing.com

CONTENTS

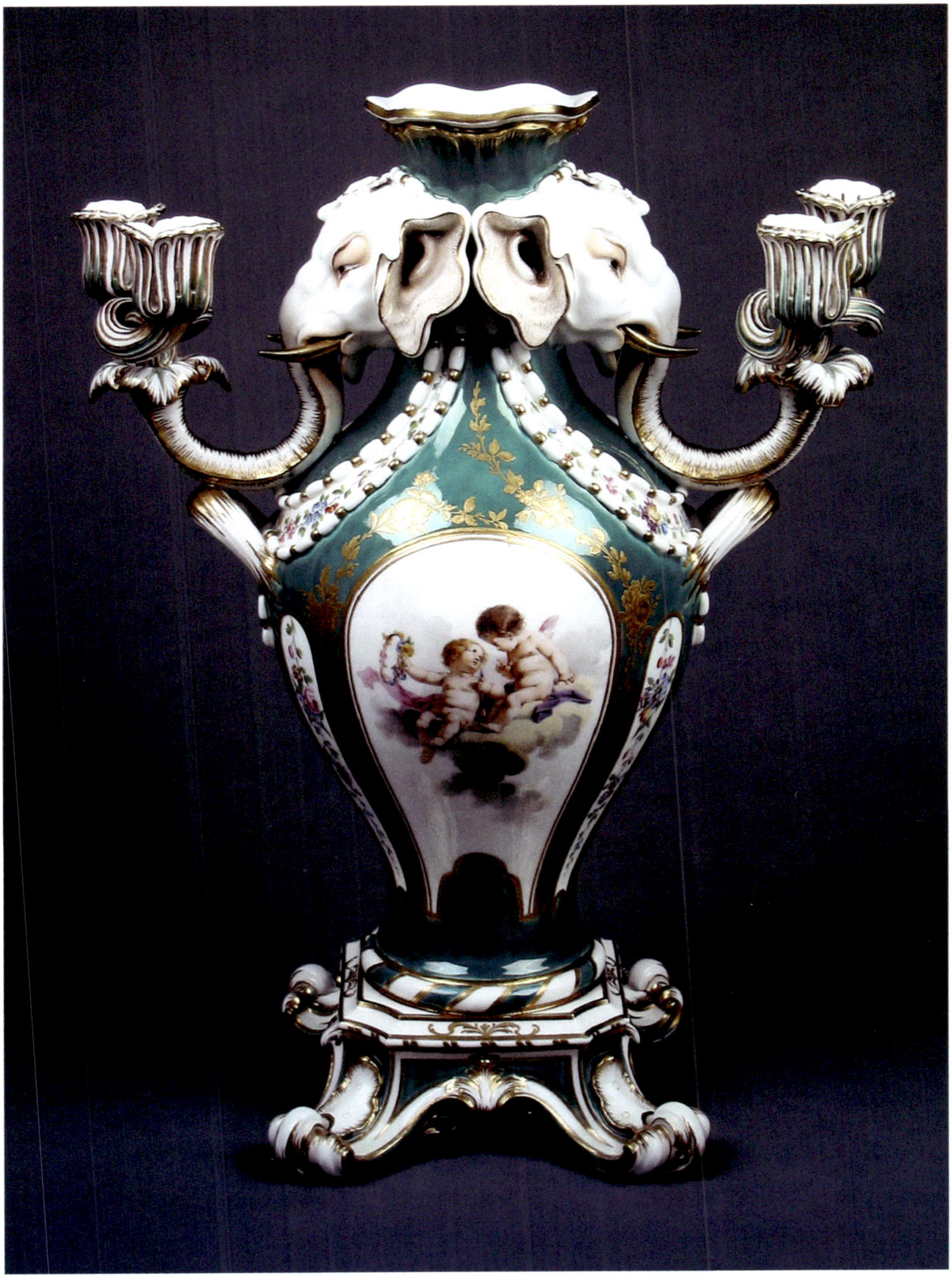

Plate 1 *Vase à tête d'éléphant*, 1756. Sèvres, soft paste porcelain, 37.6 × 38.3 cm. The Wallace Collection, London. Copyright: The Wallace Collection.

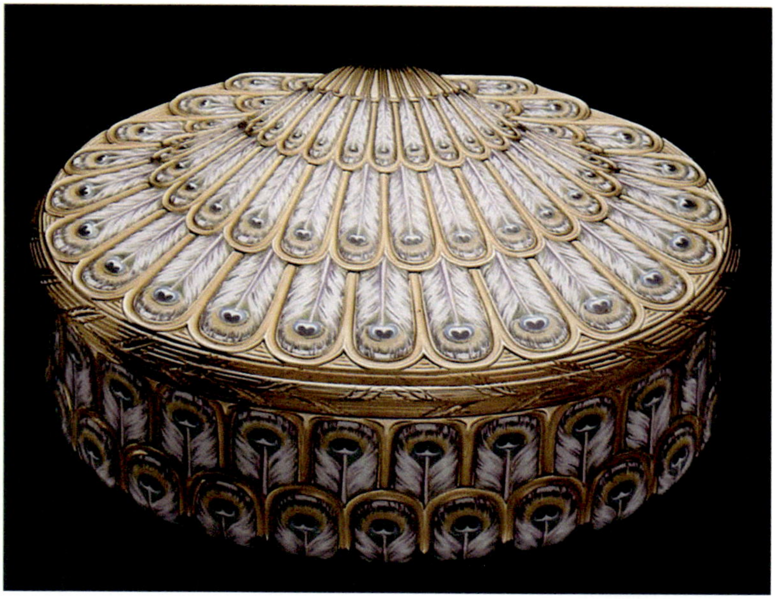

Plate 2 J. Ducrollay, *Snuff box*, *c*. 1770. Gold and enamel, 3.2 × 7.6 × 5.8 cm. The Wallace Collection, London. Copyright: The Wallace Collection.

1

INTRODUCTION: IMAGE–OBJECT–SPACE

KATIE SCOTT

The concept of the decorative arts is of modern invention. Moreover, by the time the term enjoyed common currency in the early 1900s and had a museum in Paris dedicated to its definition, 'decorative art' described a cultural activity of the past.[1] 'Decorative' arts are arts produced in artisanal, that is to say pre-industrial conditions, and they have been positioned by modern historiography at the antipodes of design. Design is something applied to objects; it manifests a division of labour in its meaning: decorative arts are, by contrast, objects to which the principles of refined manufacture and complex aesthetic elaboration are semantically intrinsic. Decorative arts, unlike design, necessarily have strong locational value; they belong to particular places[2] – in these essays, to the workshop and the domestic interior. If modernity has sometimes looked back in envy at the early modern workshop, or rather at its mythologized form of familial structure, integrated system of production and bespoke output, it has, on the contrary, cast a disenchanted look at the domestic interior. As Christopher Reed has pointed out, modernism, the avant garde, invented itself not inside the private house, but outside, on the public way; it imagined itself; as he put it, 'marching towards glory on the battlefields of culture'.[3] To this 'anti-domestic' agenda the decorative arts owe one measure of the contempt in which they are so often held, not by the art market, but by the art world and by art history. Eighteenth-century French decorative arts labour under a double indictment: by their place of destination *and* by the structures of hereditary privilege and habits of extravagance that under the *ancien régime* supposedly gave them life.

These essays do not set out, singly or collectively, to put the world of scholarship to rights. Postmodernism, in the form, for example, of recent art practice in Britain, has already rediscovered the politics of the personal, of the home, and some contemporary artists are engaged in sustained artistic dialogue with the modalities of Rococo power in which stuff, pattern and craftsmanship, power's supplement, play so critical a role. The ambition of academia, of these essays, is more parochial, more historical: to reflect upon the status of the decorative in eighteenth-century discourse and to investigate the role played by the decorative arts in shaping the professional, familial and political dreams of those whom they touched.

'From luxury to the everyday' imposes a thematic rather than a chronological order on this collection. The essays loosely divide into pairs, pendants that juxtapose this seeming binary. Mary Sheriff attends to the 'high' rhetoric and sophisticated forms of allegory in the frontispiece to Diderot and d'Alembert's *Encyclopédie* (1751–80), while Elisabeth Lavezzi analyses the 'lower', prosaic description in word and image of individual entries on trades selected for case study. Command of the elite end of the silk market by means of the emulation of high art and its practices is a strand of Lesley Miller's account of the success of Phillipe de Lasalle, while the materialization of the principles of the French Revolution in everyday things, fashioned in plain stuffs by largely anonymous makers, holds the attention of Leora Auslander. Across the period there are contrasts between these everyday objects, portrayed, by Jean-Siméon Chardin, as René Démoris indicates, to stake out a space for the representation of the bourgeois family – and the luxuries that attended, supplied and supported the *mondain* sociability of the court, personified exquisitely by the performances of Mme de Pompadour, the subject of Katie Scott's essay. Image–object–space captures, not too reductively I hope, something of the disparate perspectives on the decorative, perspectives that overlap and intersect as eighteenth-century images could engineer spaces, textual spaces, and were potentially objects, and objects often bore images on their surfaces and were necessarily spatial, and spaces were viewed and felt respectively as images and enclosure (like clothing). The narrative of this intersection is imitation, a conceptual category that recurs in different senses and contexts and creates a pattern.

IMAGE

The self-imposed task of the *Encyclopédie, ou dictionnaire des sciences, des arts et des métiers* – to gather, order and describe the sum of human knowledge – has long invited reflection on the relationship between truth, knowledge and representation, and on the alleged power of images not only to communicate fact but to change minds. Historians have been particularly concerned with the representation of the world of craft, with the difficulties of translating an oral culture and tacit knowledge into articulate and intelligible text, and with judgement of the success with which the intention to raise the status of the *arts et métiers*, avowed in the *Discours préliminaire*, was realized in the entries and illustrations devoted to particular trades.[4] The greater utility of the mechanical arts having been asserted by Jean Le Rond d'Alembert, Denis Diderot assigned to the liberal arts the responsibility of rescuing them from 'the scorn where prejudice has long since held them'.[5] It was a challenge to which the draughtsman, print-maker and secretary of the Académie Royale de peinture et de sculpture, Charles-Nicolas Cochin, seemingly responded in his design for the *Encyclopédie*'s frontispiece. Sheriff argues from a close reading of the iconography, that in the 'Sanctuary of Truth', as Cochin depicts it, priority is given not to reason but to truth's relation to imagination, the human faculty from which spring the fine arts. The figure of Imagination advances to garland Truth with flowers; thus, to decorate knowledge is, as she points out, to enhance it. Taken literally, this suggests, for Sheriff, that the arts of the book as well as the reasoning of the text played a part in enlightenment. Although, in

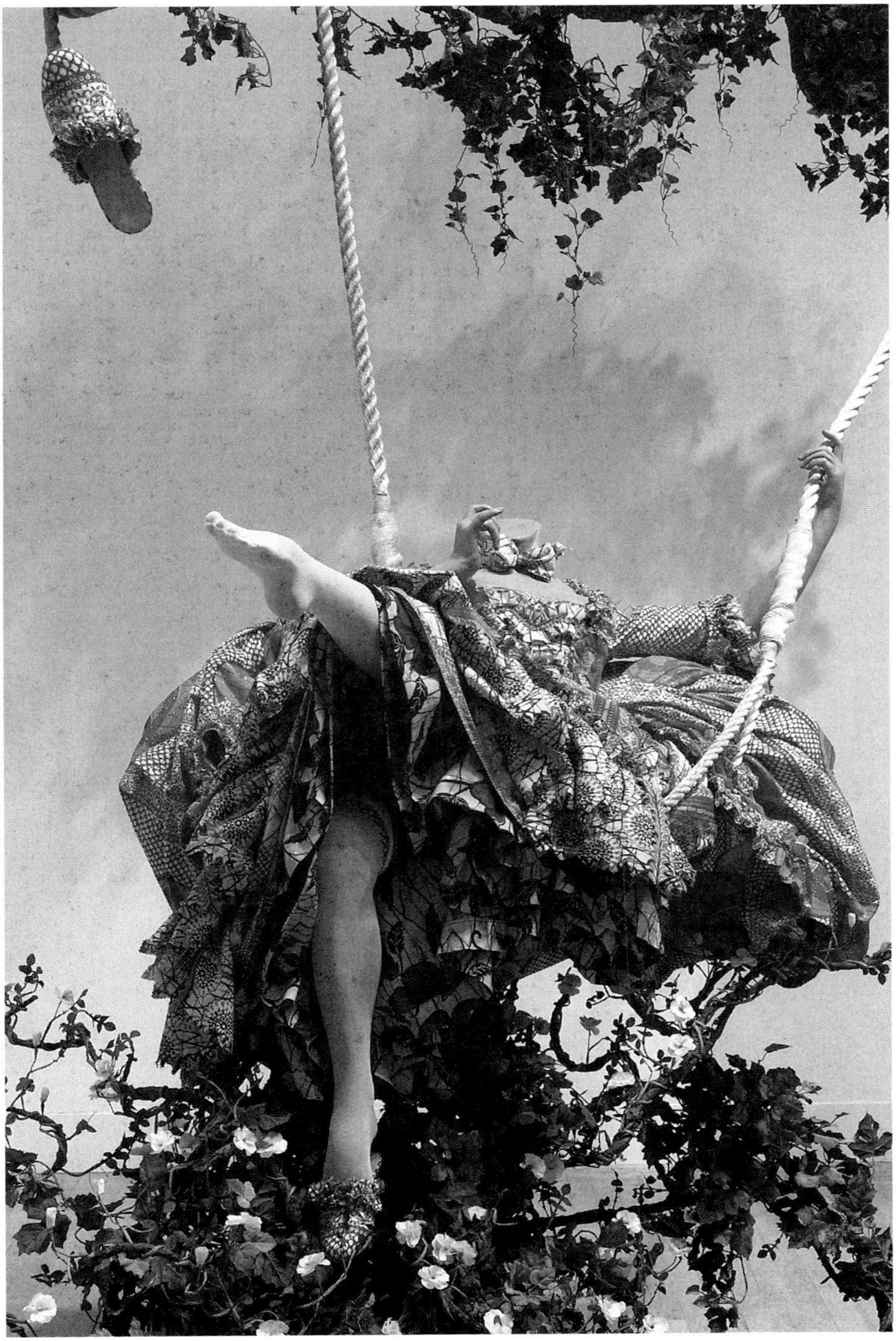

1.1 Detail of Yinka Shonibare, *The Swing (after Fragonard)*, 2001. Dutch wax, printed cotton textile, life-size mannequin, swing, artificial foliage, 330 × 350 × 220 cm. Tate, London.

d'Alembert's schematization of knowledge, mechanical arts such as paper-making, typesetting, engraving, printing and book-binding were distributed under the faculty of Memory in the province of History, their activities regarded as merely habitual and routine, Cochin 'saved' them as creative. His revisions of the frontispiece for the second edition of the *Encyclopédie* included, tellingly, the extension of the chain of arts linked to Imagination to include, among others, *Imprimerie* (printing) and *Horlogerie* (clock-making).[6]

Cochin's vindication of decoration, of ornament, was, of course, also a justification of allegory, a charged and figurative form of discourse.[7] While modern allegory was often condemned by critics as bizarre and enigmatic, for its obscurantism indeed,[8] ancient metaphor was generally thought to have originated in order to express things and ideas when words were lacking. Lavezzi's essay starts with this lack – not of verbs (to decorate) or nouns (decorator, decoration) but of categories (the decorative arts). She relates that during the Renaissance and up to the end of the seventeenth century arts such as mosaic and marquetry had been defined as 'dependent', dependent that is on one or more of the trinity of finer arts: dependent physically for material support or dependent procedurally for their appearance. The fine and 'decorative' arts were linked here not by imagination, but by imitation; for example, marquetry imitates mosaic which imitates painting. It was a relation of dependency that found expression elsewhere, notably in debates about art education. A memorandum from the late 1760s written on behalf of the Académie argued against the foundation of free drawing schools for the trades on the grounds that the Académie already fulfilled that role: only 1 per cent of its students allegedly became painters and sculptors, the other 99 per cent became goldsmiths, jewellers etc.[9] Academic education, to which the imitation of nature in the privileged form of the human figure was central, remained, in theory at least, a mainstay of the goldsmith's, the *ébéniste*'s or the silk weaver's training, subordinating them and their arts to a finer practice.

To this hierarchical order of filiation the *Encyclopédie* introduced the first stirrings of change. Lavezzi's detailed analysis of the entries on mosaic and marquetry reveals the beginnings of a break with imitation but also a shift from older, corporate definitions of the trades according to materials and tools, which established a ranking by the value of stuffs (gold-smithing before paper-making), to a qualitative definition of the processes of production (marquetry before carpentry). That is, it marked the gradual reorientation of definitions of the 'decorative arts' based on knowledge at the consumer end, to ones based on knowledge at the production end, or, as Arjun Appadurai has put it succinctly, of the re-conception of goods as *products*.[10] Lavezzi builds a case for saying that the introduction of dynamic 'microsystems' (new orders of knowledge) started to erode the Great Chain of Imitation (or Garland of Imagination) that had held art and artists to their appointed places, and in prospect licensed the 'decorative' arts to raise *themselves* by refinement.[11] To put it differently, definitions of the decorative arts in terms of a specific (refined) manner of operation secured them

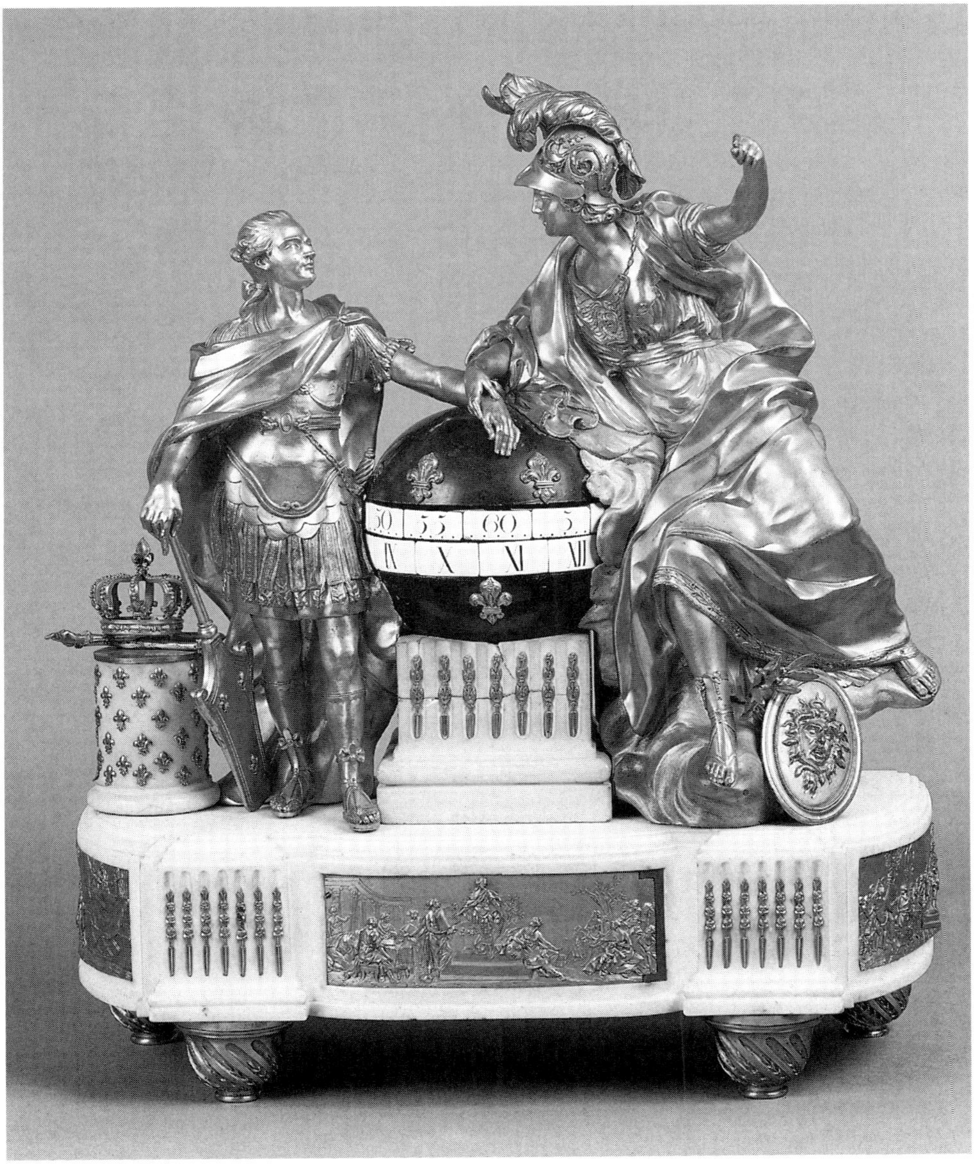

1.2 *Mantel Clock with Louis XVI and Minerva*, c. 1774. Spring-driven clock with a case of white marble and gilt and enamel bronze, 60.5 × 51.8 × 22 cm. The Wallace Collection, London. Copyright: The Wallace Collection.

autonomy and ended their dependency. Her analysis has broader implications. Like William Reddy's analysis of dictionary definitions of cloth, it suggests a cultural crisis in older ways of thinking about making even though predominant modes of manufacture remained unchanged.[12] It endorses the argument for the *Encyclopédie* as 'progressive', as moving towards what Reddy calls a 'capitalist mode of evaluating commodities' and a modern understanding of the economy as a labour market. But it does not go so far as to support William Sewell's claim for the illustrations, that they represent the mechanical arts as pure, abstract labour force.[13] The defining attention that J.-R. Lucotte assigned in his account of marquetry in the *Encyclopédie* to the particular skills of the jigsaw suggests that conflicting definitions of the mechanical arts coexisted: definition first by imitation, secondly by creative, independent skill and finally by anonymous, routine labour.

OBJECT

The *Encyclopédie* was not only a text, a collection of images and ideas, it was also an object, a substantial collection of lavish volumes, a coffee-table rather than portable book, described by Sheriff in considerable detail from its calf-skin covers to its densely inked type, an object that was produced, marketed, exchanged and finally possessed as private property. Such attentiveness to the object and its histories distinguishes scholarship that falls under the heading of material culture and which tends to define itself against histories of the object as text. The practices of (to use examples from the first two essays) book-binding and marquetry were materially conditioned by tools, techniques, raw materials, skills, regulations, markets.[14] It was no coincidence, perhaps, that the 'new' idea of the decorative should have started to emerge in the case of marquetry, an 'art' transformed after the mid-century by the importation of exotic woods from the Indes.[15] The substitution of these cheaper woods (relatively speaking) for the more costly 'mosaic' or *pietra dura* and Boulle marquetry of the late seventeenth century stimulated growth. In the expanding consumer market, skilled labour for cutting and applying the veneers became scarce.[16] Dearth doubtless drew attention to skill, to the particular, intricate skills of the *ébéniste*.[17]

Philippe de Lasalle was a Lyonnais silk designer to compare in skill, innovation and enterprise with the likes of Jean-François Oeben or Jean-Henri Riesener in the furniture trade. Miller's account of his success leaves no place for chance; rather it was achieved out of knowledge of loom technology, textile design, marketing strategy and taste, acquired over years in business. Luxury and the everyday both played a part. That is to say that Lasalle produced for both ends of the market: the bespoke end of one-off commissions for extraordinary furnishing fabrics, and the ordinary end of dress silks, produced in batches for anonymous consumers. Lasalle's strategy was one specifically suited to the dynamic, commercialized market for luxury and semi-luxury goods that developed in France in the second half of the eighteenth century.[18] Dena Goodman has demonstrated the key role played by taste (actually and discursively) in the transformation of consumption from a roughly polarized moral economy, of luxury and necessity, to a smoothly continuous commercial order, of more or less expensive fashionable goods.[19] Taste is a discrimination of the senses, especially of the faculty of sight.[20] Miller's essay, which is notably attentive to the evidence provided by the silks themselves, supports the argument for the mounting commercial importance of aesthetic value in the decorative arts. It argues for a viewer and not just a consumer of silks.[21] Miller notes, for instance, the self-conscious way that Lasalle stages imitation in his designs – imitation of nature, naturally, but also imitation of other stuffs – of fur and of painting. Such imitation is self-reflexive, amounts to an engagement with the discourses surrounding the manufacture of silks, and constitutes an invitation to an attentive viewer to read the fabric in relation to other materials, other arts and traditions. Imitation or emulation was also, of course, a commercial strategy. It ensured that success in one kind of fabric was exploited and developed by others, drawing the textile market into tight circuits of competition which the specialization of scholarship into tapestry studies, silk studies, printed-cotton studies and the like has done little to recognize. Miller argues persuasively that manufacturers like Lasalle were highly conscious both of developments in adjacent industries and of changes of taste at court and in Paris. They responded to both and their response constituted part of the fabric's meaning for informed contemporary viewers.

Where Miller's essay sets out to understand success, Auslander is concerned with failure: the apparent failure of the French Revolution to generate new furniture for the new Republic's citizenry. Standing at the centre of her essay are no more than a handful of objects, pieces of furniture whose Revolutionary origin is

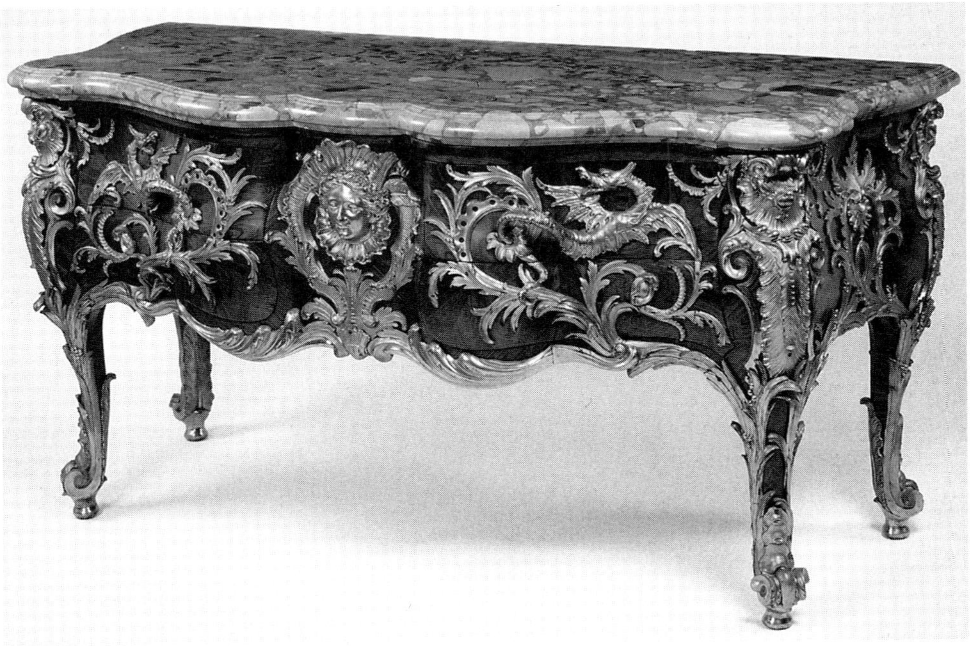

1.3 Attributed to Antoine-Robert Gaudreaus, Chest of Drawers *(commode)*, *c.* 1735–40. Oak veneered with kingwood *(bois de violet)* and mounted with gilt bronze, 93.3 × 179.3 × 81.5 cm. The Wallace Collection, London. Copyright: The Wallace Collection.

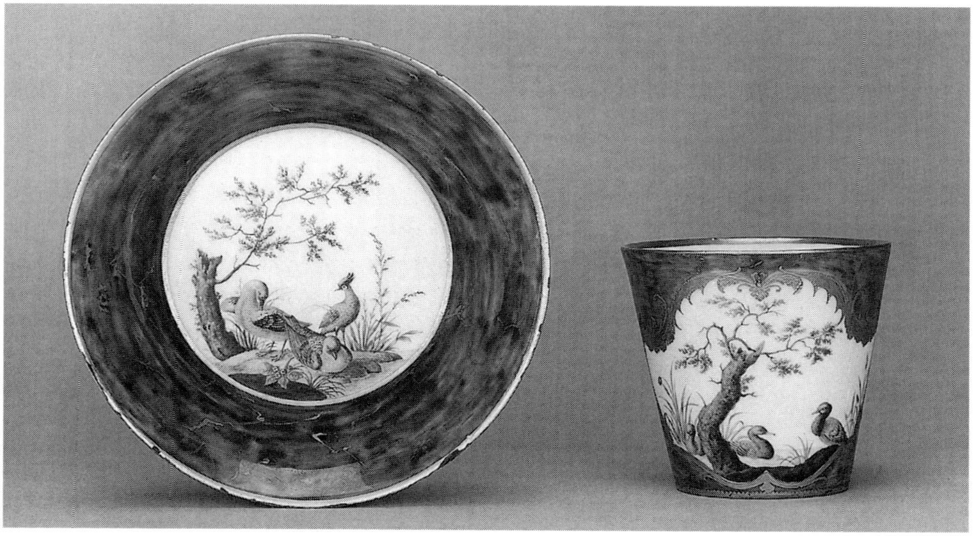

1.4 *Goblet à la reine*, *c*.1752–3. Vincènnes, soft paste porcelain, saucer, diameter 15.6 cm, cup height, 8.5 cm. The British Museum, London. Copyright: The Trustees of the British Museum.

apparent in the simple manufacture, the plain forms, the native, untreated wood and the repertoire of Republican ornaments. These *armoires*, chests of drawers, side-tables and desks would be difficult to locate on the scale of luxury to semi-luxury goods discussed above because choice of material and finish is so clearly marked by restraint – the anti-luxury of self-denial. Luxury and the everyday, understood as different registers of a language of communication, recover their moral moorings in the Revolution, and in this essay.[22] Ornament is not just a matter of symbols, allegorical figures. It is also symbolic, in the sense that ornament is figured not as an added or applied value, but as embedded (literally inlaid) in the bodies of the objects, the iconographies reworked and invented in the continuities of artisanal practice. At an historical level, Auslander challenges the revisionist case for regarding eighteenth-century France as a consumer culture on the model and scale of eighteenth-century Britain. She interprets the relative absence of decorative arts made and marked by the Revolution as evidence of the limits, and of the uneven development, of consumption in France: dress and accessories had entered the fashion system but domestic goods, decorative arts, had largely not. At a methodological level, Auslander uses the 'everyday' to address questions of power and hegemony. By setting the absence not only of furniture but of contemporary comment about it against the riot of Republican dress, and address to clothing and architecture, she argues that crude was the state's understanding and management of the relation of public and private. Revolutionary governments sought to monopolize authority in the public domain, saturating the street with symbols carried on the surfaces of its citizens and the façades of public buildings, but they seemingly left the domestic sphere to its own devices.[23] Significantly, some of the types of furniture discussed by Auslander – a desk and a dressing table – are precisely those that served to mediate passage between the inside and the outside, the home and the street. Letters, petitions, written on the slope of the desk, may even have sported one of the many Republican letterheads designed for official use.[24] In the case of the dressing table, its deeply carved top leaves no flat surface to support the vessels and utensils of the toilette and bears at its centre a *bonnet rouge*, a cap, that is, for the wearing of which no toilette is necessary. This piece of furniture, by its failure of function, urged its possessor onto the street. We are much closer here to Richard Cobb's '*la vie en marge*' than to Jurgën Habermas's 'bourgeois public sphere'.[25]

SPACE

Furniture and furnishings of all kinds occupy space and recent analysis of Paris probate inventories has done much to reveal exactly where, in the eighteenth-century interior, particular things found their place: the writing desk, for instance, apparently supplanted the *cabinet* in the bedroom or closet (*cabinet*) as an item of prestige furniture in upper bourgeois houses.[26] But furniture also constituted space: Annik Pardailhé-Galabrun defines the eighteenth-century bed as a veritable 'house within the house';[27] Orest Ranum describes how intimate interior spaces were multiplied by the transformation of furniture into rooms.[28] Cabinets (cupboards with drawers) became *cabinets* (small, private rooms).[29] Or, in the case of the desk, as Ranum puts it, 'a man who once kept a locked writing desk' could, by the eighteenth century, 'closet himself in his writing room and lock the door'.[30] Moreover, if oak-lined rooms with shelves and cupboards strongly suggested furniture for habitation, four-, six-, eight- or twelve-leaf screens faced with material of all kinds provided improvisational coverings, walls within walls, for drawing about the body.[31]

However, the shift in perspective from objects to spaces, from the decorative arts to the decorated interior, effects a change of histories; from the history of everyday things (consumption) to a history of everyday practices. Sociology has identified the interior space of the house as a primary mechanism in the internalization of the *habitus*, defined by Pierre Bourdieu as the process by which social structure is both internalized (through conscious and unconscious learning) and externalized as social practice.[32] It is thus a site where symbolic relations of class, gender and race are inscribed in the everyday and naturalized as physical patterns of behaviour. Space is not, however, prior to those social relations, it is not a given. Consequently, it does not function necessarily to reproduce the social hierarchy and repeat its ideology.[33] On the contrary, social space combines and recombines residual, dominant and new figurations – hegemony is never absolute, even under Absolutism. It is to the new, rather than the dominant or the residual, that recent eighteenth-century scholarship has been most attracted, despite Norbert Elias's highly influential study of court society, first published in 1969.[34]

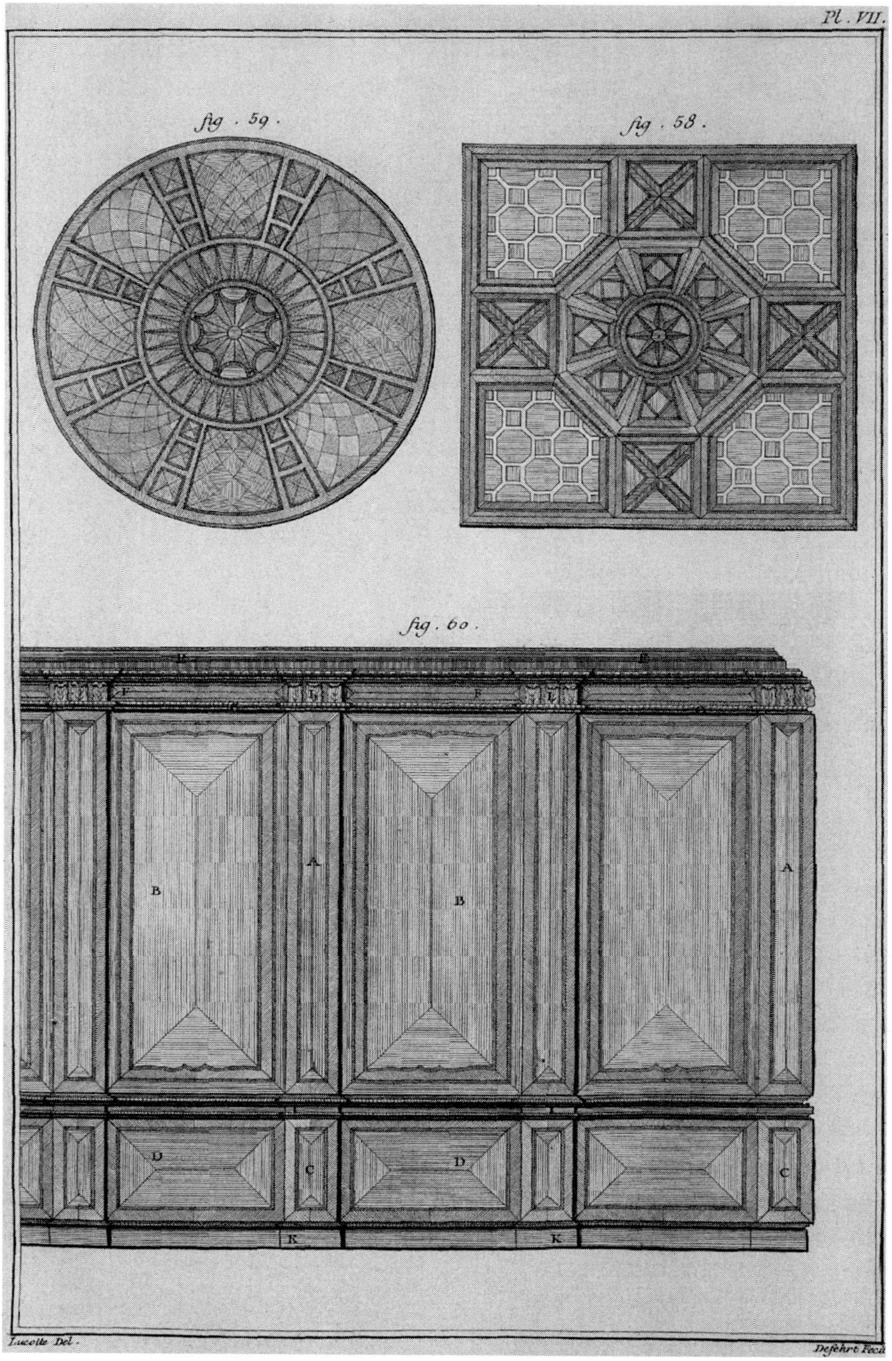

1.5 Defehrt after J.-R. Lucotte, 'Marqueterie', in *Encyclopédie, ou Dictionnaire raisonné des sciences, des arts et des métiers*, Paris, 1751–1780, *Receuil de planches*, vol. 8, plate VII. Engraving. London: The London Library.

Of interest are actual spaces and imaginary ones, and the relations between them. Pardailhé-Galabrun's *La naissance de l'intime* (1988), a study of the contents of 2,783 domestic dwellings in Paris from probate inventories, has as its cover Chardin's *The Water Fountain* (1734, Stockholm: Nationalmuseum), and while the painting does not seem obviously to bear out her findings of a consumer revolution, of increased material satisfactions,[35] it was presumably chosen for the portrayal it apparently offered of a new inwardness, a new intensification of emotional contents, identified by this historian in actual eighteenth-century interiors. Chardin's genre scenes have generated considerable debate about their place in the formation of a bourgeois rhetoric of the family, replete with locutions of family affection and domestic bliss, and their constitution of a counter-space to aristocratic households and worldly libertinage.[36] In the last essay Démoris suggests that these images offer not so much serene instances of well-regulated households and well-governed children, as scenes marked by resistance, discord and disaffection, or awash with erotic desire. Discussing the reformation of eighteenth-century social life, historians and art historians have singled out three spaces of particular consequence: the *salon* and the practices of sociability that helped to engender a Republic of Letters and mobilize public opinion; the *boudoir* and the practices of aristocratic libertinage which constituted an alternative tactic of evasion and resistance; and the spaces of the family, the arena of the pre-social, before the analytical distancing that language introduces, and in the intimacy of which the modern individual was seemingly formed.[37] Though most women in the early modern period did not build houses, such studies have shown that they played an active, at times a transformative, role in the production of the interior space which they experienced and used in ways significantly different to men.[38]

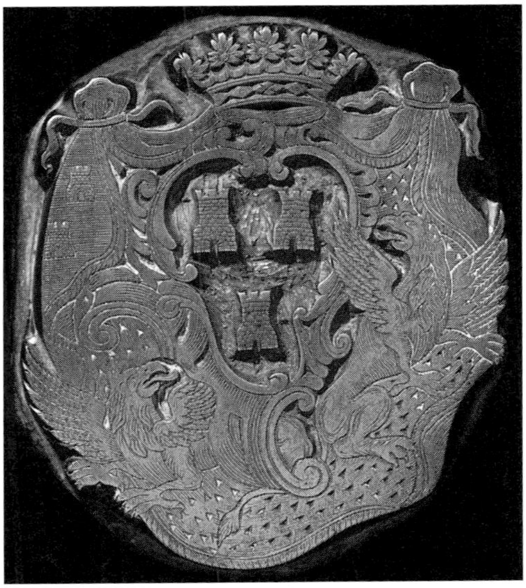

1.6 Bookbinder's stamp with the arms of Mme de Pompadour, *c.* 1750. Bronze on a wooden block, 9.5 × 8.3 cm. Victoria and Albert Museum, London.

Jeanne-Antoinette Poisson, Marquise de Pompadour was one such woman. Scott's essay shows the ways in which gender, and the role of royal mistress, led the Marquise to reconfigure the space of the baroque palace in unprecedented and possibly unexpected ways. Drawing on phenomenology, which advances a notion of space that unfolds from the body and is experienced physically through movement and touch as well as by sight, Scott reconstructs Pompadour's dynamic presence at Versailles, and the compressions and distortions of architectural space and social ritual that she effected there. Contemporaries predictably exaggerated the extent of her lubricious authority and the pleasure she took in her disorderly conduct, and Scott argues that through the interiors of her own orchestration, notably at the château of Bellevue, Pompadour in fact sought to establish a stable and viable identity for herself, goals she possibly achieved in the distribution and decoration of the hôtel d'Evreux in Paris. Her success rested on the perception of architecture as representational rather than spatial. Saint-Simon's diary offers some evidence at the beginning of the eighteenth century for the currency of the conceit of reading character in relation to architecture: the sick and aged princesse de Soubise is caricatured as 'rotting on the most exquisite furniture in the depths of the vast and magnificent hôtel de Guise'.[39] But it was in architectural theory that the idea of the house as image of its proprietor was most fully articulated. What was this identity, this respectability that Pompadour wrought through her interior? Where did these spaces place her in the hierarchy of estates and roles? She pretended to the status of *femme savante*, her libraries were spacious and well stocked, but as the *king*'s mistress she could not reign over a *salon*, could not establish an extra-public, potentially oppositional space within the state. She laid claim to maternal feeling, to her 'cottage moments', and bought paintings by and prints after Chardin's domestic interiors, but as the king's *mistress* she could scarcely identify convincingly with the role of mother, the guardian of the hearth. Her space was rather that of the *boudoir*, a space of freedom (*liberté*), of escape from prescribed social roles, as well as a place of sexual licence. In the absence of fixed ideas about her identity she proliferated through images and objects deployed in space representations of herself as lover, sultana, friend.

Michel Delon has argued that the present-day fascination with the eighteenth century is one that is rooted in this doublet of political and sexual liberality.[40] This collection argues that the means – the images, objects, spaces – are constituent elements of that ongoing fascination with a complex and conflicted century.

Notes

My warmest thanks to my co-editor Deborah Cherry for her patience, encouragement, her additions and her constructive critical comments.

1 The Musée des arts décoratifs was founded in 1905. For the dictionary definition of decorative art, see the essay by Elisabeth Lavezzi.

2 For a schematic enumeration of the different values inscribed in objects to which current scholarship turns its attention, see Mary Schoeser's introduction to *Disentangling Textiles. Techniques for the Study of Designed Objects*, eds M. Schoeser and C. Boydell, London, 2002, 3–10. I am grateful to Lesley Miller from bringing this collection to my attention.

3 C. Reed, 'Introduction', in *Not at Home. The Suppression of Domesticity in Modern Art and Architecture*, ed. C. Reed, London, 1996, 7.

4 See, for example, W. Sewell, *Work and Revolution in France*, Cambridge, 1980, 64–71; D. Brewer, *The Discourse of Enlightenment in Eighteenth-Century France*, Cambridge, 1993, 13–55; and specifically

in relation to print-making, J. Pannabecker, 'Representing Mechanical Arts in Diderot's *Encyclopédie*', *Technology and Culture*, 39:1, 1998, 33–73.

5 D. Diderot and J. Le Rond D'Alembert, *Encyclopédie*, 17 vols, Paris, 1751–65, 'Discours préliminaire', 1: xiii; 'Art', 1: 714.

6 *Diderot et l'art de Boucher à David*, exhib. cat., Hôtel de la Monnaie, Paris, 1984–5, no. 148. G. May, in 'Observation on an Allegory: The Frontispiece of the *Encyclopédie*', *Diderot Studies*, 16, 1973, 159–74, suggests a number of different readings of the relation between the mechanical arts beneath Imagination and the categories of reason, imagination, sciences and arts.

7 See A. de Baecque, 'The Allegorical Image of France, 1750–1800: A Political Crisis of Representation', *Representations*, 47, 1994, 111–43.

8 The story of Truth, of her veilings and unveilings, demands, as Sheriff makes very clear, a sophisticated command of metaphor and of the history of emblems, that is, of the images behind the image, but it is also worth noting that the form of knowledge represented by Cochin's Truth bears striking analogy to the craft lore conveyed by Walter Benjamin's storyteller via the 'slow piling one on top of another of thin transparent layers' of retellings, in the workshop or at the inns (*mères*) of the *compagnonnage*. Allegory and oral craft lore both found themselves under attack by the culture of information that was, in other respects, the *Encyclopédie*. See W. Benjamin, 'The Storyteller. Reflections on the Works of Nikolai Leskov', in *Illuminations*, ed. H. Arent, trans. H. Zohn, Bungay, 1982, 93.

9 *Mémoire sur les écoles gratuites de dessin*, 20 October 1767, Archives nationales O'1627/1767.

10 A. Appadurai, 'Introduction: commodities and the politics of value', in *The Social Life of Things: Commodities in Cultural Perspective*, Cambridge, 1986, 41–56, esp. 46.

11 On the different ways of ordering the cosmos in the eighteenth century and their relation to the *Encyclopédie*, see C.J. Koepp, 'The Alphabetical Order: Work in Diderot's *Encyclopédie*', in *Work in France*, eds S.L. Kaplan and C.J. Koepp, Ithaca and London, 1986, 229–57.

12 W. Reddy, 'The Structure of a Cultural Crisis: Thinking about Cloth in France before and after the Revolution', in *The Social Life of Things*, 261–84.

13 W. Sewell, 'Visions of Labour: Illustrations of the Mechanical Arts before, in and after the Encyclopédie', in *Work in France*, eds Kaplan and Koepp, 258–86.

14 For the new tools needed for *dentelle* decoration on the leather bindings described by Sheriff, see G. Barber, 'The Parisian fine binding trade in the last century of the *ancien régime*', in *Luxury Trades and Consumerism in Ancien Régime Paris*, eds R. Fox and A. Turner, Aldershot, 1998, 43–62.

15 M. Sturmer, '"Bois des Indes" and the Economics of Luxury Furniture in the Time of David Roentgen', *Burlington Magazine*, 120, 1978, 799–805.

16 See A. Pradère, *French Furniture Makers*, Paris, 1989, 24–5.

17 Cost was still primarily determined by materials however.

18 On the consumer culture of the *ancien régime*, see D. Roche, *The People of Paris: An Essay on Popular Culture in the Eighteenth Century*, trans. G. Lewis, Berkeley, 1987, 97–194; *A History of Everyday Things: The Birth of Consumption in France, 1600–1800*, trans. B. Pearce, Cambridge, 2000, esp. 166–249; C. Fairchilds, 'The Production and Marketing of Populuxe Goods in Eighteenth-Century Paris', in *Consumption and the World of Goods*, eds J. Brewer and R. Porter, New York, 1993, 228–48; 'Marketing the Counter-Reformation. Religious Objects and Consumerism in Early Modern France', in *Visions and Revisions of Eighteenth-Century France*, eds C. Adams, J.R. Censer and L.J. Graham, 1997, 31–52; D. Poullot, 'Une nouvelle histoire de la culture matérielle', *Revue d'histoire moderne et contemporaine*, 44, 1997, 344–57. See also C. Sargentson, *Merchants and Luxury Markets: The Marchands Merciers of Eighteenth-Century Paris*, London, 1996; N. Coquery, *L'hôtel aristocratique. Le marché du luxe à Paris au XVIIIe siècle*, Paris, 1998.

19 D. Goodman, 'Furnishing Discourses: Readings of a Writing Desk in Eighteenth-Century France', *Luxury in the Eighteenth Century: Debates, Desires and Delectable Goods*, eds M. Berg and E. Eger, Basingstoke and New York, 2003, 71–88.

20 For an account of role of the visual, of connoisseurship that attaches it to the culture of the guilds rather than the market, see Reddy, 'The Structure of a Cultural Crisis', esp. 266–7, 275.

21 Such an approach is abundantly justified by primary sources such as the *Mémoires* of the duc de Luynes which records the attentive looking of king and court on occasions when the textile furnishings of rooms were renewed. See, for example, C.-P. d' Albert, duc de Luynes, *Mémoires du duc de Luynes sur la cour de Louis XV, 1735–58*, ed. L. Dussieux and E. Soulié, 17 vols, Paris, 1860–65, 1: 404, 410–11; 7: 129; 8: 243.

22 This approach was pioneered by M. Douglas and B. Isherwood in *The World of Goods: Towards an Anthropology of Consumption*, London, 1981. See also K. Scott, *The Rococo Interior*, London and New Haven, 1995, 81–99.

23 So much so, indeed that no thought of solving the glut of accumulated Republican wallpapers, commissioned from the company Jacquemart et Bénard in 1792, was given to dispersing them on the market. For the correspondence related to

this problem, see Archives nationales, F12 2285, *dossier Jacquemard et Bénard.*

24 E. Liris, 'La République à l'en-tête des letters, 1792–1804', *République et révolution: l'exception française*, ed. M. Vovelle, Paris, 1993.

25 R. Cobb, '*La Vie en Marge*: Living on the Fringe of the Revolution', in *The French and their Revolution*, ed. D. Gilmour, London, 1998, 348–95. J. Habermas, *The Structural Transformation of the Public Sphere*, trans. T Burger, London, 1989.

26 A. Pardailhé-Galabrun, *La naissance de l'intime. 3000 foyers parisiens XVIIe-XVIIIe siècles*, Paris, 1988, 320, 322.

27 Pardailhé-Galabrun, *La naissance de l'intime*, 275.

28 O. Ranum, 'The Refuges of Intimacy', in *A History of Private Life*, vol. 3, *Passions of the Renaissance*, ed. R. Chartier, trans. A. Goldhammer, Cambridge, Mass. and London, 1989, 210.

29 See E. Harth, *Cartesian Women*, Ithaca and London, 1992, 15–33.

30 Ranum, 'The Refuges of Intimacy', 211.

31 Pardailhé-Galabrun notes that the *Dictionnaire de Trévoux* defines the screen as furniture used 'dans les chambres, auprès des portes, auprès du feu, *autour* des lits pour *se couvrir* et défendre contre le vent'. The screen is both an enclosure and a covering, an architectural form of clothing. See Pardailhé-Galabrun, *La naissance de l'intime*, 375.

32 P. Bourdieu, *Outline of a Theory of Practice*, trans. R. Rice, Cambridge, 1977, 72–95, esp. 90–1. Bourdieu compares this learning to apprenticeship.

33 See H. Lefebvre, *The Production on Space*, trans. D. Nicholson-Smith, Oxford, 1991.

34 N. Elias, *Die höfische Gesellschaft*, trans. E. Jephcott as *The Court Society*, Oxford, 1983. See especially chap. 3, 'The structure of dwellings as an indicator of social structure'.

35 See Pardailhé-Galabrun, *La naissance de l'intime*, 348–65; D. Roche, *A History of Everyday Things*, chap. 6.

36 See especially C. Duncan, 'Happy Mothers and Other New Ideas in French Art', *Art Bulletin*, 55, 1973, 570–83; S. Maza, 'The "Bourgeois" Family Revisited: Sentimentalism and Social Class in Pre-Revolutionary French Culture', in *Intimate Encounters*, ed. R. Rand, Hood Museum of Art, Dartmouth College, 1997, 39–47.

37 On the *salon* see, for example, D. Goodman, *The Republic of Letters*, Berkeley, 1994, and from a more art-historical perspective, P. Radisich, *Hubert Robert and the Spaces of Enlightenment*, Cambridge, 2000; on the *boudoir*, see M. Delon, *L'Invention du boudoir*, Paris, 1999, and M. Sheriff, *Fragonard and the Art of Eroticism*, Chicago and London, 1990, 95–116; on the family, see note 35 above, and R. Démoris, *Chardin: la chair et l'objet*, Paris, 1991, 71–105.

38 See M. Merleau-Ponty, *Maurice Merleau-Ponty: Basic Writings*, ed. T. Baldwin, London 2004, esp. the essays in parts 5–6, 247–324.

39 L. de Rouvroy, duc de Saint-Simon, *Mémoires de M. le duc de Saint-Simon*, eds A. de Boislisle, et al., 43 vols, Paris, 1879–1930, 17: 75.

40 M. Delon, *Le Savoir-vivre libertin*, Paris, 2000, introduction.

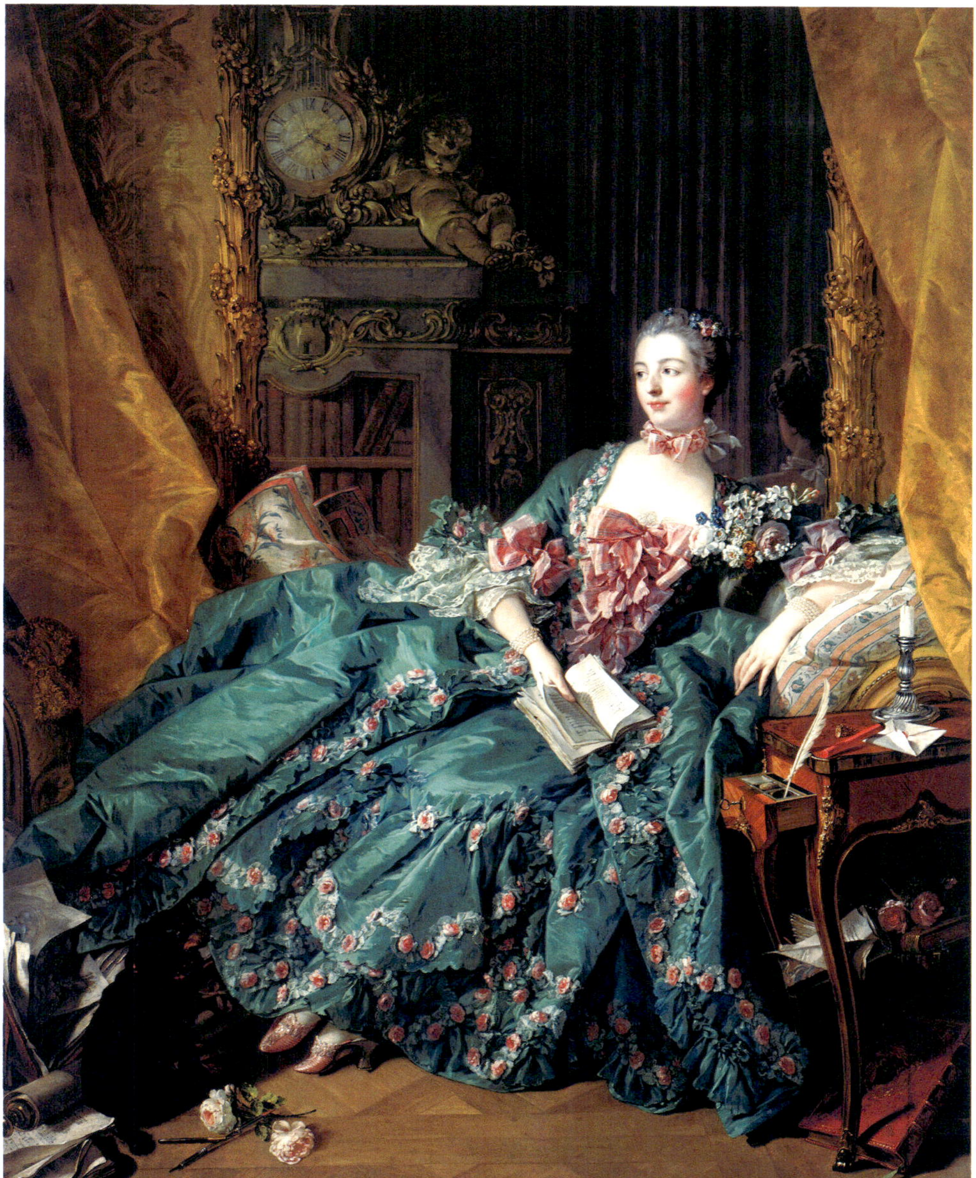

Plate 3 François Boucher, *Portrait of Madame de Pompadour*, 1756. Oil on canvas, 201 × 157 cm. Munich: Collection of the HypoVereinsbank AG at the Alte Pinakothek, Munich. Photo: ARTOTHEK.

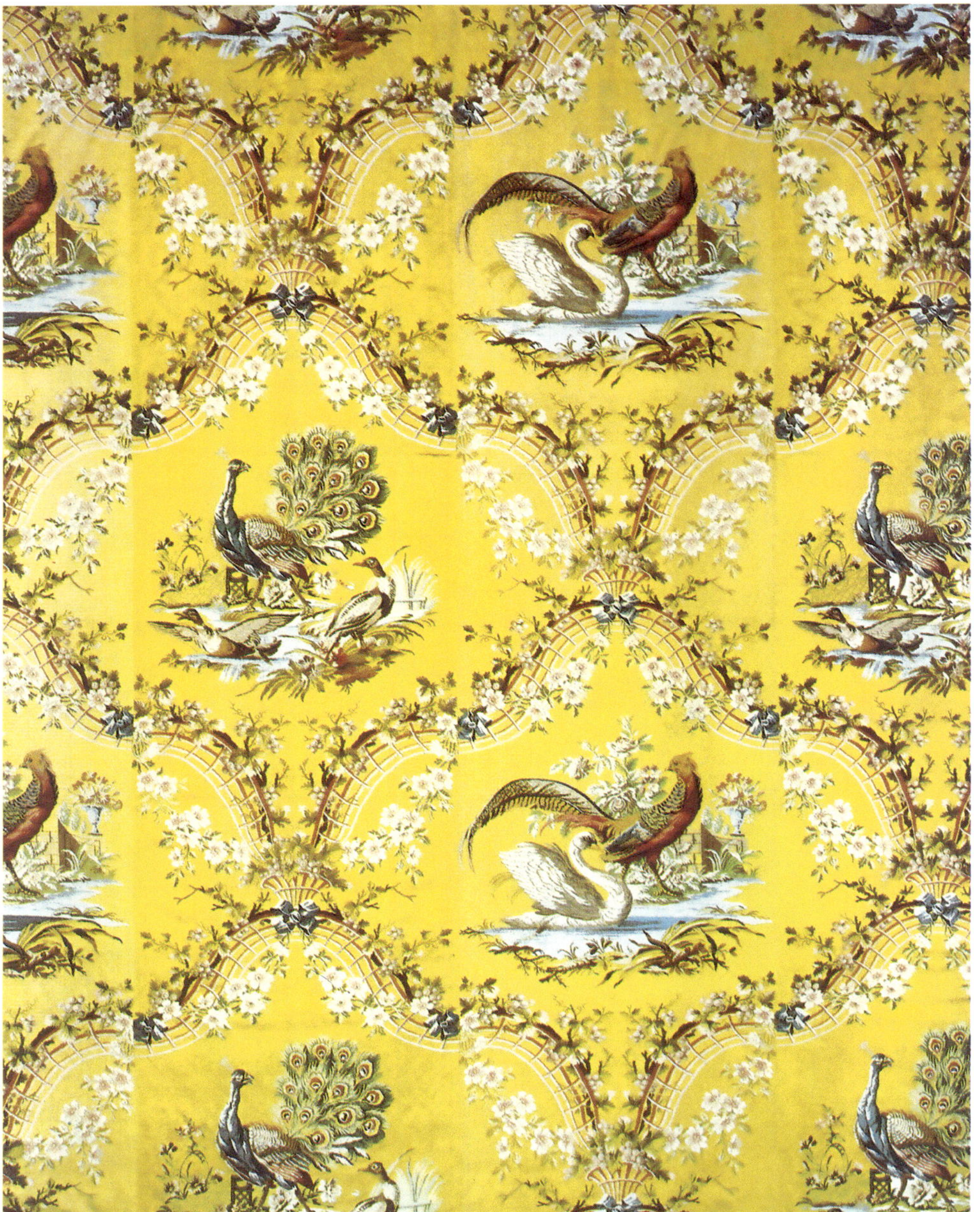

Plate 4 Philippe De Lasalle, seamed panels of 'The Pheasant and Peacock of China', prepared for a wall-hanging, *c.* 1773. 3.12 × 3.04 metres. Length of repeat: 1.48 metres. Tassinari et Chatel Archives. Photo: Courtesy of Musee des tissus, Lyons.

2

DECORATING KNOWLEDGE: THE ORNAMENTAL BOOK, THE PHILOSOPHIC IMAGE AND THE NAKED TRUTH

MARY SHERIFF

POMPADOUR'S BOOKS

Collecting books was fashionable among the elite of eighteenth-century France. Becoming erudite was not. Even as they gathered books, supported *philosophes*, and performed physics experiments in their *cabinets*, elite women and men generally found erudition tedious and boring. Collecting, however, had long been part of elite culture, and the well-to-do acquired books as avidly as they amassed coins, natural history specimens and paintings.[1] Among those with impressive libraries was Jeanne Antoinette Poisson, marquise de Pompadour (1721–64) who from 1745 to 1764 was the powerful mistress of Louis XV. As is the case for other book collectors, both men and women, it is impossible to know how many of the texts she actually read. But it is clear that she had a taste for fine bookbindings. Many books in Pompadour's library were sumptuously bound, stamped with her coat of arms, and decorated with ornamental motifs.[2] A portrait sketch by François Boucher (*c.* 1750; Paris: Musée du Louvre) shows the marquise standing at a clavichord. In the right foreground a deluxe volume is visible, its cover prominently displaying Pompadour's coat of arms, which identifies the sitter and marks the book as her possession.

Not only did Pompadour collect books, but she also had herself portrayed with them. In Boucher's portrait sketch the deluxe volume in the foreground is a counterpoint to the crowded bookcase that stands behind the marquise. In a later image of 1764, François-Hubert Drouais shows an older Pompadour at work on her embroidery seated before an elegant case filled with books (London: National Gallery of Art). And Boucher's celebrated portrait shown at the Salon of 1757 (plate 3) represents the sitter reclining in her boudoir, a small volume in her hand. Behind her is a well-stocked bookcase.[3]

In none of these portraits is the artist at pains to show what texts the sumptuous bindings contain. This trait distinguishes them from the monumental pastel by Maurice Quentin de La Tour, completed in 1755 (plate 2.2). Here the artist

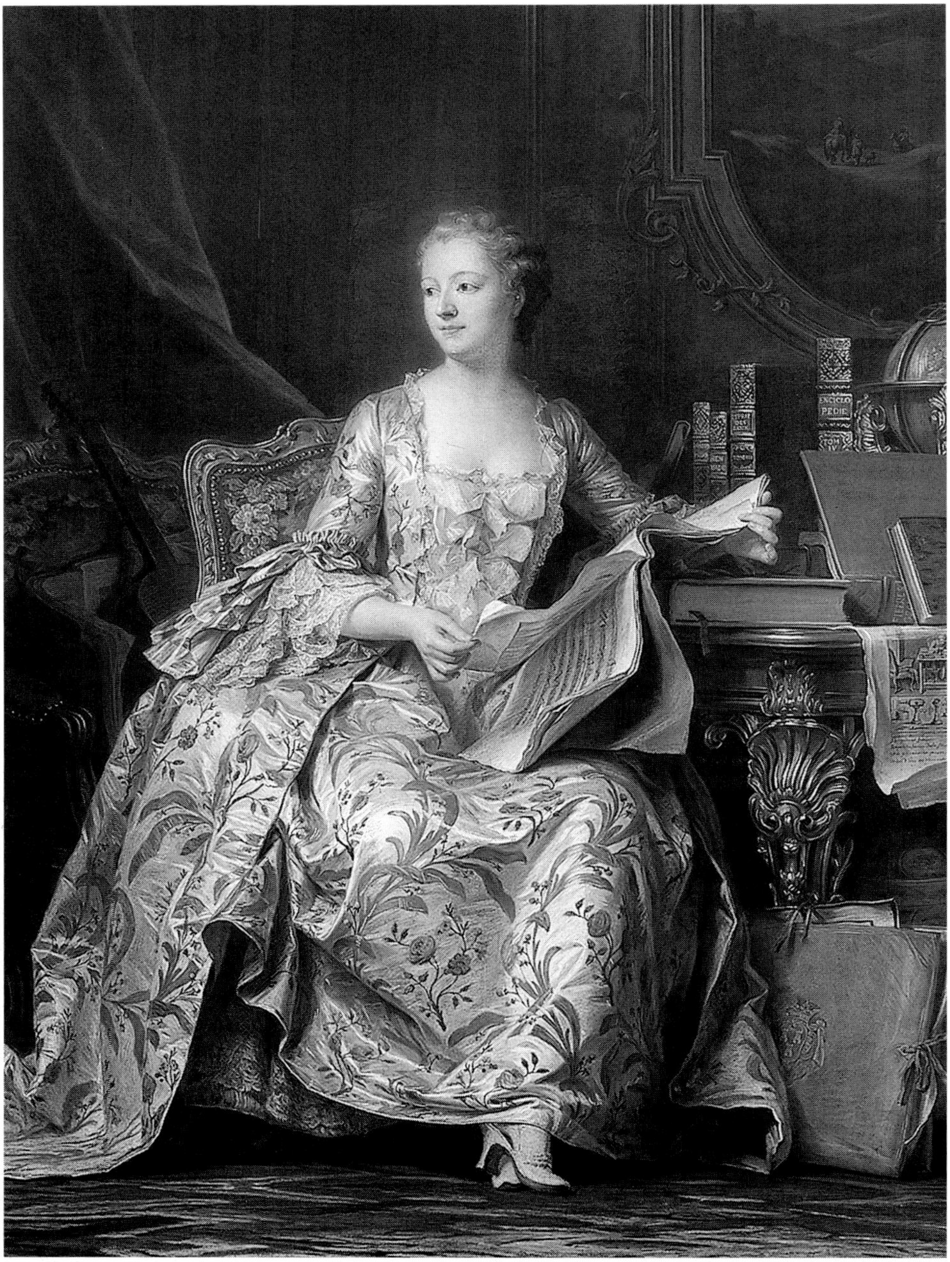

2.1 Maurice Quentin de La Tour, *Portrait of Madame de Pompadour*, 1755. Pastel with highlights in gouache on blue-grey papers backed on canvas, 177.5 × 133 cm. Paris: Musée du Louvre. Photo: Réunion des musées nationaux, Paris/Art Resource, New York.

presents Pompadour thumbing through a sheaf of music, while on her desk are copies of Voltaire's *La Henriade* (1728), Charles de Secondat, baron de Montesquieu's *L'Esprit des lois* (1748), Battista Guarini's *Il Pastor Fido* (*c.* 1590), and volume four of the *Encyclopédie* in the Paris folio edition made for '*les grand seigneurs*' and libraries.[4] This volume is the largest of all those assembled, and its title the most legible. Scholars have speculated as to why erudite tomes are evident in this fashionable woman's space. They have pointed out that, in La Tour's portrait, the *Encyclopédie* and other titled texts function as symbolic objects, seen either as part of Pompadour's self-fashioning or as attesting to her actual erudition.[5]

In contrast to these studies, this essay investigates what the *Encyclopédie* has in common with those unnamed books that line Pompadour's bookcases, rest on her marquetry tables, or lie in *beau désordre* on her parquet floors. Here the *Encyclopédie* is analysed as both a text of knowledge and a decorated book. A concern with the relation of the book to knowledge and ornament leads me to open the *Encyclopédie*, not just to read its text, but to interpret the embellishments that adorn its interior spaces. Prime among those embellishments is the allegorical frontispiece, which shows Reason trying to uncover Truth even as Imagination moves to decorate her. When the allegory is read alongside texts and images that relate truth to imagination, decoration, fable and time, a new picture of truth emerges, one that paints truth as enhanced, rather than tainted, by artful embellishment. This eighteenth-century vision of truth guides a return to Pompadour's portrait and the search for knowledge in the visual arts.

THE BOOK AND ITS DECORATION

Looking closely at two portraits of Pompadour – Boucher's painting of 1757 and La Tour's pastel of 1755 – it is clear that superb artisanal work is displayed in each. Pompadour's costume shows the weaver's skill and the art of fashion. Boucher lavishes attention not only on the fabric's rustle and sheen, but also on the lace, ribbons and rose garlands that adorn the marquise. La Tour's dress is likewise beribboned, and it, too, has elaborate lace sleeves; but here the roses are woven into the fabric amid serpentine gold fronds. No less exactly displayed in each work are the furniture-making trades. La Tour is at pains to show the rocaille motif of the table leg and Boucher picks out the marquetry in Pompadour's writing table, a piece made by the master *ébéniste* Bernard II van Risenburgh.[6]

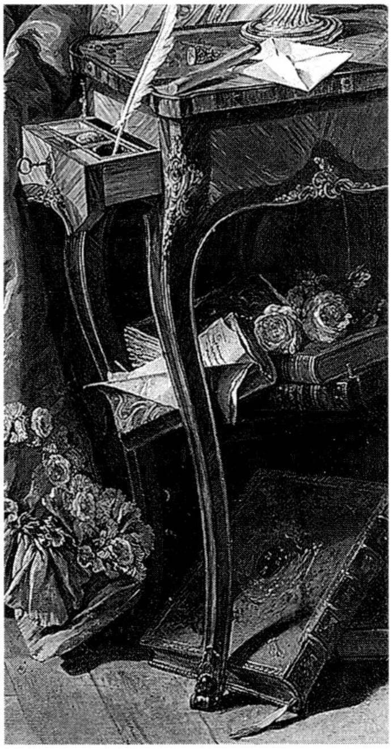

2.2 Detail of François Boucher, *Portrait of Madame de Pompadour*, Munich: Alte Pinakothek. Photo: Staatsgemäldesammlungen.

And in each painting the other accessories – writing implements, drawing tools, beribboned portfolios and engravings – are portrayed in detail and distributed with pleasing informality.

The volume Boucher that places with apparent carelessness beneath Pompadour's writing table (plate 2.2) shows the bookbinder's art: the red morocco cover is adorned with her coat of arms and gilded with *dentelle*. Above lies a brochure whose marbled cover is bent back and caught between the table leg and other leather-bound volumes. Roses adorn these books just as they cover Pompadour's body and frame her drawing implements. Less obviously perhaps, the books in La Tour's composition also function as ornamental accessories arranged for their decorative value. They seem 'less obviously' ornamental, bidding viewers to divide their attention between the text and the book, between reading the title and seeing the decorated object. The inclusion of a title lends an air of truth as well as a point of specificity to the object that La Tour represents. Neither effect, however, diminishes the book's decorative function. La Tour's *beau désordre* may be more controlled than that of Boucher, but his arrangement is no less elegant (plate 2.3), and he is careful to show not only the titles, but also the elaborate *dentelle* borders on the spines of Pompadour's books. *Dentelle* is a form of ornamentation that mimics lace work, and in La Tour's image lace also decorates the edges of Pompadour's bodice, the edges of her cuffs and, most conspicuously, the underskirt, which is visible only because La Tour depicts her dress as carelessly caught up. Like her ornamented books, the marquise is edged in lace, and even the gold patterning on her robe resonates with the gilded decoration of the bindings.

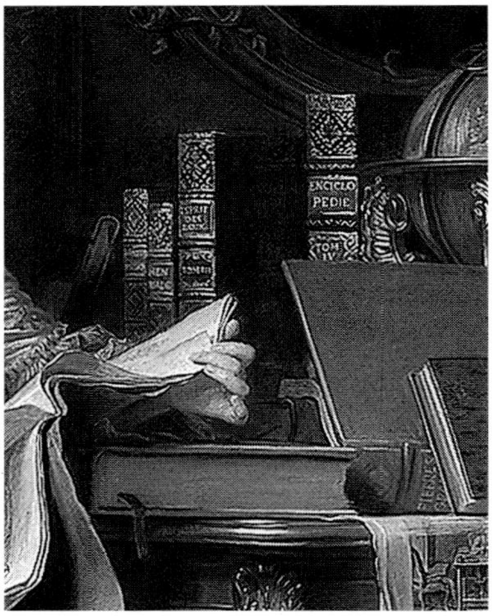

2.3 Detail of Maurice Quentin de La Tour, *Portrait of Madame de Pompadour*. Paris: Musée du Louvre.

Resting on a shelf or a table was part of the book's decorative mission. In *L'art du relieur-doreur de livres* (1772) René Martin Dudin (1725–1807) explained the 'Decorations of cover':

> The more or less elaborate embellishments give a pleasing exterior to a book and make it an ornament in libraries. It is for this reason that individuals go to great lengths in this respect and load their books with *dentelle* or lacework borders. Others order gilding.[7]

Less sumptuous than leather binding was marbled paper. Marbled paper had no purpose save to be ornament, and its job, as noted by the *Encyclopédie*, was to please the eye.[8] Marbled papers were also customary in leather-bound volumes, and they appeared between the cover (or board) and the book's first page.[9] Marbled paper was the first ornament of the book's interior, as it was, incidentally, for many volumes of the *Encyclopédie*.

In La Tour's portrait of Pompadour, the *Encyclopédie* functions as a decorative and decorated object; it is both part of the painting's embellishments and one of its symbolic motifs. Admittedly, more sumptuously bound and ornamented books were produced at the time, but the idea that this compendium of knowledge – the kind of text that would seem most resistant to ornament – is decorated and functions as decoration, gives cause for reflection.

If, for artists and their patrons, books often functioned as decorative objects, for the encyclopedists the book was first and foremost a text, judging by the entry on '*livre*', which begins, 'a writing composed by an intelligent person on some point of science for the reader's instruction and amusement'.[10] Here the book is defined as non-fiction writing, and its goals – to educate and entertain – are notably aristocratic. Eighteenth-century elites wanted knowledge to be amusing as well as informative, and to be acquired without apparent effort. To continue, the reader finds a second definition: the book is also a 'composition by a man of letters' that can be either a personal account or an invented fiction.[11] Following the brief consideration of the book as text, however, comes a much longer one of the material object, as the entry traces the history of book-making from writing on stone tablets to contemporaneous methods of production. In view of this emphasis on the book's manufacture, it is useful to recall that Jean le Rond d'Alembert contested the hierarchy that would give the text priority. In the *Discours préliminaire de l' encyclopédie* (1751), he stresses that the superiority of the liberal over the mechanical arts is unjust because it is achieved by social prejudice: the routine of the manual arts has been left to the lower classes, and these arts thus remain despised. He goes on to argue that any actual advantage afforded the liberal arts because of their intellectual demands is counterbalanced by the superior usefulness of the mechanical arts.[12] Nothing is said, however, about decorating the useful or creating the decorative, goals that were the object of many crafts engaged in luxury trades.

Decoration, however, also had a use, and perhaps an unjust one, for it encoded social distinction. This use is clear in the writings of architect and theorist Jacques-François Blondel, who, as Katie Scott has shown, viewed ornament as giving a demonstrable shape to the values attached to certain social orders.[13] Blondel contributed the entry on decoration as an architectural term to the *Encyclopédie*, and there he argued that decoration is the 'most interesting part of architecture although considered the least useful relative to commodiousness and solidity'.[14] Decoration, he argues, separates those buildings that are merely useful – factories, barracks, hospitals, poorhouses and the homes of those who work in commerce or the mechanical arts – from the more noble buildings that demand magnificence displayed – churches, palaces of sovereigns, houses of *grands seigneurs* and triumphal arches.

It seems no coincidence that Blondel drew attention to the book's interior decoration in describing his first publication, *De la distribution des maisons de plaisance et de la décoration des édifices en général* (1737–38).

> I have extended my careful attention to those elements that are only accessories. The vignettes, the *culs-de-lampe* or tail pieces, the *lettres griffes* with which these two volumes are embellished, joined to the beauty of the newly cast letters, to the *reglets*, to the choice of paper and to the printing announce to persons of art that every effort has been made to push this enterprise to the highest degree of perfection.[15]

On the one hand, Blondel implies that a book's illustrations – for example, the vignettes – are in the same category as the typeface and the quality of the paper. On the other, he is aware of the printed object's sensual nature and, as Antoine Picon points out, it is 'as if knowledge and its supports, the book and its ornamentation were inseparable'.[16] Given Blondel's theories of decoration, one can conclude that the perfection of his book's ornament reflects the status and nobility of his project and profession, and the superiority of learning and theory to practice. Decorating the book, taking care with its ornamentation, is also a way of both showing its status and honouring the book, in the sense that to decorate means to cover with honours. Might the same not be said about the deluxe folio edition of the *Encyclopédie* with its fine paper acquired at prestigious mills and its type ordered from the most elegant founder in Europe?[17]

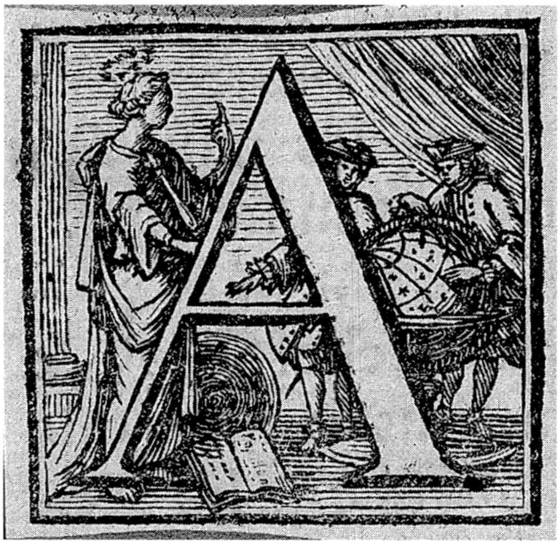

2.4 Illuminated letter from Denis Diderot and Jean le Rond d'Alembert, *Encyclopédie, ou dictionnaire raisonné des sciences, des arts et des métiers, par une société de gens de lettres*, Paris, 1751, vol. 1. Engraving. Chapel Hill: University of North Carolina at Chapel Hill, Rare Book Collection. Photo: courtesy of University of North Carolina Photographic Services.

Despite d'Alembert's defence of the strictly useful arts, the *Encyclopédie* was not only elegantly printed, it was also decorated. Subscribers honoured the importance of the work – and their own status – by choosing expensive leather bindings and gilt *dentelle* ornaments, and displaying the book as part of an impressive – and decorative – collection. Painters represented the *Encyclopédie* as beautifully bound and as part of the embellishment that ennobled a sitter and the artist, reflecting the status of the one and the talent of the other. And the editors commissioned interior ornaments that would add to the beauty and prestige of their product. The *Encyclopédie* had several sorts of interior embellishments. Illuminated capital letters mark the point at which the entries are alphabetized under a new character: an illuminated

'A', for example, signals the start of the entries beginning with that letter (plate 2.4). Such decoration recalls a long tradition of illuminated manuscripts, both sacred and secular, stretching back to the Middle Ages. In this tradition the decorated letters mark the beginning of a section, but they also provide a space for fanciful grotesques and graceful arabesques or enclose a narrative or allegorical scene. The illuminated 'A' that decorates the *Encyclopédie* follows the latter course, twice representing the science of astronomy. On the right side of the capital 'A' two men in contemporary dress study a celestial globe, while, on the left, the allegorical figure of Astronomy stands by to designate and oversee their intellectual pursuit. If illuminated letters indicate the start of an alphabetical series, *culs-de-lampe* indicate a section's end. An engraved allegory is repeated on the title page of each volume and an allegorical headpiece appears at the beginning of each volume's entries. These embellishments suggest that artistic imagination was at work in the *Encyclopédie* right from the start.[18] Moreover, even in the published prospectus, provision was made for a more significant decoration – a frontispiece to the multi-volume production. Charles Nicholas Cochin the Younger designed that frontispiece, but only in 1765, well after the first volume appeared, and Benoit Prevost engraved it in 1772 (plate 2.5). For the *Encyclopédie* Cochin invented an allegory that gives yet another valence to decoration, for it invites consideration of the role of decoration in searching for knowledge and truth. Its reflection on that role, moreover, illuminates the function of a frontispiece as well as its relation to architecture and ornament.

Since the seventeenth century, the standard relation of frontispiece to text had been like that of façade to building interior; one contemplated the frontispiece before entering the text.[19] Indeed, the French word '*frontispice*' is etymologically related to '*façade*'. As an architectural term, '*frontispice*' denotes the main façade of a monumental building, while in typography the term indicates either the large title page of a book, or an illustrated plate placed before or facing the title page.[20] The frontispiece prepares readers for what they will find in the chapters arrayed behind it, and in theory it is intimately related to a book's contents. For the *grands seigneurs,* a frontispiece, like the façade of a grand *hôtel,* functioned as an ornamental entrance, and, as such, it was necessary to their exquisite editions.

THE FRONTISPIECE

There was a lapse of more than twenty years between the first volume of the *Encyclopédie*, which appeared in 1751, and the arrival of the frontispiece in 1772. Subscribers could have the frontispiece belatedly bound into their volumes, following or not the instructions of the editors as to placement.[21] Some of those subscribers likely knew something of the frontispiece before receiving it, because Cochin exhibited his drawing at the Salon of 1765, where the allegory was explained briefly in the *livret.*

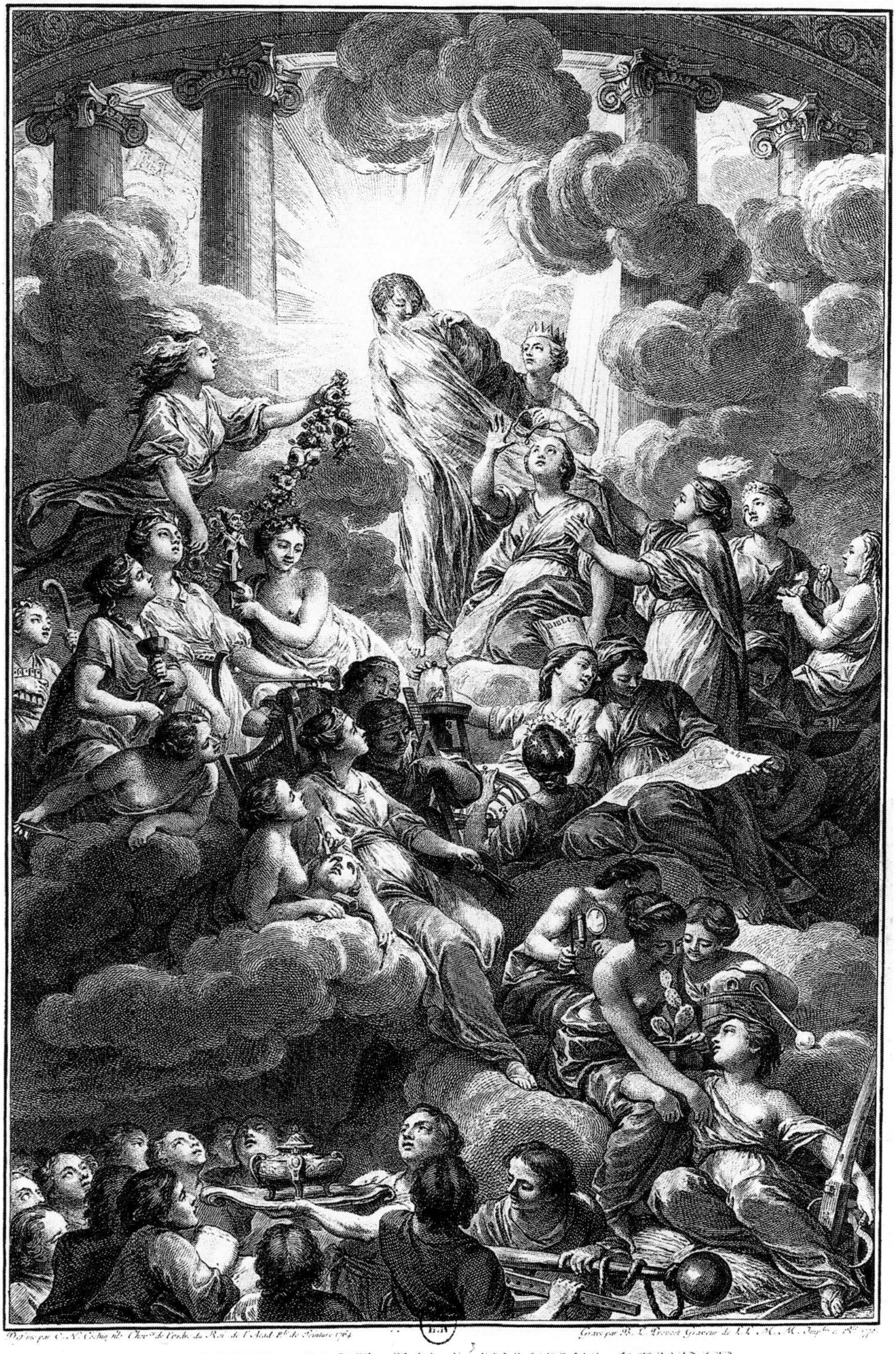
FRONTISPICE DE L'ENCYCLOPEDIE.

One sees the sciences occupied with uncovering Truth. Reason and Metaphysics try to raise her veil. Theology awaits her light from a ray that comes from the heavens; near to her are Memory and Ancient and Modern History. Beside and below are the sciences. On the other side, Imagination approaches with a garland to ornament [*orner*] Truth. Below her are the different forms of poetry and the arts. At the bottom are several Talents that derive from the sciences and arts.[22]

Looking at the allegory with this description in mind, notice that the métiers are placed at the bottom of the scene and apparently pay tribute to the arts and sciences distributed in the 'sanctuary of truth', as the space was called in the description that accompanied the frontispiece.[23] Cochin seems to ignore d'Alembert's call for equalizing the applied and fine arts, and his work endorses the standard hierarchy upheld by the Académie Royale de peinture et de sculpture, which Cochin served as an officer. That institution insistently separated itself from craft guilds, but at the same time argued for a connection between the fine arts and the crafts. The perfection of the 'noble' arts helped to elevate craftsmanship and thus to ensure the quality of French commercial goods.[24] But more important here than the relation between the fine and applied arts is that between truth and imagination. In relation to truth, imagination is recognized and labelled as an ornamenting function, and indeed, in the frontispiece, Imagination rushes to embellish Truth (plate 2.6) with a rose garland that she might have lifted from Pompadour's gown.

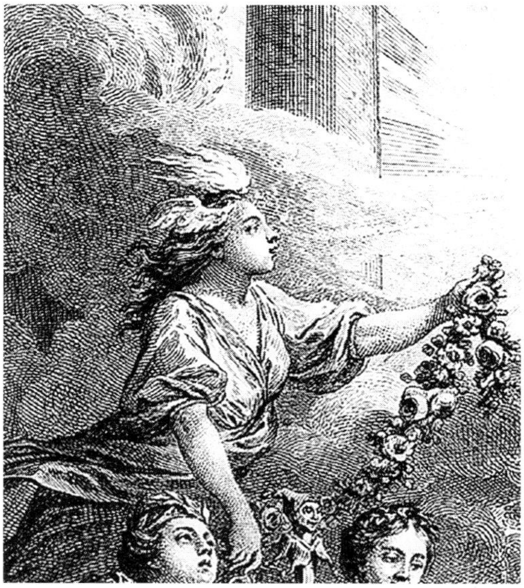

2.6 Detail of Imagination, in C.-N. Cochin, *Frontispiece*, from Diderot and d'Alembert, *Encyclopédie*. Paris: Bibliothèque national de France.

Every description of Cochin's allegory published in the eighteenth century affirmed imagination's role as decorator. A separate page issued with the fron-

2.5 (facing) Benoît-Louis Prévost, after Charles-Nicholas Cochin the Younger, *Frontispiece*, 1772, from Denis Diderot and Jean le Rond d'Alembert, *Encyclopédie, ou dictionnaire raisonné des sciences, des arts et des métiers, par une société de gens de lettres*, Paris 1751–77, vol. 1. Paris: Bibliothèque national de France. Photo: Bibliothèque national de France.

tispiece proclaimed: 'to the left one sees Imagination who prepares herself to embellish [*embellir*] and perfect [*couronner*] truth.'[25] And Diderot in his Salon criticism remarked: 'At the top one sees Truth between Reason and Imagination; Reason tries to tear away her veil, as Imagination prepares to embellish her.'[26] Giving imagination the function of embellishing truth appeals directly to Etienne Bonnot, abbé de Condillac (1714–80), whose *Essai sur l'origine des connaissances humaines* (1746) the encyclopedists endorsed in the *Discours préliminaire*. Condillac explains in his *Essai* that to make truth beautiful, imagination embellishes it with the most appropriate ideas, and he continues: 'Imagination is to truth what *parure* is to a beautiful woman. It should lend every help to set her off to best advantage.'[27] Here truth is figured as a beautiful woman and imagination as her adornment, but earlier Condillac deemed imagination 'a coquette whose only desire is to please, who draws on her fancy rather more than her reason', and 'whose power ends where that of analysis begins'.[28] It is notable that this discussion of imagination comes from the only section of the essay that uses figures – the ornaments of language – to analyse a mental power, and imagination is the only power that is overtly sexed and gendered through ornament. In both Condillac's theory and Cochin's allegory, pleasure, ornament, imagination and truth merge with the beautiful female body.

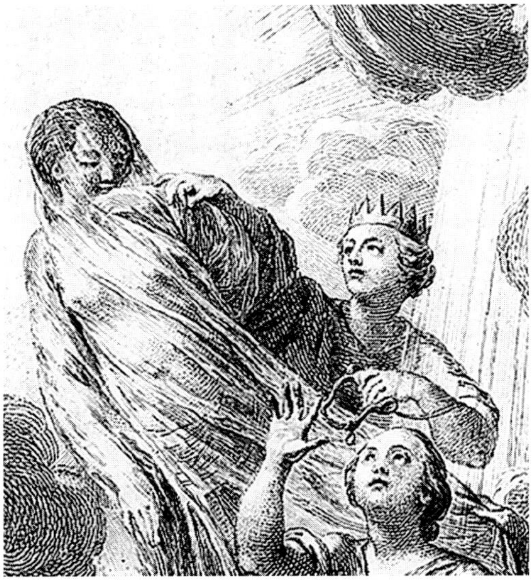

2.7 Detail of Reason, in C.-N. Cochin, *Frontispiece*, from Diderot and d'Alembert, *Encyclopédie*. Paris: Bibliothèque national de France.

In regard to the feminine character of Imagination and her special import in Cochin's allegory, it is significant that the 'sanctuary of truth' is decorated in the Ionic order. Since Vitruvius, the Ionic column and capital had been considered imitations of the female form. The shaft's slenderness and grace recapitulated a woman's proportions, its flutes the folds of a matron's robes; the capital with its volutes figured a woman's curls. Blondel also saw the Ionic order as feminine, and the orders as giving their character to the whole building.[29] The same might be said of this frontispiece, where femininity is appropriated for the artist's imaginative and decorative powers.

With attributes, pose, expression and action, Cochin's Imagination not only allies herself with decoration, but also with invention and enthusiasm – the established components of artistic genius. This alliance depends on the instability of allegorical figures, which offered a wide scope for interpretation, given the

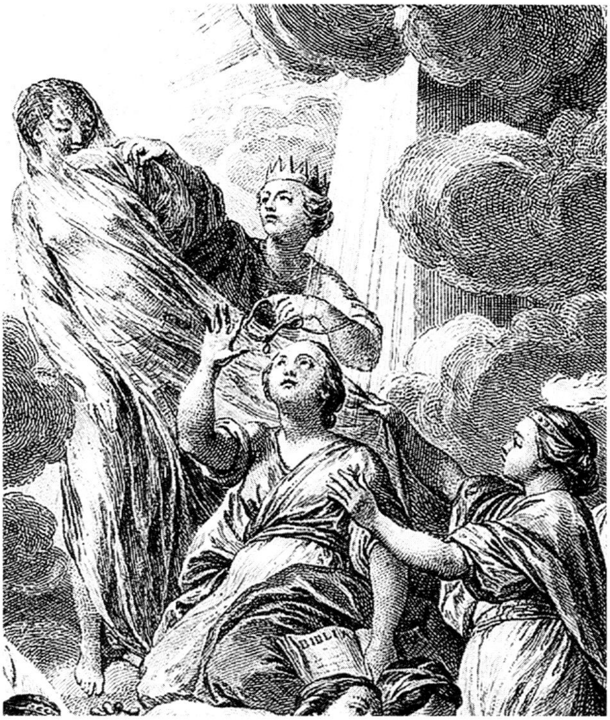

2.8 Detail of Truth, Metaphysics and Religion, in C.-N. Cochin, *Frontispiece*, from Diderot and d'Alembert, *Encyclopédie*. Paris: Bibliothèque national de France.

number of emblem books varying that tradition. Although Imagination's attributes are clear – a flame emerging from her head and wings on either side of her temple – she actually does not accord well with the figure in *Iconologie par figures* to which Cochin contributed.[30] The illustration shows Imagination as a young woman with wings on either side of her head and small creatures (not flames) popping up from her crown. Although her hair and drapery seem to move, this Imagination is immobilized in the classic pose of inspiration. In the frontispiece, no objects coming full-blown from Imagination's brain are visible, and she moves across the field vigorously, her hair and drapery thrown back, her mouth open wide. In the flame that does spring from her head, and in her furious movement, Imagination slides into the allegorical figure of *Enthousiasme poétique*, as described in Jean-Baptiste Boudard's *Iconologie françoise* of 1759.[31] But she is not exactly Enthusiasm either, for the laurel crown is missing. A confusion of enthusiasm and imagination may be precisely the point, for there was a strong theoretical connection between enthusiasm's passion and imagination's energy in Condillac's writings, in the *Encyclopédie*, and throughout eighteenth-century aesthetic theory. Enthusiasm was the spark that ignited the imagination, set ablaze its inventive capacities.[32] Thus imagination's decorative mission is here impelled by enthusiasm and enabled by invention.

A complex figure, Imagination plays a leading role in Cochin's allegory, and she also appears to be the privileged partner of Truth, despite two widespread

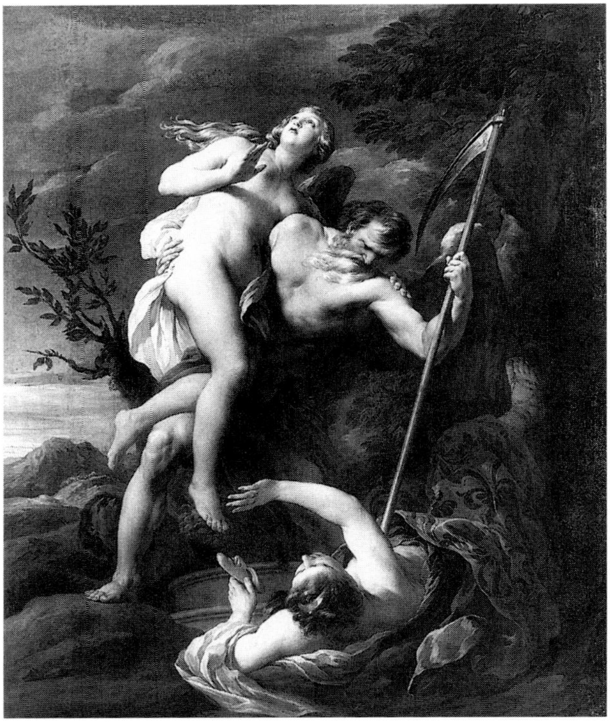

2.9 François Lemoyne, *Time Revealing Truth*, also called *Time Saving Truth from Deception and Envy*, 1737. Oil on canvas, 183 × 149 cm. London: Wallace Collection. Photo: by kind permission of the trustees of the Wallace Collection, London.

beliefs: that imagination, especially in concert with passion or enthusiasm, readily produced false notions, and that ornament hid or disguised truth. Imagination is placed in the uppermost register of the composition near Truth. Her excited movement draws attention. Can the same be said about Reason, whose theoretical relation to truth was less problematic for the Encyclopedists? On the left of Truth, crowned Reason (plate 2.8), holding the bit and reins that control Passion, is placed above all others; yet she is pushed into the background, her body hidden behind Truth. She is even less visible than Religion who, from her kneeling position, attracts the eye with her large, open Bible and raised right arm. Also prominent but in a lower register is Metaphysics, the central science associated with Reason, who with Reason tries to remove Truth's veil.

In showing Reason and Metaphysics pulling at Truth's veil, the allegory plays on the conventional one of 'Time unveiling Truth', which shows an old man – Father Time with his scythe – seeming to take the draperies from a woman in various states of undress. In Cochin's allegory, however, Time is represented as a winged old man crouching behind Metaphysics at the right-hand edge of the composition. Here Time supports History, or more precisely History's work, for the open book on which she writes is balanced on Time's bent back. Although Cochin denies Time the honour of unveiling truth, his new allegory depends on the old tradition that he has transformed.

'Time unveiling Truth' expresses the idea that time will wear away all 'decoration': all the misunderstandings, personal interests and superficial ornaments that surround the kernel of truth and render it imperceptible. When finally revealed, Truth is naked and unadorned, as we see in an anonymous eighteenth-century drawing now in the Auckland Art Museum, which copies Bernini's *Truth Unveiled* of 1646–52 (Rome: Galleria Borghese). Here Truth is a nude woman holding a sun disc in her hand and resting her left foot near an orb. Along with her nudity, both the disc and orb are Truth's recognizable markers; the sun's light is the medium through which truth is revealed and her foot on the globe shows that truth is above ordinary things.

The theme was taken up in the visual arts throughout the eighteenth century, and artists embroidered scenes around the basic action of unveiling truth. In Jean-François de Troy's *Time Unveiling Truth* of 1733 (London: National Gallery), for example, the artist has enhanced the theme by adding additional allegorical figures. At the left side of the composition, the four cardinal virtues – Fortitude, Justice, Temperance and Prudence – kneel in homage to Truth as she is unveiled by Time. Truth's garment has already dropped below her breasts, and viewers may anticipate its final fall. Old man Time, naked and winged, swoops across the top of the composition, holding his scythe in one hand and lifting the drapery from Truth with the other. At the same time Truth reaches over to unmask Fraud, seated to her right. Figured as an older woman swathed in dark drapery and clutching a mask, Fraud contrasts with the youthful open-faced Truth, whose white cloak has already dropped low enough to reveal a radiant body beneath. Further strengthening the contrast between Truth and Fraud is the difference in how each responds to being revealed. Truth appears to acquiesce to her unveiling, even to welcome it; Fraud, on the other hand, resists, and tries to push Truth away.

In Cochin's *Frontispiece*, however, Truth is not revealed. Truth differs from type not only because she is completely veiled, but also because she appears to resist her uncovering (plate 2.8). So firmly does Truth cling to her drapery that Metaphysics resorts to using Religion's body for leverage, pushing against her breast with one hand the better to exert the force necessary to remove Truth's garment. Truth, however, refuses to be stripped bare. Her right arm is crossed over her body; it rests just below her neck and she appears to struggle against Reason, who grabs the drapery at her wrist. Apparently, this Truth does not want to be unveiled, and she is loath to take the bit of Reason.

Something of the violence attendant to uncovering Truth, as well as the supposed opposition of truth and ornament, is evident in paintings like François Lemoyne's *Time Saving Truth from Deception and Envy* (1737, plate 2.9). Time here is figured as a vigorous and bearded old man who carries off Truth rather than revealing her. The relation between Time and Truth resonates with the image of the rape of the Sabine women, or of Pluto carrying off Persephone, and these references give a particularly sexualized cast to the abduction.[33] In Lemoyne's conception, Time is not only kidnapping Truth, he is also about to dispatch the figure of Deception, a finely dressed woman holding a mask, who has fallen to the ground. This allegory of Deception suggests that dress, finery and ornament, as much as deception, are opposed to truth. And by extension, that imagination, as an adorning function, is somehow truth's enemy. It also calls to mind the commonplace eighteenth-century truism that beauty masks evil, that flowers hide the lurking serpent.

Even more than this well-worn adage, Lemoyne's violent dispatching of Deception also implies a fear of ornament and artifice – a fear of all Truth's others. In this case, Deception's garments are identical to those worn by Hercules in Lemoyne's *Hercules and Omphale* of 1724 (Paris: Musée du Louvre) to signify that the great male hero has given himself to feminine things. Those silky brocades that wind around his body bring to mind the clothing worn by women like Pompadour, women whose elegant dress and captivating looks might dissimulate a dangerous character.[34] Thus while Time saves, or rather kidnaps, one aspect of woman, he beats back another, aggressively thrusting his scythe into her. He has already vanquished Envy, who is barely visible as she falls in Time's wake. Envy, too, had her association with women because common wisdom held that jealousy was a passion that women were prone to experience and often to experience violently.[35] But what about Truth? She looks up and turns away from Time with an imploring expression, as if she needs to be saved from, not by, this violent old man. Perhaps she does not want to witness the destruction of ornament, artifice and deception. Perhaps it was not her choice to be stripped and abducted.

Cochin's Truth seems to be in much less danger. What need she fear with Time relegated to the furniture of history and Imagination rushing to the rescue, rose garland at the ready? Imagination here is not opposed to Truth. Should Reason and Metaphysics succeed in stripping away the veils, Imagination will create other seductions, other ornaments. Truth will never be naked, at least not in this allegory.

Cochin's image suggests not only that imagination serves truth by adorning her, but also that imagination is truth's preferred partner. The artist further explored the adorning function of imagination in an image closely related to the *Encyclopédie* frontispiece, which Augustin de Saint-Aubin engraved in 1770 (plate 2.10). This work illustrates a famous line from the poet and theorist Nicolas Boileau Despréaux (1636–1711): 'Only the True is Beautiful.' Here beautiful Truth is embellished with jewellery, drapery and flowers; rather than Time stripping her bare, Cochin's design shows Imagination and the arts completing Truth's toilette. On the right, two winged genii with the flame of imagination bursting from their heads adjust the folds that cover Truth, while just below her a female figure surrounded by emblems of the literary genres puts a final touch on the garland that encircles her body. Beneath Truth's attendants are the great men – painters, writers, perhaps even philosophers (is that Plato pointing upwards?) – in the process of representing Truth. And Cochin's figure seems cast as the vision of Beautiful Truth that they both imagine and copy. Their collective fantasy also engages the spectators at the bottom of the composition, who react emotionally to the beauty of Truth's representation.

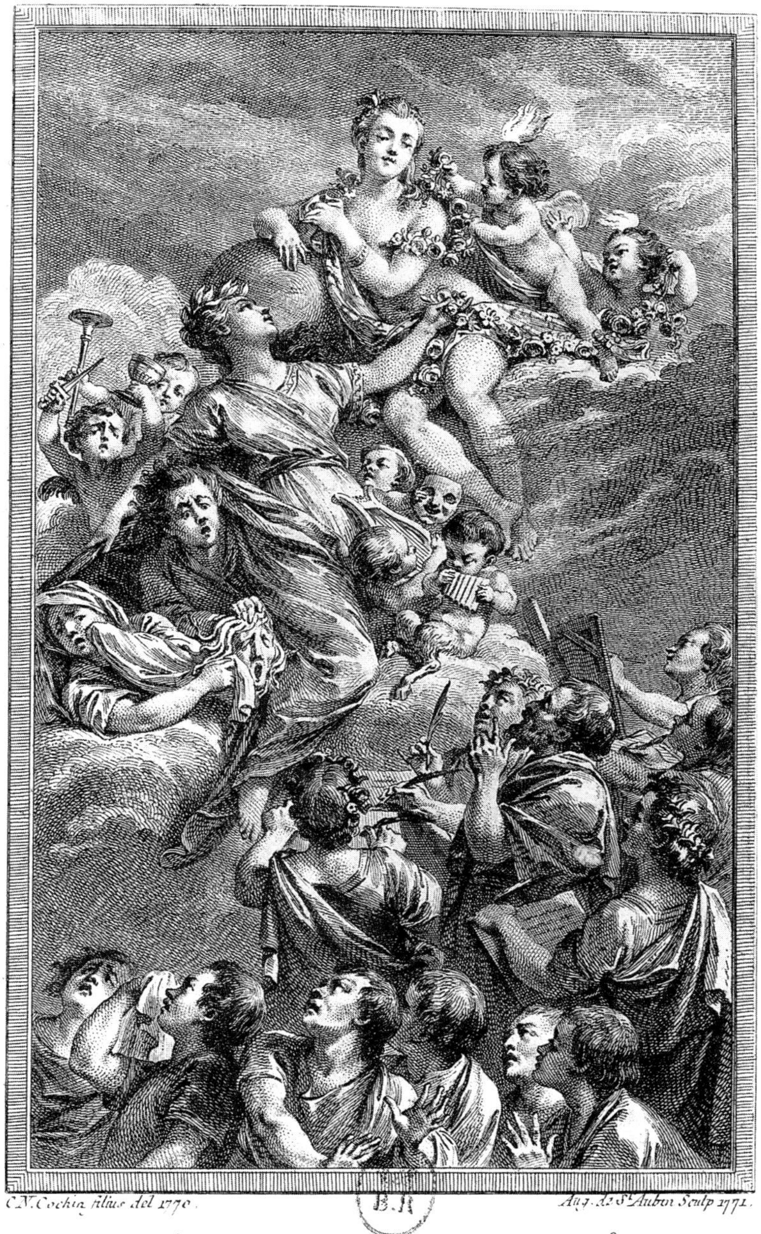

2.10 Augustin de Saint-Aubin, after Charles-Nicholas Cochin the Younger, *Rien n'est beau que le Vrai*, or *Only the Truth is Beautiful*, 1770–71. Engraving. Paris: Bibliothèque national de France. Photo: Bibliothèque national de France.

Given that Cochin's allegory illuminates Boileau's adage, it seems only appropriate that the composition ties together Truth, Beauty, Imagination and Ornament. One might expect the *Encyclopédie*'s frontispiece to privilege Reason's relation to Truth, but this is not the case. In addition, the frontispiece presents a picture of knowledge different from that represented in the chart published as part of the *Encyclopédie*'s front matter (see plate 3.3). D'Alembert called this chart an 'encyclopedic tree' that gathered together all knowledge from a single point of view.[36] Rooted in Condillac's philosophy, this tree grew from the premise that all knowledge came from a different aspect of the mind acting upon sensation. Assuming that the action of different mental faculties produced different kinds of knowledge, the chart brackets the various offshoots of history, philosophy and the fine arts into three separate columns, each headed by a specific power of mind. History is the realm of memory, philosophy relies on reason, and the fine arts – collectively grouped under the name Poetry – depend upon imagination. 'Poetry' here does not refer to a specific art form, and d'Alembert claims that the term should be understood as synonymous with invention.[37] He notes elsewhere in the *Discours préliminaire* that all the fine arts together can be called 'Painting' because their productions are portrayals or imitations. Unlike historical fact and philosophical theory, knowledge in the fine arts is an imitation of nature created through the workings of imagination.[38]

Cochin's image uses a very different visual language from d'Alembert's chart and respects neither its ordering of knowledge nor its hierarchies. The chart figures a tripartite division of 'Human Understanding' and employs a quasi-mathematical notation of brackets and columns to separate offshoots into sets and subsets. The frontispiece, on the other hand, represents neither a tripartite division nor an orderly separation and arrangement. The figures are loosely divided into two, rather than three, major groups, and these are positioned – although not exactly – below either Imagination or Reason. Obviously, no one would expect a visual allegory shown at the Salon and claiming a place as high art to abide by the diagrammatic schema that the encyclopedists devised. Still, an artist as skilled and experienced as Cochin could have arranged his figures to suggest d'Alembert's overall plan, but he does not. In fact, a close look at the composition will show that while maintaining some relation with the *Discours préliminaire*, Cochin hardly follows the divisions that d'Alembert proposes.

In the frontispiece the arts are not separated from the sciences, but flow into them, thereby confusing the distinction between imagination and reason. Painting, for example, eases her foot onto the cloud that bears the weight of Botany with her cactus. Near the centre of the image, Architecture's arm touches the hand of Astronomy with her astrolabe and starry crown. Even if one looks inside, rather than between the loosely formed groups, Cochin appears to ignore d'Alembert's system. Coming from 'particular physics', Botany and Chemistry (with her retort and furnace) sit together with both Agriculture, who belongs to a subcategory of 'botany', and Optics, whose family is 'mixed mathematics'. Had

Cochin wanted to conform to d'Alembert's tree, it would have been simple enough, especially as there is a sameness to the figures, whose variations of pose, costume and expression are usually unrelated to the science or art that they represent. A quick change of attribute, the switching of a plough for an astrolabe, and one figure becomes another.

The clear separation between realms of knowledge in the *Encyclopédie*'s chart suggests that different mental operations create different sorts of knowledge. In the *Discours préliminaire,* however, difference implies hierarchy. D'Alembert conceives of history and philosophy – stemming from memory and reason – as occupied with analysing both material and immaterial things. The fine arts dependent on imagination he views as only concerned with the material. Not only does d'Alembert tie imagination to the material world, he also amplifies its limitations when he outlines the 'talents' of those who pursue the different branches of knowledge. Memory is the talent of the historian, who is concerned with facts; wisdom belongs to the philosopher; and artists have pleasure as their portion. Pleasure in itself was certainly not a negative; contemporary art theorists argued that the goal of art was to please and seduce, precisely by inducing attractive illusions or moving the emotions.[39] But pleasure separated from the goal of wisdom has a lesser position in the encyclopedists' universe. When Diderot wanted to defend the arts, he did so by hailing those subjects that were both pleasurable and morally edifying.

Cochin's *Frontispiece* suggests how fictive is the incompatibility of image and idea, pleasure and wisdom, ornamenting and revealing truth. With its figures acting out a drama of veiling and unveiling Truth, Cochin's *Frontispiece* conveys not simply an action but an idea, and not simply one idea, but many. Cochin presents his audience with a sensuous and decorative picture of knowledge. D'Alembert's system, however, implied that one could not make a sensuous picture of knowledge, because a consideration of knowledge would be an idea, but not an image, an analysis but not an imitation. Yet Cochin's *Frontispiece* functions as image and idea. It is an ornament that reveals and beautifies truth, and it simultaneously offers visual pleasure and philosophic ideas. In relation to the systematic chart, this visual allegory transgresses the boundary that contains the imitative arts.

Another *discours préliminaire*, the one that prefaced the *Iconologie par figures*, speaks to the significance of visual allegory:

> In poetry, in painting, in all the arts that speak to imagination and whose end is to instruct and please, it is always under the veil of allegory that ethics presents to men consoling truths and useful principles. History often borrows the same language to preserve the memory of an event, to consecrate a heroic deed, to immortalize a generous action.[40]

Allegory, this discourse contends, is one of the most perfect inventions of the human spirit. And allegory in this sense casts her veil over Cochin's entire *Frontispiece*, which honours and celebrates allegory as truth.

If the veil of allegory drapes Cochin's Truth, it is a veil everyone can see through – at least partially. What is gained by covering Truth with a veil so nearly transparent that it both covers and reveals? Is it that Truth is seductively veiled to ignite Reason's desire: the desire to see that provoked Zeuxis to try to lift the veil Parrhasios painted? The desire to know, which led Freud's little boy to peek up his mother's skirt? In Cochin's allegory, Reason and Metaphysics are captivated by their passion to know all, by their desire – which reason supposedly keeps in check. And the *Frontispiece* makes Truth a coquette, arousing and resisting desire. Imagination participates in this game of inciting Reason by decorating Truth, by making her attractive. Although d'Alembert ignored decoration's power to attract, it did find its way into several *Encyclopédie* entries. Take, for example, these articles:

> *Embellir*: to embellish is artfully to add forms or accessories to objects that in themselves would be without interest, thereby rendering them captivating, pleasurable, precious, etc.[41]

> *Ornement*: that which serves to embellish something. The important rule is that the essential and principal parts should transform themselves into ornaments, so that the spectator, who thus sees the useful acting as a base for the pleasurable, is affected as delicately as possible.[42]

Without Truth's veil, without the ornaments of imagination, would Reason give Truth a second glance?

The problem of decorating and revealing Truth is taken up in two other images that relate to Cochin's allegory. In *Iconologie par figures* Truth is represented as a celestial virtue, nude because 'she has no need of ornament.'[43] This conception obviously differs from that implied by the figure who adorns the *Encyclopédie's* frontispiece. Nevertheless, this standard Truth is worth a second look because in *Iconologie par figures* she is paired with Fable. Although throughout the *Iconologie* such pairings often suggest an opposition, this is not the case here exactly. Fable is allied with Truth in that she is 'an ingenious fiction that conceals a useful lesson'.[44] At the same time, Fable shares attributes with Deception: she is described as richly dressed and decorated, and one of her attributes is the mask. But as the description also suggests, Fable's embellishments are like the veil of allegory, a veil that both hides and reveals truth. It is because she dons this veil that Fable is akin to the Truth of Cochin's *Frontispiece*.

The kinship between Truth and Fable, moreover, was the first tale told by the poet Claude Joseph Dorat in his collection of *Fables nouvelles* in 1773. The story opens with Truth decrying Fable's audacity: why should Fable think that they are equals? Truth proclaims that she existed before time and can endure all catastrophes. Fable replies that she recognizes Truth's power and realizes that she is but Truth's shadow. Nevertheless, Fable calls herself 'a delightful shadow' and one unlike Truth's mirror, which is a 'frightening accessory'. Fable argues that naked truth has had her day: 'When man is corrupted, you must be veiled. My august sister, the age of gold is past, do not go around preaching in the nude if you want

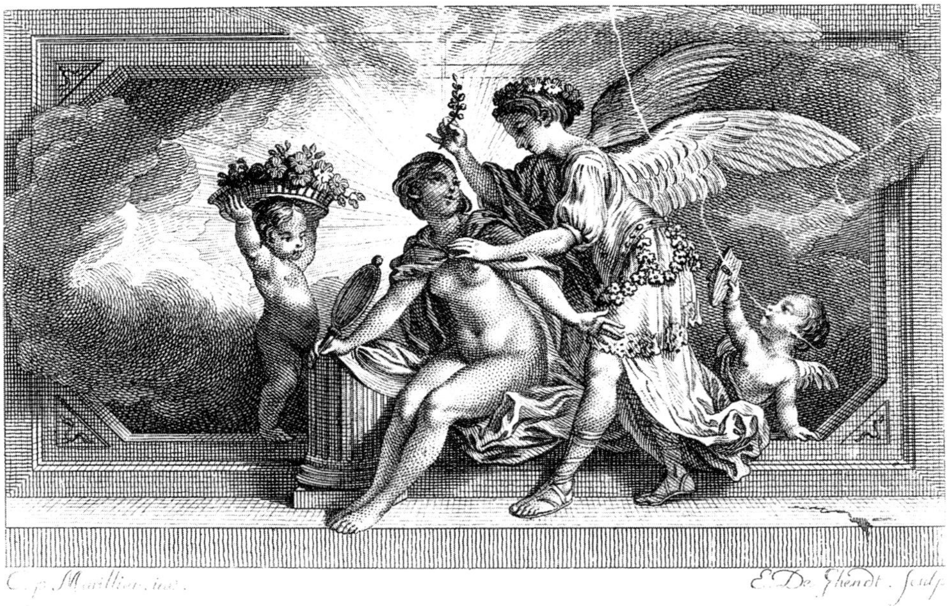

2.11 Emmanuel-Jean Nepomucene de Ghendt, after Clément Pierre Marillier (1740–1808), *Truth and Fable*, from Claude Jospeh Dorat, *Fables nouvelles*, The Hague, 1773. Engraving. Chapel Hill: University of North Carolina at Chapel Hill, Rare Book Collection. Photo: courtesy of University of North Carolina Photographic Services.

to enlarge your court.'[45] And she reminds Truth that even Venus pleases more when she has a few clothes on. Fable then proposes that the two unite; she will be Truth's '*dame d'atour*', or handmaid, and embellish her. In Clément Pierre Marillier's illustration (plate 2.11) one sees Truth being adorned, a Truth that calls to mind Cochin's figure in the rays of light that dispel the clouds around her head. Here Fable adorns Truth, and Fable herself is already decorated with garlands. As Truth's *dame d'atour*, Fable chooses flowers from one cupid's basket to ornament Truth while a second cupid holds a theatrical mask, which emphasizes Fable's relation to both Truth and Duplicity. The nakedness of Marillier's Truth can be seen beneath her embellishments, but in a way that differs from Cochin's strategy of veiling while unveiling. Whereas Cochin used a transparent garment to veil Truth, Marillier prefers a cape that reveals most of, although not all, Truth's body. Fable, on the other hand, is entirely dressed, and one is not sure how closely Truth will approximate Fable when her toilette is complete.

If Marillier's engraving suggests that Fable will cover Truth with adornments, Cochin's encyclopedic allegory leaves little room to imagine that Reason will, once and for all, reveal naked Truth. In Cochin's allegory, Reason cannot thwart Imagination's advance. Decorating Truth is here as urgent a task, perhaps even more urgent, as removing her veils. While I make no claims for Cochin's intentions, his composition pushes History and Memory to the side, relegates Reason to the background and gives Imagination a clear field.

DECORATING POMPADOUR

Although the volume of the *Encyclopédie* that La Tour placed on Pompadour's table in 1755 is undoubtedly without its frontispiece, the allegory that Cochin later designed poses questions for anyone seeking the 'truth' that underlies La Tour's portrait. With most of the Salon critics who wrote about the work, viewers today can admire the perfection and finish of his ornaments, which look so real, so true to life. These include the garments that clothe the marquise and the objects that surround her, including her decorated and titled books.[46]

Today interpreters are apt to imagine that La Tour selected particular decorations – like the *Encyclopédie* volume – as signs of some 'truth' about the sitter's actual or imagined person, and one anonymous Salon critic, calling himself the 'Partisan of Good Taste', more or less agreed. He argued that to put Pompadour next to the *Encyclopédie* was to demand that she assume a demeanour not appropriate for a decorative woman, but suitable for a serious *philosophe*. In this critic's estimation, La Tour did not embellish Pompadour enough: she needed more make-up, more finery, and a beautiful smile to decorate her face.[47] Although the passage reads as a criticism of La Tour, it also implies that Pompadour is not what she appears to be. This anonymous critic takes the *Encyclopédie* as text, ignoring not only its status as decorated object and its role in the portrait as decoration, but also the possibility that a noble patron's ownership decorates, in the sense that it honours, the books she owns. Stripping away these decorative functions does not reveal truth, even if the critic presents himself as unmasking La Tour's 'bold scheme' of presenting Pompadour as a *femme philosophe* rather than as a beautified woman.[48] One cannot deny that aspects of this pastel, such as Pompadour's pose, can be interpreted as suggesting a *femme philosophe*. The point is rather that the Partisan of Good Taste eliminates from the portrait certain 'truths' about books, patrons and ornaments, all the better to cover the image (and perhaps his dislike of Pompadour) with assumptions about the incompatibility of beautiful womanliness and serious learning, of ornament and knowledge.

But what truth, what true Pompadour, can anyone now find beneath the decorative elements of La Tour's portrait? Can anyone, with the help of time, strip away all passion, all interest, all superficial ornament and reveal the naked kernel of truth? Or is the search for truth less an unveiling and more an embellishing? Or is it some of each? Gazing into Cochin's sanctuary of truth, I see a complex interplay of decoration, imagination, enthusiasm, reason and truth. Unlike the *Encyclopédie*'s schematic chart, Cochin's allegory does not clearly separate the reasonable sciences from the arts of imagination. Atop his jumble of the arts and sciences one finds, as Diderot put it, 'Truth between Reason and Imagination'. Or, perhaps better said, Truth somewhere between Reason and Imagination. And in Cochin's *Frontispiece* it appears that as Reason acts, Imagination is on the move. The fable I derive from this allegory of truth emphasizes the embellishments that even those who seek knowledge through objective research and reasoned analysis add to whatever truth they find or make. Cochin's allegory suggests – if only inadvertently – that despite the best efforts of reason to rein in passion and strip away interest, imagination – driven by its enthusiasms – will inevitably embellish truth. Imagination acts in spite of reason, and even without realizing it, we are decorating Pompadour with our own favourite flowers.

Notes

Sincere thanks to Katie Scott for inviting me to participate in this volume; her astute comments have greatly improved the essay. I am grateful to my research assistant, Deborah Selinger, for her help in locating sources.

1 For an extended and important discussion of these issues, see Katie Scott, *The Rococo Interior*, London and New Haven, 1995, 166–76.

2 Ewa Lajer-Burcharth has written provocatively about the implications of books and reading in relation to Pompadour. See 'Pompadour's Touch: Difference in Representation', *Representations*, 73, Winter 2001, 54–88. Isabelle de Conihout discusses book collecting in 'Madame de Pompadour bibliophile', in *Madame de Pompadour et les arts*, ed. Xavier Salmon, Paris, 2002, 268–79.

3 Other portraits of Pompadour with books include an undated work by François-Hubert Drouais, *Madame de Pompadour as a Vestal Virgin* (Montréal: David Stewart Museum) as well as two other works by Boucher: a version of the Louvre sketch at Waddesdon Manor, dated to *c.* 1759, and a portrait set out of doors, 1758, in the Victoria and Albert Museum. These are illustrated in Salmon, ed., *Madame de Pompadour et les arts*, 144–66.

4 Robert Darnton, *The Business of Enlightenment: A Publishing History of the Encyclopédie 1775–1800*, Cambridge, Mass., 1979, 33 and 273–4.

5 On Pompadour as a *femme savante*, see Elise Goodman, *The Portraits of Madame de Pompadour: Celebrating the Femme Savante*, Berkeley, 2000. For studies of Pompadour's self-construction, see Melissa Hyde, 'The "Makeup" of the Marquise: Boucher's Portrait of Pompadour at Her Toilette', *Art Bulletin*, 82, September 2000, 453–75. Also, Lajer-Burcharth, 'Pompadour's Touch'.

6 Salmon, ed., *Madame de Pompadour et les arts*, 148.

7 René Martin Dudin, *The Art of the Bookbinder and Gilder*, trans. Richard MacIntyre Atkinson, Leeds, 1977, 52.

8 *'Marbreur de Papier'*, in Denis Diderot and Jean Le Rond d'Alembert, *Encyclopédie, ou Dictionnaire raisonné des sciences, des arts et des métiers, par une société de gens de lettres*, 17 vols, microfiche facsimile of 1751–80 edn, Zug, Switzerland, 1979, 10:72.

9 Dudin explains that 'Although strictly speaking the marbling on covers of books is no more than decoration and in no way strengthens our bindings, our eyes are so used to seeing it there that the work would seem unfinished if absent.' (52) On the history of marbled paper, see Marie-Ange Doizy, *De la dominoterie à la marbrure, histoire des techniques traditionelles de la décoration du papier*, Paris, 1996, and Richard J. Wolfe, *Marbled Paper: its History, Techniques and Patterns*, Philadelphia, 1990.

10 'écrit composé par quelque personne intelligente sur quelque point de science, pour l'instruction & l'amusement du lecteur.' *'Livre'*, in *Encyclopédie*, 9:601.

11 *'Livre'*, in *Encyclopédie*, 9:601.

12 Jean le Rond d'Alembert, *Discours préliminaire de l'encyclopédie*, Paris, 1965.

13 Scott, *The Rococo Interior*, 103.

14 'la partie de l'Architecture la plus intéressante, quoique considérée comme la moins utile relativement à la commodité & à la solidité.' Jean François Blondel, *'Décoration, terme d'Architecture'*, in *Encyclopédie*, 4:702.

15 'J'ai étendu mes soins jusqu'aux choses qui n'étoient qu'accessoires, les Vignettes, les Culs-de-Lampe, les Lettres Griffes dont ces deux Volumes sont embellis, joints à la beauté des Caractères fondus à neuf, aux Reglets, au choix du Papier & à l'Impression, feront sentir aux personnes de l'Art qu'on s'est efforcé de pousser cette entreprise jusqu'au plus haut degré de perfection.' Jean François Blondel, *De la distribution des maisons de plaisance et de la décoration des édificés en général*, 2 vols, Paris: 1737–8; reprinted Farnborough, 1967, 2:v.

16 Antoine Picon, *French Architects and Engineers in the Age of Enlightenment*, trans. Martin Thom, New York, 1992, 47.

17 Darnton, *The Business of Enlightenment*, 274.

18 I am grateful to Katie Scott for this insight.

19 Marc Fumaroli, *L'école du silence*, Paris, 1998, 421.

20 *'Frontispice'*, in Paul Robert, *Le nouveau petit Robert*, revised by Josette Rey-Debove and Alain Rey, Paris, 1995, 979.

21 The example of the 1751–1765 edition found in the University of North Carolina Library lacks a

frontispiece, but instead has a page with the words 'Frontispice de l'Encyclopédie' inserted where a frontispiece would have been placed.

22 'On y voit les Sciences occupées à découvrir la Vérité. La Raison & la Métaphysique cherchent à lui ôter son voile. La Théologie attend sa lumière d'un rayon qui part du Ciel: près d'elle la Mémoire & l'Histoire ancienne & moderne. A côté & audessous sont les Sciences. D'autre part, l'Imagination s'approche avec une guirlande, pour orner la Vérité. Au-dessous d'elle sont les diverses Poésies & les Arts. Au bas sont plusieurs Talens qui dérivent des Sciences & des Arts.' *Explication des peintures, sculptures et gravures de messieurs de l'Académie Royale*, Paris, 1765, 39. There are only a few essays devoted to the frontispiece: Georges May, 'Observations on an Allegory: The Frontispiece of the *Encyclopédie*', in *Diderot Studies*, 16, 1973, 159–74. Christian Michel comments briefly in *Diderot & l'Art de Boucher à David*, Paris, 1984, 494 and in *C.N. Cochin et le livre illustré au XVIIIe siècle*, Geneva, 1987, 284–6.

23 *Encyclopédie, ou Dictionnaire raisonné des sciences, des arts et des métiers, par une société de gens de lettres*, Paris, 1751, n.p.

24 For a discussion of the relation between the fine arts and commerce, see Mary Sheriff, *The Exceptional Woman. Elisabeth Vigée-Lebrun and the Cultural Politics of Art*, Chicago, 1996, 83–90.

25 'A gauche de la Vérité on voit l'Imagination qui se dispose à couronner et à embellir la Vérité.' *Encyclopédie, ou Dictionnaire raisonné*, n.p.

26 'On voit en haut la Vérité, entre la Raison et l'Imagination: la Raison qui cherche à lui arracher son voile, l'Imagination qui se prépare à l'embellir.' Denis Diderot, 'Salon de 1765', in *Oeuvres complètes*, 25 vols, Paris, 1990, 14:319.

27 'L'imagination est à la vérité ce qu'est la parure à une belle personne; elle doit lui prêter tous ses secours pour le fair paraître avec les avantages dont elle est susceptible.' Etienne Bonnot, abbé de Condillac, *Essai sur l'origine des connaissances humaines*, in *Oeuvres complètes*, Paris: 1821–22; reprinted Geneva, 1970, 1:102.

28 'C'est une coquette qui, uniquement occupée du désir de plaire, consulte plus son caprice que la raison.' And 'Son empire finit où celui de l'analise commence.' Condillac, *Essai sur l'origine des connaissances humaines*, 1:100.

29 Picon, *French Architects and Engineers in the Age of Enlightenment*, 90.

30 Hubert Gravelot and Charles Nicolas Cochin, *Iconologie par figures*, 4 vols, Paris, 1791; reprinted Geneva, 1972, 3:1. This work was begun by Hubert Gravelot (1699–1773) and completed by Charles-Nicolas Cochin, fils (1715–1790) and Charles-Etienne Gaucher (1741–1804).

31 Jean-Baptiste Boudard, *Iconologie tirée de divers auteurs*, 3 vols, Vienna, 1766; reprinted New York, 1976, 2:37.

32 Mary D. Sheriff, *Moved by Love: Inspired Artists and Deviant Women in Eighteenth-Century France*, Chicago, 2003, chap. 1.

33 For example, Gianlorenzo Bernini's *Pluto and Persephone*, 1621–22, Rome: Borghese Gallery.

34 For attitudes towards Pompadour, see Thomas Kaiser, 'Madame de Pompadour and the Theaters of Power', *French Historical Studies*, 19, Fall 1996, 1025–1044.

35 Diderot comments on the strength of woman's jealousy in *Sur les femmes* in *Qu'est-ce qu'une femme?'* ed. Elisabeth Badinter, Paris, 1989, 166.

36 D'Alembert, *Discours préliminaire*, 57.

37 D'Alembert, *Discours préliminaire*, 57.

38 D'Alembert, *Discours préliminaire*, 57.

39 For example, Jean-Baptiste, abbé du Bos makes pleasure the central goal of the arts in his *Réflections critiques sur la poésie et sur la peinture*, 1719.

40 'Dans la poésie, dans la peinture, dans tous les arts qui parlent à l'imagination, & dont le but est d'instruire & de plaire, c'est toujours sous le voile de l'allégorie que le morale présente aux hommes des vérités consolantes, des préceptes utiles, & l'histoire emprunte souvent la même langage pour conserver la mémoire d'un évènement, consacrer un fait héroïque, immortaliser une action généreuse.' Gravelot and Cochin, *Iconologie*, I:v.

41 'c'est ajoûter avec art à des objets qui seroient peut-être indifférens par eux-mêmes, des formes ou des accessoires qui les rendent intéressans, agréables, précieux, etc.' *'Embellir'*, in *Encyclopédie*, 5:555.

42 'ce qui sert à parer une chose, quelle qu'elle soit. Le grand principe c'est que les parties essentielles & principales se tournent en ornemens; cars alors le spectateur qui voit l'utile servir de base à l'agréable, est affecté le plus doucement qu'il est possible.' *'Ornement'*, in *Encyclopédie*, 11:657.

43 Gravelot and Cochin, *Iconologie*, 4:119.

44 Gravelot and Cochin, *Iconologie*, 4:119.

45 'Quand l'homme est corrumpu, tu dois être voilée/Ma très auguste soeur, l'âge d'or est passé/Ne vas point prêcher ainsi nue/si tu prétends grossir ta cour.' Claude Joseph Dorat, *Fables nouvelles*, The Hague, 1773, fable 1.

46 *Mercure de France*, for example, noted that La Tour had made a painting of the greatest beauty, with details and ornaments well finished (November 1755), 182. *L'Année littéraire* praised the light effects and details rendered in such a way as to be perfectly illusionistic. Elie Catherine Fréron, *L'Année littéraire*, 16 vols, Paris, 1751–89, 1755, 54.

47 Estève, *Seconde lettre à un partisan du bon goût*, Paris, 1755, Deloynes, vol 6, pièce 75, 5–6.

48 Estève, *Seconde lettre à un partisan du bon goût*, Paris, 1755, Deloynes, vol 6, pièce 75, 5–6.

3

THE *ENCYCLOPÉDIE* AND THE IDEA OF THE DECORATIVE ARTS

ÉLISABETH LAVEZZI

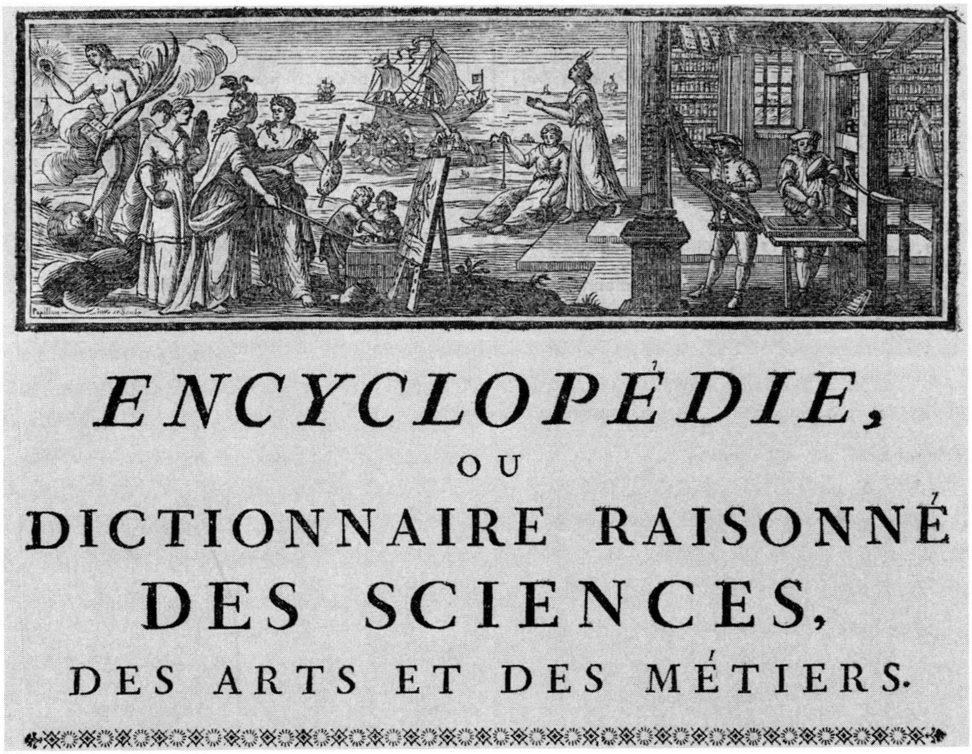
ENCYCLOPÉDIE,
OU
DICTIONNAIRE RAISONNÉ
DES SCIENCES,
DES ARTS ET DES MÉTIERS.

3.1 Jean-Baptiste-Michel Papillon, Headpiece from the title page of volume 1 of the *Encyclopédie, ou Dictionnaire raisonné des sciences, des arts et des metiers*, Paris, 1751–1780. Woodcut. London: The London Library.

In the eighteenth century the phrase 'decorative arts' did not exist, nor the idea that it now expresses. Nevertheless, those arts that are today so-called – such as cabinet-making, weaving, metalwork, or porcelain – were practised with exquisite refinement. Despite their presence, these arts were neither named nor conceptualized as 'decorative', and thus they were absent, as such, from the tree of knowledge and the entries that together constitute Denis Diderot's and Jean le Rond d'Alembert's *Encyclopédie ou Dictionnaire raisonné des sciences, des arts et des metiers* (1751–80).[1] This essay contends that 'decorative art' is more than a simple descriptor or qualifier, one tag among many (mechanical arts, applied arts, minor arts, crafts, design). Its emergence marked the surfacing of a particular sphere of activity and a particular order of knowledge, and ultimately registered a shift of attention from objects to processes and to labour. The first faltering steps of this shift are explained here through the juxtaposition of the 'Enlightened' texts and plates of the *Encyclopédie* with the Renaissance writing of Vasari and the Baroque opinion of Félibien, and through the definition of two arts, mosaic and marquetry. Not until the nineteenth century did the separate constituents of decoration and art, severally present in the *Encyclopédie*, come together in the term 'decorative art(s)'.

Maximilien Littré's was apparently the first dictionary (1877) to record the phrase 'decorative art'; even then it did so under the heading DÉCORATIF[2] rather than ART. ART referred to 'beaux-arts', 'liberal arts' and 'mechanical arts'. The reluctance to consider the 'decorative arts' as equivalent to these other arts did not forestall debate in the nineteenth and twentieth centuries;[3] the unwillingness to use this aesthetic category is marked, in fact, by the proliferation of other, more or less synonymous, phrases: 'minor arts, applied arts, industrial arts, design'. Definitions of 'decorative art[s]' given in dictionaries have often been tautological and have generally failed to distinguish them from the mechanical arts, the liberal arts and the beaux-arts.[4] Étienne Souriau, for example, explained in 1990 that 'Today we call "decorative arts" those activities which organise the architecture of the interior by creating furniture, wall-hangings, panelling, flooring ... with everyday or elite living in mind.'[5] In ART, he defined them in opposition to the beaux-arts and assimilated them into the minor arts. Lastly, in MINEUR he set forth the two premises upon which their lowly status depended: 'The first is that of an inferiority of the artisan, a manual worker in relation to the artist who practises a liberal art.' 'The second is that of an inferiority of arts applied to utilitarian objects in relation to the noble arts which have only aesthetic value as their end.' *The Oxford Companion to the Decorative Arts* (1975) proposes a conventional definition: 'those arts which are made to serve a practical purpose but are nevertheless prized for the quality of their workmanship and the beauty of their appearance'.[6] Paul Rouaix's *Dictionnaire des arts décoratifs* of 1890 was the first of its kind in France and provides a comprehensive list of those arts from *ameublement* (furniture) to *vitraux* (glass).[7]

Did the *Encyclopédie* anticipate the concept of 'decorative arts'? Did it create some of the conditions that fostered its emergence? In answering these questions I will not be analysing the notion of the decorative arts as expressed in the *Encyclopédie*, but rather the conditions that prepared the way for its conceptualization. Nor will I be reconstructing the history of its formation, but speculating on certain aspects of its pre-history – because details read with hindsight (by present-day readers conversant with the idea of the decorative arts) may be interpreted as precursory signs.

'*DÉCORATEUR*' AND '*DÉCORATION*' IN THE *ENCYCLOPÉDIE*

The *Encyclopédie* aspired above all to be a useful work, open to consultation on almost any matter. In re-reading it today it is worth remembering that even though all the articles belonging to the same field came under the editorial control of Denis Diderot, the same author did not necessarily write them all. The aim of utility, in the form of a comprehensive body of fact, did not, therefore, necessarily deliver a united body of opinion. Indeed, the multi-authored nature of the enterprise often gave rise to tensions between and within entries.[8] When a single term had different meanings in disparate contexts, the entry eschewed a comprehensive overview providing instead differently authored parts, such as decoration in poetry, theatre and architecture. This kind of polyphony marks its style of writing, and they are pertinent to this account. Sharply juxtaposed bodies of textual and visual evidence generate an argument by forced contrast or unmediated conjunction. Capitalization of the subject of entries is retained here to remind the reader of the authoritive but fragmented nature of the discourse under study.

DÉCORATEUR, written by Louis de Cahusac, was defined in the restricted sense of designer for the theatre and public festivals.[9] Although the theatre is not within the scope of this study, two features of this entry stand out because they have since been applied to practitioners of the so-called 'decorative arts'. First, the set designer is defined as '*experienced* in drawing, painting, sculpture, architecture and perspective' (4:700). This definition takes up conventional wisdom, according to which the set designer must know all the arts of design, but it adds one qualification; by recourse to 'experience' it implies that, in the formation of knowledge, practice surpasses theory in importance. Secondly, the set designer is said to 'invent *or* [...] execute'; the alternative is surprising. The verbs refer back, of course, to invention and execution, two dimensions of painting that the painter *must* undertake; but the 'or', which splits this complementary duo, restricts the set designer to one or the other. Moreover, in the case of 'to invent', invention is understood in conjunction with experience (conventional practice), thus considerably weakening the status of the analogy of the set designer as painter. The set designer's role model (the painter) was more distantly removed than may first have appeared. Though the set designer 'executes and composes works of painted architecture' (4:700), and though 'to compose' invokes 'composition', another dimension of painting, de Cahusac means 'to place the works on the stage or to arrange them at festivals'. Thus, DÉCORATEUR articulates an ambivalent relationship to the pictorial prototype: it borrows it, divides it, and alters its focus. These semantic shifts and tensions are also to be found in the case of some of those arts thereafter defined as decorative.

Moving from the 'actor' to the action of DÉCORATION, what can be learned from the three authors – de Cahusac, Jean-François Marmontel and Jacques-François Blondel – who defined it for the *Encyclopédie*? In relation to literature, the writer Marmontel explained that decoration represents the place of dramatic action; it follows the principles of architecture, perspective and design and aims at the imitation of nature's beauty; again, painting constitutes a significant model (4:700–1). De Cahusac, writing on the set design (*décoration*) of the opera continued in the same vein: 'invention, design and painting form its three principle elements.' But by adding that 'the set-designer, whatever genius one can attribute to him, only invents according to the outline given' by the poet (that is to say, according to the plot), he reiterated a prejudice that the set designer is a mere collaborator of the second order (4:701). These two subsections of the entry reinforce the idea that decoration – in literature and at the opera – was doubly subordinate: in *borrowing* from the arts of drawing, it cannot be their equal; in coming into play *after* the poet's intervention, it has to be executed in keeping with his invention.

The third subsection by Blondel (remembered principally for his writings rather than his buildings) concerned architecture. His entry on ARCHITECTURE had in fact referred the reader to DÉCORATION, among other cross-references. As Mary Sheriff indicates elsewhere in this volume, decoration was an important element of architecture and it laid claim to four types of space: the façade, the garden, the theatre and the domestic interior. The last instance was a matter of 'interior decoration' and concerned 'the richness of the materials, the magnificence of the furniture, sculpture, painting, bronzes, mirrors'; such enumeration of objects suggests a relation between interior decoration and those arts later termed decorative, but a relation that fell somewhat short of assimilation because the latter are both more numerous and differently conceived. Blondel's list may also appear heterogeneous: fine arts (painting and sculpture) mixed with arts that, in accordance with common usage, the *Encyclopédie* qualified as mechanical (the arts of furniture, bronze-making and mirror manufacture).[10] Did this heterogeneity generate the conditions that would foster the reordering of knowledge in the direction of the idea of the decorative arts?

An answer is suggested by the remark: 'we understand by this noun (*décoration*) *the most* interesting element of architecture *despite* its consideration as *the least* useful.'[11] The paradox is due, among other things, to the way in which Blondel modified the usual formulation of the end of art as 'useful and pleasing'. By substituting 'interesting' for 'pleasing', he introduced the perspective of the artist alongside that of the viewer: decoration, which is of little use to those who occupy the interiors, is very interesting to the artist and to the architect. By substituting 'despite' for 'and', by introducing inversely proportional superlatives ('the most/the least') and by revising a statement (to understand/to consider), he bore witness to a feature specific to decoration that distinguished it from the other components of architecture. Whereas architecture defines itself by its utility, decoration, one of its constituents, turns its back on necessity and distances itself from it. If, according to Blondel, decoration belonged to architecture, his paradoxical formulation allows one to suppose that he may have doubted it; moreover, the adjective 'interesting' is sufficiently vague to provide decoration with the means of detaching itself from architecture. The complexity implicit in this definition, according to which decoration's specificity borders on autonomy, announces the emergence of the idea of the decorative arts and constitutes one of the necessary conditions for it. Does the *Encyclopédie* contain other indications of the same order? A comprehensive answer is beyond the scope of this essay, but some observations are offered on cases where the encyclopedic discourse falters.

FORMULATING KNOWLEDGE IN THE *ENCYCLOPÉDIE*

Jean le Rond d'Alembert, after having explained the 'genealogy and interrelations of our knowledge' in the *Discours préliminaire* (1751) of the *Enyclopédie*, then modified his reasoning: abandoning diachrony for synchrony, he adopted a 'general perspective'.[12] He reverted to a distinction between sciences and arts:[13] 'Speculation and practice constitute the principle difference that distinguishes the Sciences from the Arts';[14] the arts being 'purely practical have the execution of something as their aim', the sciences being 'simply speculative limit themselves to the examination of their object and to the contemplation of its properties.'[15] Jean-Baptiste-Michel Papillon alludes to the dichotomy in his design of the *Dictionnaire*'s headpiece (plate 3.2): figures of Theory (her dividers upon her brow, open to the heavens) and Practice (her dividers in her hand, tracing forms upon the ground) occupy the centre of a composition in which Minerva presides over the representation of knowledge and printers attend to its reproduction and dissemination. But this binary division is at the same time brought into question by a particular category of knowledge mixed by nature: it 'uses speculative study of its object to extrapolate the purpose one can make of it in practice' and corresponds to the liberal arts. A duality is thus replaced by a trilogy: sciences, liberal arts and mechanical arts.[16] Next, within the parameters of the liberal arts, d'Alembert circumscribes the category of the fine arts, characterized by the 'imitation' of nature.[17] This way of rationalizing knowledge does not afford anything original, and the entries in the *Encyclopédie* devoted to those arts now called decorative were largely classified amongst the mechanical arts. However, the incorporation of the idea of the fine arts, expounded by the abbé Charles Batteux in 1746,[18] shows that the categorization of knowledge was sufficiently elastic to incorporate microsystems, albeit with some adjustments. Had the decorative arts existed as a category, it is likely that they, too, would have had a place in this prefatory discourse because its narrative was synchronic, took account of mixed cases and embraced the new.

The division of knowledge performed by the *Discours préliminaire*, though not foundational to the encyclopedic system, was nevertheless occasionally present; thus, the mechanical arts were categorized under the branch of history, and the fine arts under the branch of poetry. Where would the decorative arts have featured? The question is less meaningless than it may first appear; it is not a matter of imagining an answer but of noting that, if the question is raised at all, it is because something *in* the system makes it pertinent.

Diderot and d'Alembert tabulated their division of knowledge in a 'Système figurée' and acknowledged their debt in this to Francis Bacon from whom they borrowed the idea of an arrangement by reference to the faculties of human understanding (plate 3.3): Memory from which arises history, Reason from which philosophy, Imagination from which poetry, in the broader sense of fiction. They felt free to modify the borrowing by addition – of 'a very great number of things [. . .] which [they] owe not in the least to Bacon' – and redistribution – 'All the

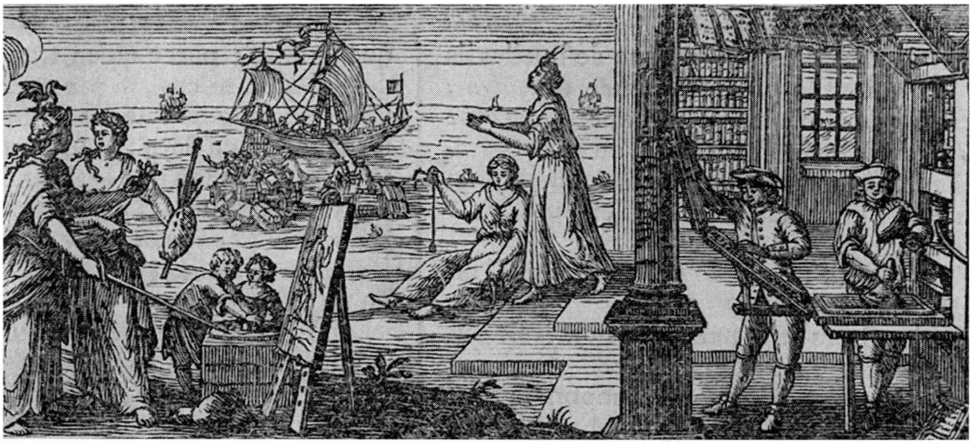

3.2 Detail of Jean-Baptiste-Michel Papillon, Headpiece, *Encyclopédie, ou Dictionnaire raisonné des sciences, des arts et des metiers*. The London Library.

encyclopaedic trees necessarily resemble one another; only the order and the arrangement of the branches distinguishes them.'[19]

If Bacon arranged 'History, Poetry and Philosophy' sequentially,[20] the editors of the *Encyclopédie* reversed the order of Reason and Imagination. D'Alembert justified this as follows. First, imagination [poetry] was redefined and limited to the creative faculty: 'We take imagination in a *nobler* and *more precise* sense, meaning the talent of *creation through imitation*.'[21] Secondly, the three faculties were classed according to their progressive complexity, understood in terms of the cumulative anterior stages, and by the addition of a new feature; thus imagination annexed 'Reason and Memory'[22] and secured a monopoly on creation through imitation. This progression from the simple to the complex instituted a scale of values. Shifting and redefining imagination allowed it to be grafted onto the branch of the fine arts. The *Encyclopédie* famously mounted a defence of the mechanical arts, but also elevated the status of the creative imagination and, with it, the 'fine arts'.[23] Precisely because the *Encyclopédie* adopted new things and

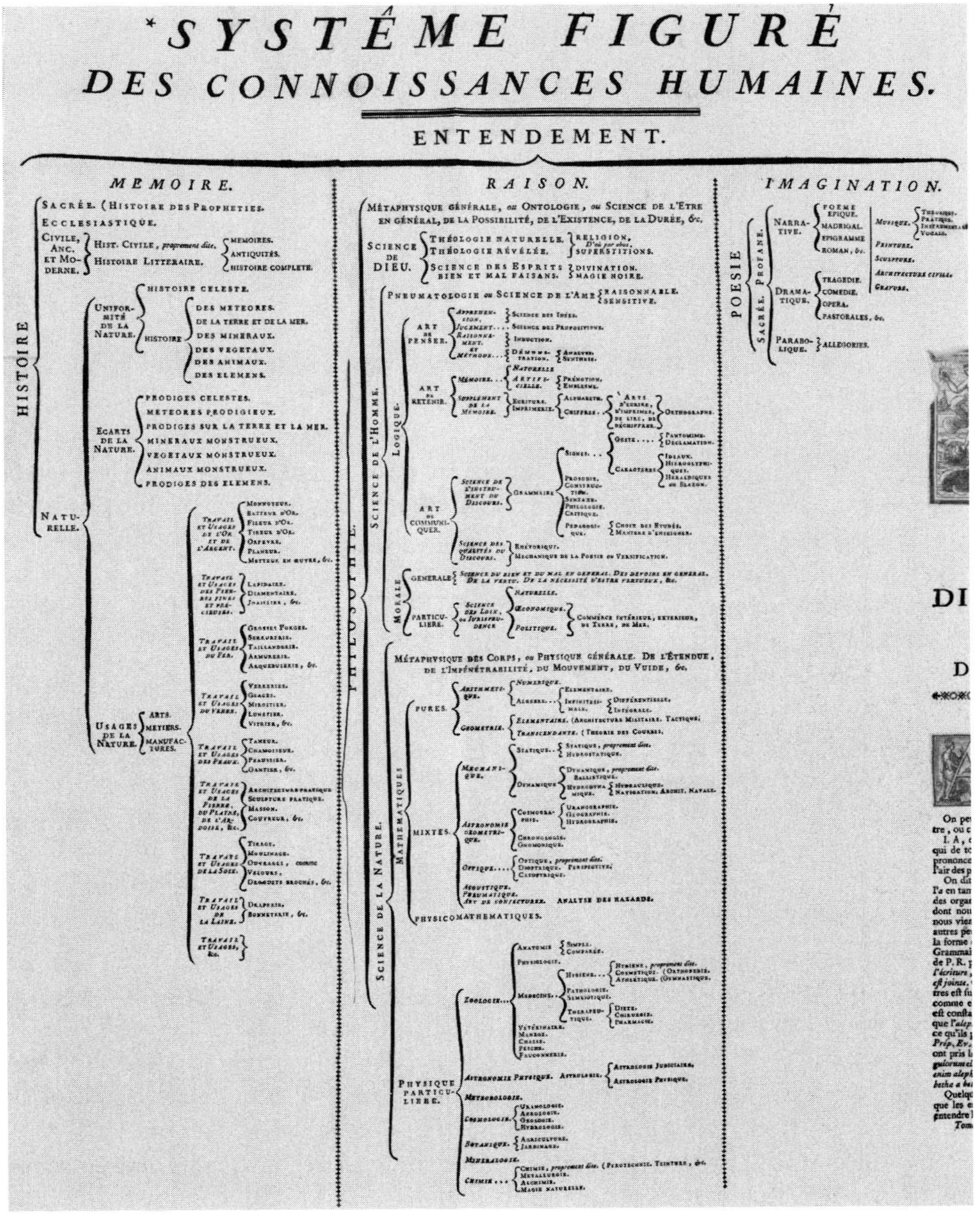

3.3 'Système figuré des connoissances humaines', *Encyclopédie, ou Dictionnaire raisonné des sciences, des arts et des métiers*, Paris, 1751–1780, vol 1. London: The London Library.

incorporated redistributions, its 'tree' was potentially flexible, organic and simultaneously responsive to cumulative and evolutionary change.

It adopted, for instance, the microsystem of the fine arts that Batteux had established in *Les beaux-arts reduits à un même principe* (1746) and which the *Encyclopédie* could ignore only at the risk of elaborating a tree of knowledge that was already obsolete. Paul Oskar Kristeller has explained the debt to Batteux: he 'distinguished the beaux arts – whose end is pleasure – from the mechanical arts, and drew up the following list of the former: music, poetry, painting, sculpture and dance.'[24] Kristeller demonstrates how the *Encyclopédie* took up Batteux's system, modified it and established another slightly different system: 'although certain turns of phrase and the retention of the principle of imitation attested to his dependence on Batteux, d'Alembert differed from him [...] in including architecture amongst the imitative arts [...] The *Encyclopédie* [...] was to codify the system of the fine arts in following and surpassing Batteux.'[25] He notes that while Batteux retained dance, d'Alembert excluded it and instead added architecture. In the mid-eighteenth century the idea of the fine arts comprised a fixed core of those arts that featured on both authors' lists with a soft periphery that varied by author (arts sometimes retained, sometimes dismissed). This hesitation is implicit in the *Encyclopédie* itself, for Diderot opened a space of indecision in the figurative system: not only did he retain print-making which d'Alembert had excluded from the *Discours préliminaire*, but he also refused, by means of an 'etcetera',[26] to close the list of the arts pretending to the elevated status of fine art. The contradictory status of engraving, included in/excluded from the fine arts in the *Encyclopédie*, shows that its list was not definitive. Through these slight discrepancies fissures begin to appear in the *Encyclopédie*'s system.

Architecture's inclusion in the category of the fine arts can be explained by the legacy of a tradition that associated it with painting and sculpture, that of the arts of drawing. The relative heterogeneity of the 'poetry' branch was not a result of the simple addition of architecture to the fine arts, but of their configuration as the three arts of design. In the 'Introduction to the Three Arts of Design', at the beginning of the chapter 'Of Painting' in *Le Vite*, Vasari dubs drawing 'the parent of our three arts, architecture, sculpture and painting'[27] thus uniting the three in a common source of origin. In the seventeenth century the trio was adopted in France; and André Félibien brought together architecture, sculpture and painting for discussion in a single work, *Principes de l'architecture, de la sculpture, de la peinture et des arts qui en dépendent* of 1676.[28]

However, the *Encyclopédie*'s combination of Vasari's trio (united by design) and Batteux's system (formed according to the imitation of 'la belle nature') was not without a heterogeneity which gave rise to reservations. Thus, d'Alembert remarked that 'architecture [...] limits itself to imitating, through the assembly and the union of the different bodies it employs, the symmetrical arrangement which nature observes *more or less approximately* in each individual [...].'[29] And Diderot repeated in the *Explanation*: the architect 'only imitates nature *imperfectly* by the symmetry of its structures.'[30] Of course, the fine arts imitate nature, but one of them does so 'imperfectly', or 'more or less approximately': the imitation of nature was a requirement that played its part fully or conditionally. The *Encyclopédie* was, at the cost of friction, capable of combining small groups of ideas in such a way that consideration of a category based on first principles could stand alongside one not so defined.

THE DEPENDENT ARTS: MOSAIC AND MARQUETRY

In Félibien's *Principes* the three arts of drawing form a close unity to which others are related more loosely – 'the arts which depend upon them', as the title of Félibien's work indicated. 'Dependence'[31] was similarly used by Blondel in ARCHITECTURE, when he referred explicitly to entries on 'arts which depend on architecture, such as SCULPTURE, PAINTING, GILDING, MASONRY, CARPENTRY, JOINERY etc.', and it remains implicit in DÉCORATION, where he enumerated the components of the interior. The following hypothesis can thus be advanced: that the idea of the dependent arts was the precursor of the idea of the decorative arts.

A point of clarification is necessary; it might be tempting to suppose that the idea of interior decoration was synonymous with that of the decorative arts, but this conclusion would be rather premature. If it is true that these two ideas not only had common referents but also articulated in themselves the beautiful and the useful, in which resided their specificity, it is no less true that ways of thinking of interior decoration in the eighteenth century were dependent on certain assumptions. Not the least among them was the belief that decoration *belonged* to architecture, one of the trio arts of drawing, the existence of the category of dependent arts, arts which were thus conceived without thought of their autonomy; and the fact that one art, such as joinery, was annexed to architecture and another, such as marquetry, to painting, without their similarities seemingly counted as significant.[32] It will be necessary to remain alert to the perspective implied by the articulation of these ideas and the prejudices that support them, as my hypothesis is refined: these assumptions about place and belonging acted to defer the emergence of the *idea* of the decorative arts, an idea which, in spite of its ambiguity, takes autonomy as a necessary and sufficient condition of its existence. It is implausible that one word should replace another without consequence. Rather than analysing all arts dependent on interior decoration, itself an element of architecture, indeed of the arts of design, two instances – mosaic and marquetry – along with shifts of their meaning in Vasari, Félibien and the *Encyclopédie* will be traced. Far from providing a general definition of artistic dependence, what follows offers focused analysis of these particular cases.

When Vasari introduced the plan of his chapter on painting, he used the verb '*dipendere*' (to depend) to designate the relationship between that art and its satellites: 'Ultimately, in talking about painting, I shall speak [. . .] of any thing that upon it depends; mosaics of all kinds, enamels, tapestry, and finally reproductive prints.' (38) However, as he passes over in silence the exact meaning of dependence, the analysis of an example may provide clarification.

Mosaic, a paradoxical case, is of particular interest. Introduced as dependent on painting, occupying chapters 29–31 of *Le Vite*, it first appears in chapter 6, devoted to architecture. Can an art thus depend on two forms of drawing simultaneously? In fact, mosaic did not sustain the same dependence on architecture as it did on painting. In the chapter devoted to mosaic in part one, on architecture, Vasari claimed that, originally, the Ancients imagined tiling floors with different stones arranged in patterns in order to please. This first stage constituted a sort of prehistory, and proto-mosaic formed a type of flooring in the service of architecture. Its particularity lay in its will to charm. At a second stage, according to Vasari, the medium of mosaic became precious and mosaic emerged as a speciality of baths. Most importantly, colours now accompanied line, which up until then had alone been used, and seen from afar, its colours gave such an impression of continuity – 'imitating painting with various kinds of colours' (59) – that henceforth mosaic was used on walls and archways. By moving into colour and assuming verticality, mosaic took painting as its model. As a result it moved from dependence on architecture to dependence on painting. But in the process a change in the meaning of dependence had occurred: from an art in the service of architecture, it became an art which took painting as its model. This transfer and this transformation were fundamental to mosaic's re-conceptualization and its status, for mosaic seemingly got the upper hand on painting by its superior solidity.

Stage three: mosaic proliferates. There was an expansion in the range of materials used (glass and eggshell as well as marble) and in pictorial models (grisaille, or the imitation of sculpture, was added to the polychrome of painting). It was only at this point that Vasari invited the reader to make the transition from the part on architecture to that devoted to painting. Abandoning the preformed, he turned his attention to the accomplished mosaic (in the sense of a work both complete and completed well) and defined the meaning of its dependence on painting: it required design as intellectual activity as much as drawing as manual reproduction. 'In this type of work both practical experience and great judgement are necessary, along with a thorough understanding of the art of design.' (87) Furthermore, it borrowed as analogy the cartoon (whose method and use is explained in chapter 16) from fresco painting. In this case, to depend on painting meant to borrow its lines and colours, its thought and a method. If proto-mosaic served architecture, mosaic copied painting: the dependence is as much polysemic as polymorphous.

Marquetry, the second case, and grisaille tiling, two branches related to mosaic, revived the question of dependence as imitation. Whilst the latter directly imitated painting, the former, more complex, only had painting as a model via the intermediary of mosaic because, as Vasari expresses it, marquetry is 'similar to mosaic *and* painting' (89). This imitation at one remove – marquetry imitates mosaic which imitates painting – distanced the dependent art from the art which furnished the prime model and weakened the link of dependence; which is why marquetry, retaining only the letter, and not the spirit of painting, required 'more patience than draftsmanship' (90). Loan without guarantee is the risk run by second-degree dependence. On the one hand, a *mechanical* art works its way towards an *art* of drawing by taking it as a model; it undergoes a metamorphosis and a promotion, as Vasari's account of the formation of the mosaic shows. On the other hand, an art that takes as its model an art that has in turn taken one of the arts of drawing as a model, can fail in its project of imitation and be defined by that failure. It was in line with its direct or mediated relation to the model that a dependent art failed or succeeded, justified its promotion, or established its mediocrity. Sometimes status-enhancing, sometimes demeaning, dependence was always ambivalent.

According to the analysis offered above, the arts that depend on the arts of drawing were divided into at least two groups, according to the meaning assumed by dependence. One group included those which served the arts of drawing, the other those which imitated them; it is the second group which is relevant to this essay. Dependence, as Vasari used it, without explicit definition, delimited in the particular cases of mosaic and marquetry a mixed zone which covers, according to the *Encyclopédie*'s classification, part of the mechanical arts and part of the fine arts; this zone comes under the former category through its requirement of manual labour and it participates in the latter in the imitation of their effects. This reinforces the hypothesis that the so-called dependent arts that imitated an art of drawing (painting, sculpture, architecture) prefigured the decorative arts, all the more so as certain arts, which were first classed as dependent arts by Vasari and later classed as decorative arts, constituted a single set.

By entitling his work *Principes de l'architecture, de la sculpture, de la peinture et des arts qui en dépendent*, Félibien was referring to the Vasarian arrangement of the three arts of drawing and their dependencies. Félibien, who borrowed the verb 'to depend' from the Italian author, enlarged its frame of reference, because he applied it not only to the satellites of painting (as did Vasari) but also to those of the other two: sculpture and architecture. In the preface, he defined the meaning of dependence: the dependent arts 'are *as though* subordinated'[33] to one or more of the three arts of drawing. Does the case of mosaic support this?

Félibien, who often paraphrased Vasari, also modified him in several places. The first change to note is the detachment of mosaic from architecture. Contrary to Vasari, Félibien did not mention mosaic in chapter 17 ('Paving and Tiling') of Book I, on architecture, but introduced it in chapters 11–14 of Book III, on painting. This was to insist that mosaic depends uniquely on painting. In chapter 11, 'Of Mosaic', Félibien summarized Vasari's chapter 6 on ornamental tiling in architecture and chapter 29, where Vasari explained mosaic in terms of painting. The second change concerns the radicalization of certain propositions. Having established the principle of human progress, Félibien used the invention and development of mosaic to illustrate it, subject to two conditions: it was necessary for painting to be constituted as such and for the desire for its survival to give rise to creativity. That which for Vasari constituted the triumph of mosaic – its longevity compared to painting – became for Félibien its aim.

His account unfolds in three stages. In the first, ornamental tiling arranged in patterns suggested a reduction in the size of tiles and the exploitation of their colour: the mosaic as process is elaborated. Mosaic does not achieve the status of a dependent art until stage two, with the intervention of the artist: 'such a beautiful invention gave *painters* the desire to make something more substantial.' (438) Two consequences followed. One was a fundamental shift: mosaic, having become a mural decoration, was henceforth 'seen from afar and from the front'. The other involved technical progress: pieces of enamel and glass were manufactured in order to obtain more colours 'which imitate painting better'. Consecration, the third stage, occurred when the fixed *a-priori* aim was achieved: 'this work surpasses all forms of painting which time effaces and destroys whereas, on the contrary, time embellishes mosaic, which survives for so long.' (439) The account of mosaic's invention and of its orbit of painting is followed by a description of it in which painting again plays the role of model. Thus, the colours of the manufactured glass were broken down into shades 'as in mixing the colours on the palette in order to paint in oils'; the pieces were arranged in a certain order 'as in painting in fresco'; finally, '[. . .] in order to compose a mosaic, first one makes a cartoon, or a drawing which one traces [. . .] in parts as when one is painting in fresco.' (440–1) Certain works are 'as finished as frescoes' and 'one can never see the end of it.' (441) Reference to painting is thus fundamental to mosaic's definition.

The case study of mosaic allows dependence or 'subordination' to be given a fairly precise meaning, the implications of which are many. Painting must have prior existence in order to give birth to mosaic – chronology is doubled by conditional logic. Painting provides a model that mosaic uses. On the one hand, mosaic appropriates the role of the painter – his or her identity as an agent. On the other, it assumes various characteristics of painting, such as ornamental function, spatial disposition (vertical and at a distance), division and classification of colour, and the procedure of tracing from the cartoon. By seeking to copy the model as faithfully as possible, the dependent art improves upon it, goes beyond it, even though this reversal remains confined to a material quality – solidity. If Vasari provided the rational grounding of the ideas, Félibien elaborated upon the notion of dependence by recourse to a comparison which, in relating the dependent art to a model and not just a support, conflated dependence and subordination. Was a hierarchy of arts not taking shape?

For Félibien three arts are linked to mosaic. *Rocaille*, or shell-work (chapter 13), a second-degree dependent art that prompted the praise of Thetis's grotto at Versailles; pictorial mosaic (chapter 12), which depended directly on painting – these are 'pictures which seem to be painted' (444) – and marquetry. Of course, the cabinet-makers (workers who practised marquetry, as distinct from the joinery of veneer, which is classified in architecture, chapter 19) used 'woods of different colours to imitate painting' (450–1) and cut out shapes following the design which 'sometimes [they] wash and put in colour' (453), but that did not suffice to elevate them to the rank of painting. Félibien adopts one of Vasari's uncertainties; he judges that 'this work requires patient rather than learned workers, because it requires a lot of time.' He qualifies Vasari's reflection by establishing two types of worker, one who 'follows the designs he is given' and one who has more ability in 'drawing, and some knowledge of painting' (450); the extra skill notwithstanding, never in his eyes is the cabinet-maker a painter. He does not cloud the issue with ambiguities: 'When these same workers represent some figure naturally [. . .] *they call* it painting in wood. And those who work in that manner *pretend* that these types of works are equal to canvases and *describe themselves* as painters and sculptors in mosaic.' (452–3) The representation of nature, even the depiction of the human figure, does not alter marquetry's nature – it remains a dependent art.

Finally, Félibien notes, unlike Vasari, that marquetry decorates 'tables', 'beds' and 'other furniture' (450). The information is vital, because this art, which is governed by the pictorial model, makes objects that are destined for use. From which observation an implicit consequence arises: the worker who makes this type of furniture has a unique status; without being a painter he can have knowledge of painting, and he has to make furniture without limiting himself to the purely practical. He practises a mechanical art in a way that is partially the concern of one of the fine arts; in short, he oscillates between the 'no more' and the 'not yet'. The case of marquetry on furniture, where the subordination to painting necessarily combines with guardianship of the functional, is particularly revealing of the status of the dependent arts. Weakly determined by Félibien, this very indeterminacy was – because of its flexibility – a potential advantage.

If Félibien's discourse leaves us anticipating a problem, it also reveals its limits: he introduced the marquetry worker under the yoke of painting, without thought of the objects he made as such. The idea of dependence produced a discourse on marquetry which ignores furniture's own requirements. The *Encyclopédie* modified this approach and contributed to the development that led, more than a century later, to the idea of decorative art. For Félibien, marquetry, even though it was broadly thought of as depending on painting, betrays a detail that, through the *Encyclopédie*, points the way towards that autonomy necessary to the decorative arts so defined.

MOSAIC AND MARQUETRY IN THE *ENCYCLOPÉDIE*

The conventional distribution of the arts of drawing and the dependent arts recurs in certain entries of the *Encyclopédie* but it coexists with another conceptualization.[34] MOSAÏQUE consists of two parts, the first by J.-R. Lucotte, the second by the abbé Louis de Jaucourt (10: 745–50). The latter introduces 'mosaic in painting' without explicitly employing the phrase 'dependent art' and while recycling old ideas. De Jaucourt explains why mosaic is annexed to painting without

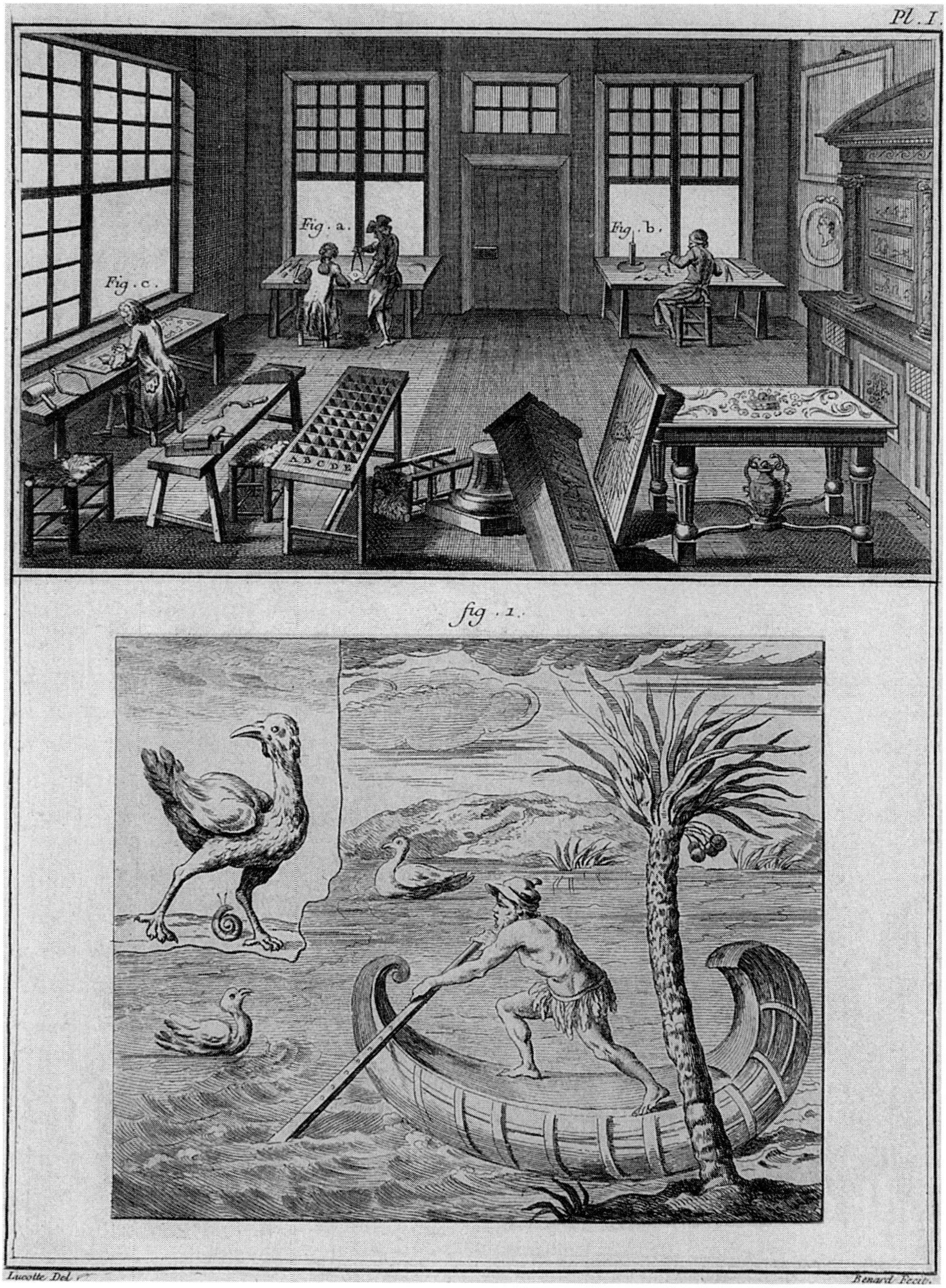

3.4 Benard, after J.-R. Lucotte, 'Mosaïque', *Encyclopédie, ou Dictionnaire raisonné des sciences, des arts et des métiers*, Paris, 1751–1780, plate 1 from vol. 8, *Receuil de planches*. Engraving. London: The London Library. The caption notes that the upper part 'represents a workshop where several artisans work on mosaic; those at *a* are occupied in tracing the little pieces of marble according to the places where they will be deployed; another *b* is busy polishing them and a third *c* is assembling them to create pictures, portraits, etc.'

being assimilated by it: it is a 'type of painting' that has recourse to cartoons (10:749). And yet it has been abandoned because 'it is impossible to imitate with stones and pieces of glass [. . .] all the subtleties of the brush.' (10:750) Something of its alleged crudeness is evident in the design of 'a landscape representing a fisherman on a boat on the Nile' that illustrates MOSAÏQUE (fig. 1, here plate 3.4): perspective and scale are not respected – the birds are too large in relation to the man and do not recede into the distance – and the boat is a stylized motif.[35] However, according to de Jaucourt, the failure of mosaic was due to a more fundamental fault: the 'lack of union and accord of colours'. Consequently, he says, 'it only produces its effect (only) from a distance.' (10:750) This conclusion is paradoxical because the cause to which failure is attributed by de Jaucourt (the necessity of distant viewing), was, for Vasari, an important reason, which had contributed to its having become a dependent of painting. Notwithstanding its banality, the part written by de Jaucourt shows that mosaic, as an art which depends on painting, fails. To consider an art as the unsuccessful imitation of a model necessarily brings about an impasse; de Jaucourt's remarks suppose that dependence should be understood as an essentially evaluative and largely non-definitional category, and, consequently, that mosaic had been unable to adapt.

Lucotte, meanwhile, totally altered the approach to mosaic, an art that he classed as mechanical. He defined it by describing the three stages of its production, and recalled, finally, that mosaic tends to 'create pictures representing [. . .] all sorts of designs imitating painting' (10:745). In relegating painting to the background, Lucotte indicated that he did not approach mosaic, fundamentally, as a dependent art – even if, in an historical section, it was still designated as 'a way of painting' (10:745). He reiterated the couplet of tiling and mosaic but instead of following Vasari's account, in which one begot the other, he arranged them synchronically: the mosaicists, who practise the 'art of making paintings in stones', are related to the paviours or stone-cutters who make 'sections of paving' (10:745). In order to describe mosaic, he gave priority to the knowledge of types of marble and referred to two other entries for which he was responsible, MASONRY and STONE-CUTTER: mosaic and stone-cutting are branches of masonry, defined as the use and manner of employing stone (9:803). Mosaic was a mechanical art, a category that was linked – by definition, that is – by its materials, its methods and its works, to masonry and stone-cutting. Of course, the boldness of the encyclopedic enterprise – which aimed to elevate the status of the mechanical arts – is evident in this reasoning, but it amounts to more than that, as that would be to deny that the pictorial model endures in mosaic, even though it has been relegated to the background, and that, as has been seen, creative imagination has a price.

If de Jaucourt, anchored in the past, saw mosaic – still – as a dependent art, but one that failed necessarily, Lucotte, attached to the present, saw it as a mechanical art, but one that continued to imitate one of the arts of drawing. No classification fits. The coexistence and concurrence, within the same entry, of two versions of the same referent is symptomatic of an anxiety accelerating into crisis.

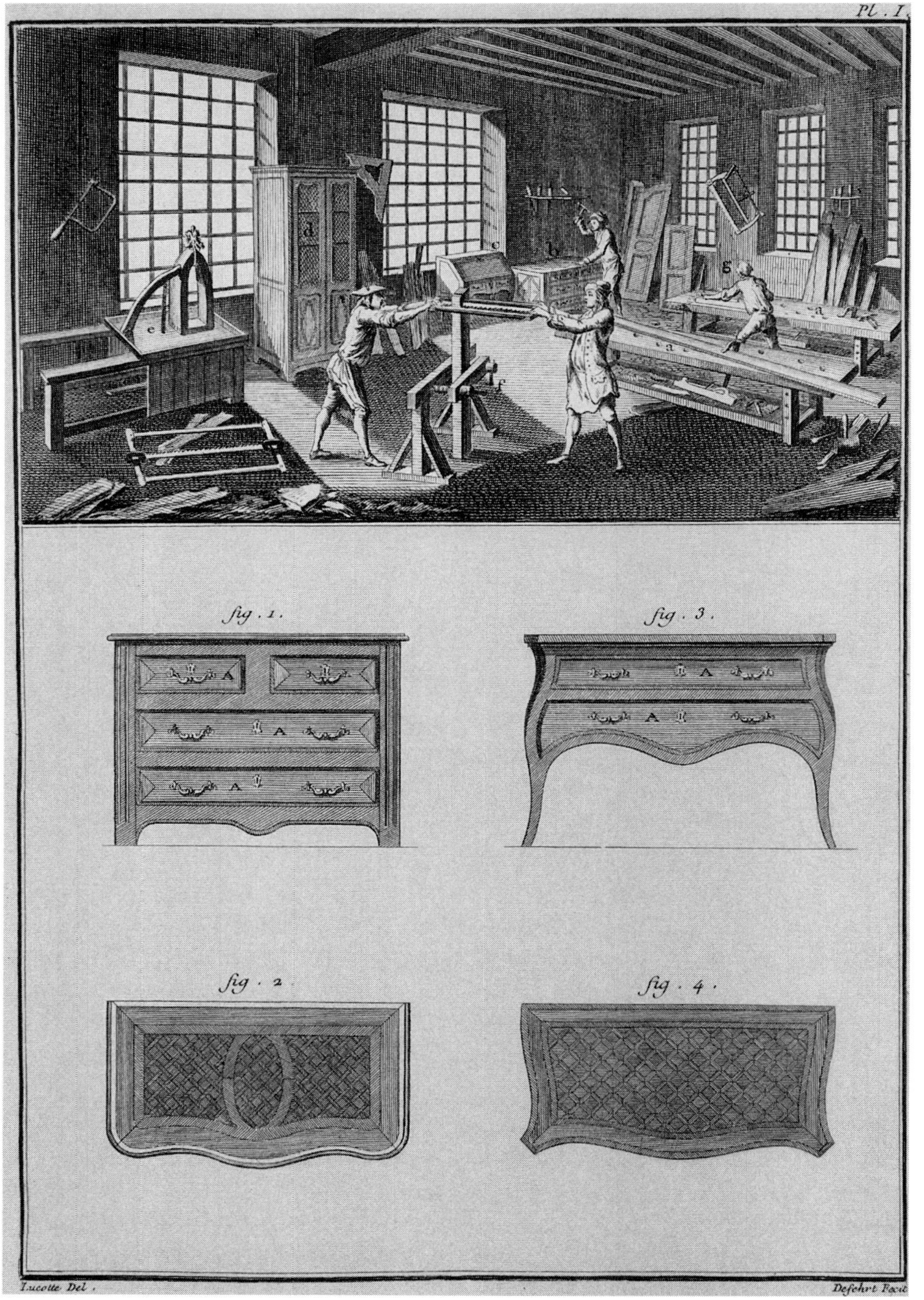

3.5 Defehrt, after J.-R.Lucotte, 'Marquéterie', *Encyclopédie, ou Dictionnaire raisonné des sciences, des arts et des métiers*, Paris, 1751–1780, plate 1 from vol. 8, *Receuil de planches*. Engraving. London: The London Library.

Lucotte was also the author of MARQUETRY (see plate 3.5), JOINERY and STONE-CUTTING (see plate 3.6), arts that, along with mosaic, are grouped together (see table 3.1).

Art	Material	Process	Mode of Assembly	Aim
JOINERY (in general)	3/ woods of different types	1/ cutting, finishing	2/ and assembling with neatness and delicacy	4/ for *les menus ouvrages*
JOINERY (in particular or joinery *d'assemblage* or *menuisier*)				1/ has for its aim the decoration and *revetement* of appartements, for which knowledge of drawing is necessary
MARQUETRY (generic)	2/ woods, metal, glass and precious stones of different colours		1/ to assemble neatly and delicately 3/ in sheets, strips and divisions onto other much more common bases	4/ to make furniture, jewels and all that contributes to the embellishment of appartements.
STONE-CUTTING	1/ the use and methods of using marbles of different types and qualities	2/ the art of cutting and polishing	3/ and assembling with neatness and delicacy	4/ according to the works for which they are destined
Mosaic	2/ a quantity of precious stones of different colours	1/ the art of cutting and polishing	3/ and making a suitable choice between them, assembling them in small sections of different shapes and sizes, on a '*stuc*' prepared for this purpose	4/ to make pictures representing portraits, figures, animals, stories and landscapes, flowers, fruits and all sorts of designs that imitate painting

Table 3.1 Comparative definitions of Marquetry, Joinery and Stone-cutting (the numbering represents the order of the phrases within the sentence)

A comparison of the definitions of those arts for which Lucotte was responsible with that of CARPENTRY by Blondel leads to the following observation: just as carpentry is described as an 'art of assembling different pieces of wood for the

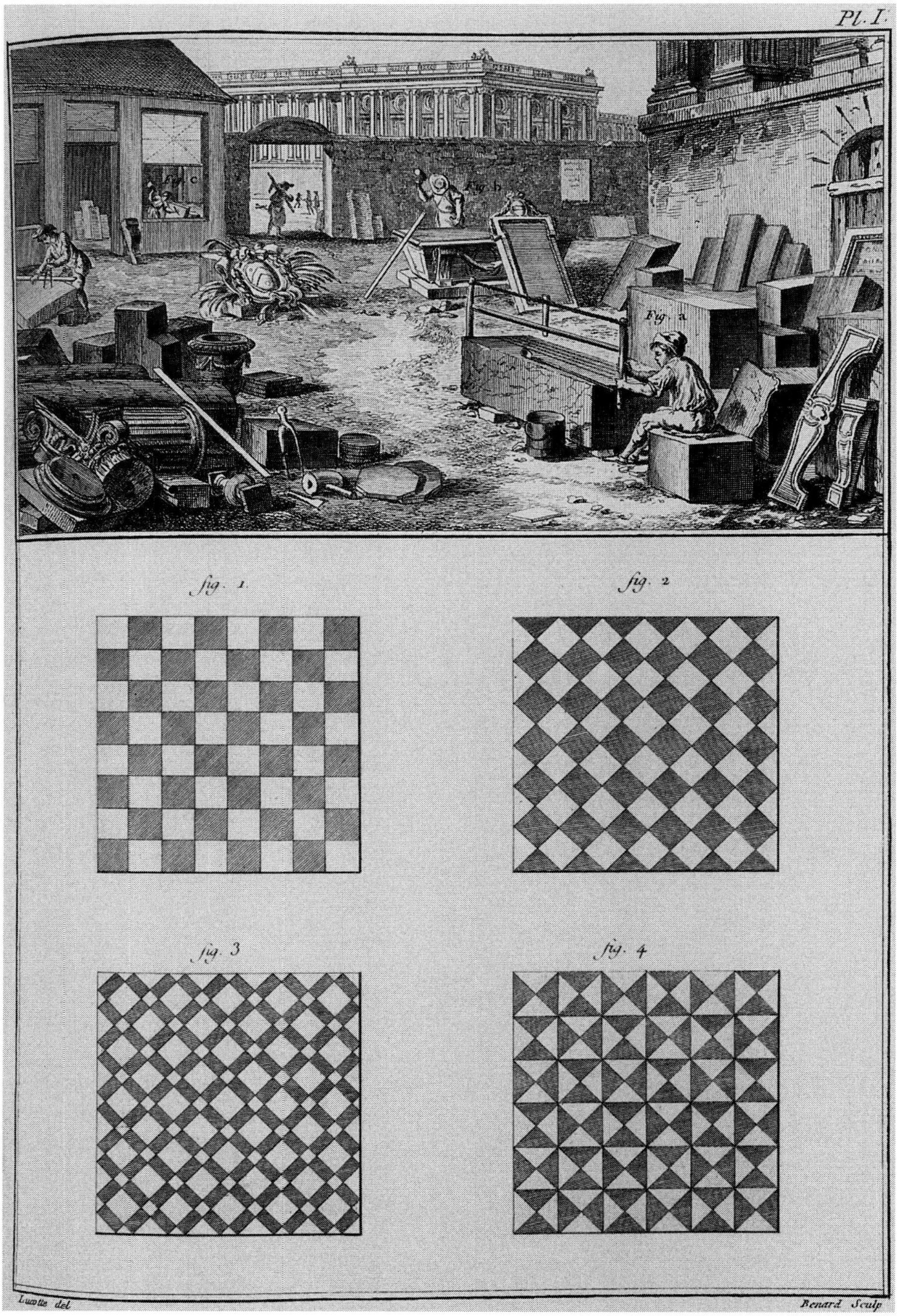

3.6 Benard, after J.-R.Lucotte, 'Marbrerie', *Encyclopédie, ou Dictionnaire raisonné des sciences, des arts et des métiers*, Paris, 1751–1780, plate 1 from vol. 5, *Receuil de planches*. Engraving. London: The London Library.

construction of buildings', so, too, marquetry, joinery, stone-cutting and mosaic are all described as 'arts of assembly' (3:214). The attention paid by the *Encyclopédie* to the mechanical arts, even when conceived as dependent, makes it impossible to read this as a coincidence. However, it is difficult to know if a preliminary discussion took place between Blondel and Lucotte, possibly with Diderot as an intermediary, or if, by his own initiative, Lucotte established his definitions in keeping with those of Blondel. Whatever the nature of the draft stage, given the alphabetical order (the distance between 'C' for *charpenterie* and 'M' for *marqueterie* is considerable) and the difference in the authors' status, it is likely that Lucotte wrote in the wake of Blondel. In these entries, the definitions of 'mosaic, marquetry, joinery and stone-cutting' as 'arts of assembly' not only link them with carpentry, but also establish this feature as a requirement of the genus.

This generic area constitutes the first level of a microsystem. Its second level, that of sub-genres, concerns the presence or absence of distinct modes of assembly. If carpentry is an art of assembly without variety, marquetry, joinery and stone-cutting are arts of 'neat and delicate' assembly.[36] The description of mosaic does not make explicit this double qualification, but assumes it ('to assemble in *small* parts' the pieces of marble deemed suitable). The skeleton of this microsystem can be completed thanks to JOINERY. Joinery is defined by its resemblance and opposition to carpentry: while both arts of assembly, the latter is crude and without variety, whereas the former assembles precisely and with the double qualification of neatness and delicacy. A third level is added by Lucotte: joinery subdivides into two sorts, that of assembly whose object is the decoration and covering of interiors (panelling, parquetry etc.) and that of veneering (onto ordinary objects of joinery) in the form of either marquetry or cabinet-making (*ébénisterie*). This ordering may be expressed in tabular form and it comprises Lucotte's first microsystem of the arts of wood, which is expressed in table 3.2.

<table>
<tr><td>Level 1</td><td>Process and material</td><td colspan="3">Assembly of wood</td></tr>
<tr><td>Level 2</td><td>Scale and mode of production</td><td>CARPENTRY (crude and without variation)</td><td colspan="2">JOINERY (with delicacy and neatness, in small)</td></tr>
<tr><td>Level 3</td><td>Complementary process</td><td></td><td>JOINERY: VENEERING = cabinet-making, marquetry</td><td>JOINERY: ASSEMBLY = revetment of walls</td></tr>
</table>

Table 3.2 Microsystem 1 – The Arts of Wood

Marquetry, however, gives rise to another microsystem. The introductory definition of marquetry as an art of neat and delicate assembly refers to level 2 of the first microsystem but breaks with its logic, which confines it to a single substance (wood), in order to establish another order according to a different criterion: that of choice of material. Each type of material ('woods, metals, glass and differently coloured precious stones' [10:137]) corresponds to three forms of marquetry: the 'assembly of wood' or marquetry (proper) or cabinet-making; the assembly of 'enamels and glass' (5:537); and the assembly of 'stones and marbles' or mosaic (10:745). Consequently, marquetry has two meanings – a generic sense ('art of neat and delicate assembly') and a specific sense ('art of neat and delicate assembly of wood'). A second microsystem takes shape.

The continuation of the entry on MARQUETRY (not as a genus but as a species, cabinet-making, or marquetry, an art which, besides assembling a body, covers it with small pieces) orders itself into three parts: 1) knowledge of woods, 2) their 'assembly' and 3) knowledge of the products. It divides itself into two 'modes' of production – the third level of the second microsystem. The first is achieved by 'join[ing] woods together', the second by using 'metal divisions' (see plates 3.4 and 3.7). The first mode produces a further division between 'frames, panels, flowers of one colour' on the one hand and 'flowers, fruits and even figures that imitate *paintings*' on the other. The second approach, which makes use of metal compartments, also subdivides into two: instances where the metal 'serves as a base', and instances where the wood does so (which becomes the content of the fourth level). This second microsystem can be tabulated as follows:

Level 1	GENUS assembled with delicacy	MARQUETRY					
Level 2	SPECIES material	Cabinet-making or marquetry = wood veneer on ordinary joinery				Glass and enamels	Stone and marble = mosaic
Level 3	MODE wood alone or not	Wood alone		Wood and metal			
Level 4	TYPE distribution	Mono chrome	Poly chrome	Metal base	Wood base		

Table 3.3 Microsystem 2 – The Arts of Delicate and Precise Assembly

The comparison of Félibien's conceptualization with that of Lucotte allows assessment of the latter's innovations. First, Lucotte's order gets rid of the qualitatively inflected binary – subordinating arts of drawing and subordinated or dependent arts – and puts in its place descriptive criteria, such as process, mode and material. This substitution has three consequences. Joinery, which depends on architecture, and marquetry, which depends on painting – according to

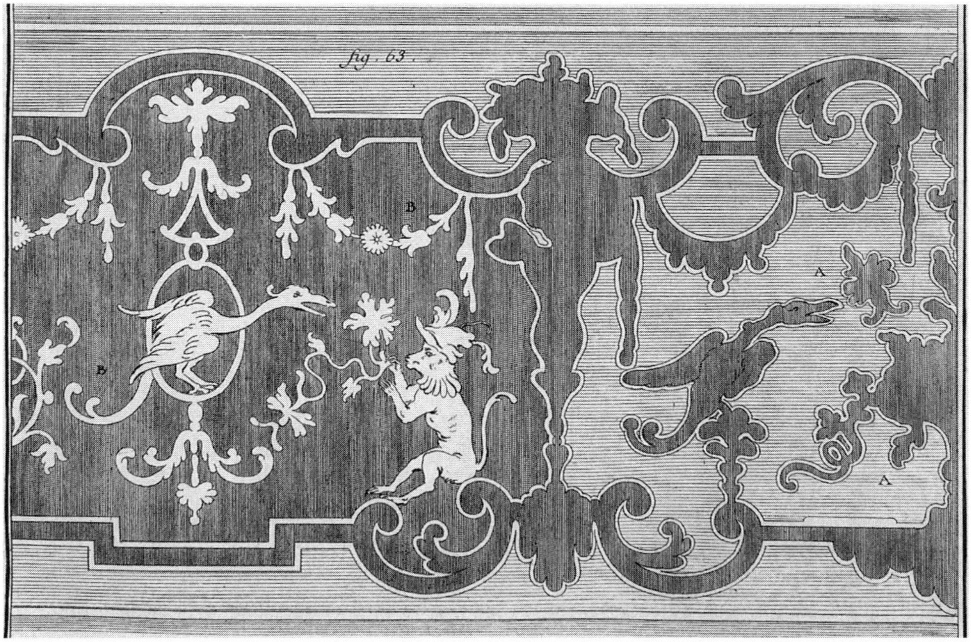

3.7 Defehrt, after J.-R. Lucotte, 'Marquéterie', *Encyclopédie, ou Dictionnaire raisonné des sciences, des arts et des métiers*, Paris, 1751–1780, plate VIII, fig. 63, from vol. 8, *Receuil de planches*. Engraving. London: The London Library.

Félibien – are reunited by Lucotte in a microsystem (table 3.2) and considered in relation to one another.

The engraved plates, for which Lucotte was also responsible, justifies this *rapprochement*; those dedicated to 'joinery in furniture' (I–XVII) and those which illustrate 'cabinet-making/marquetry' (I–VI) represent, in effect, objects in common: pieces of furniture. Certain plates show components for assembly into a body; others display surfaces of an assembled body showing its decoration (plate 3.8). Wooden panelling is depicted in plates illustrating marquetry and those showing architectural joinery (plate 3.9). The rationale for thinking of joinery and marquetry as two species of the same genus, and as autonomous in relation to the arts of drawing, is thus echoed in the plates.

In Lucotte's second microsystem, painting does not play a role until the last level: level 4. Indeed, in the historical section of MARQUETRY, Lucotte acknowledges that there existed 'ways of producing excellent works in mosaic, which *imitate painting* to the point that many *think of them as* actual painting and have *given them the name* of painting in wood, painting and sculpture in mosaic' (10: 138). He thus paraphrases Félibien, but repeats the passage where the seventeenth-century author had expressed a personal reluctance to assimilate marquetry to painting. In establishing assembly as the most wide-ranging criterion in his second microsystem, he places the worker's activity as the defining feature of the genus.

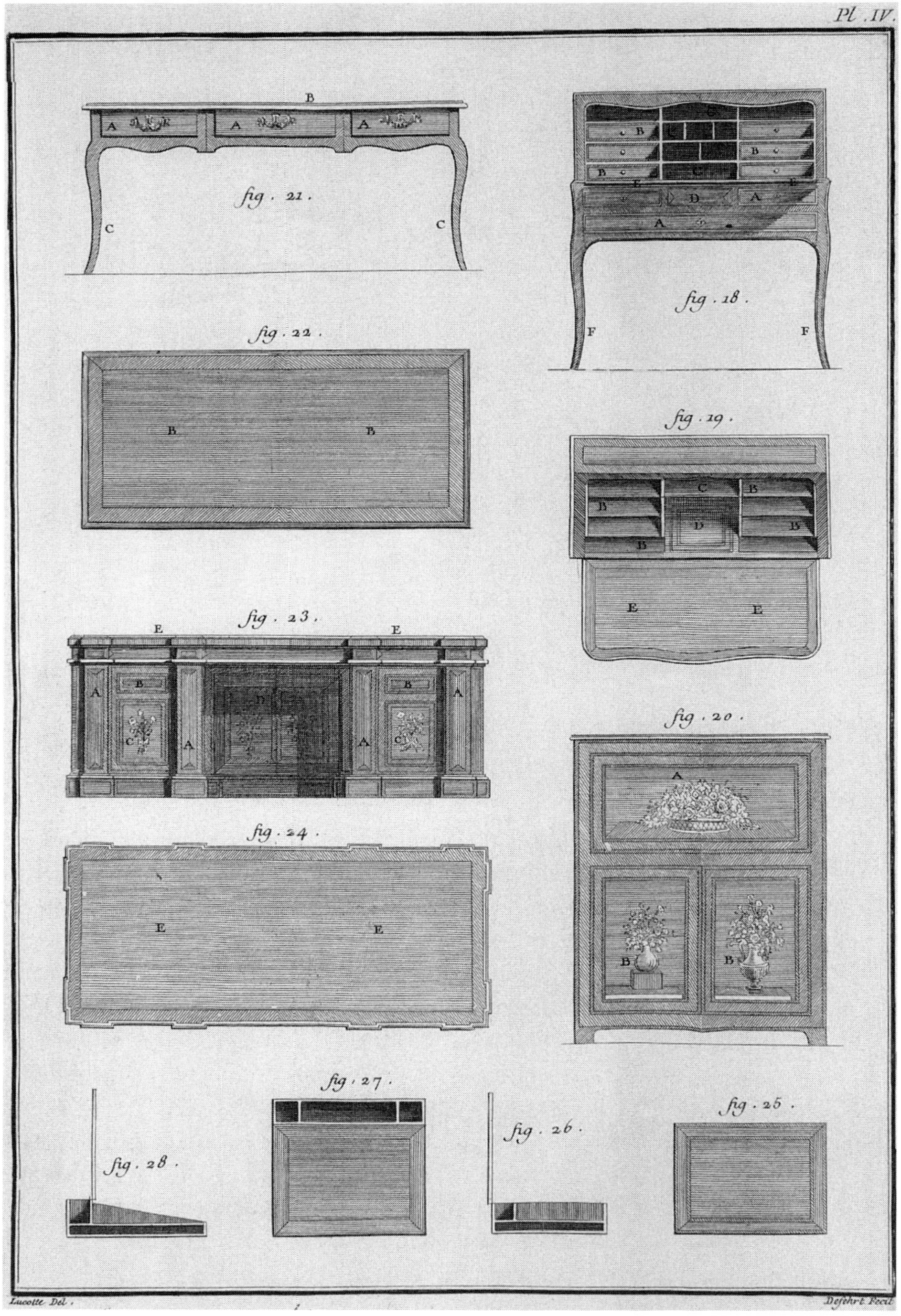

3.8 Defehrt, after J.-R. Lucotte, 'Marquéterie', *Encyclopédie, ou Dictionnaire raisonné des sciences, des arts et des métiers*, Paris, 1751–80, plate IV, from vol. 8, *Receuil de planches*. Engraving. London: The London Library.

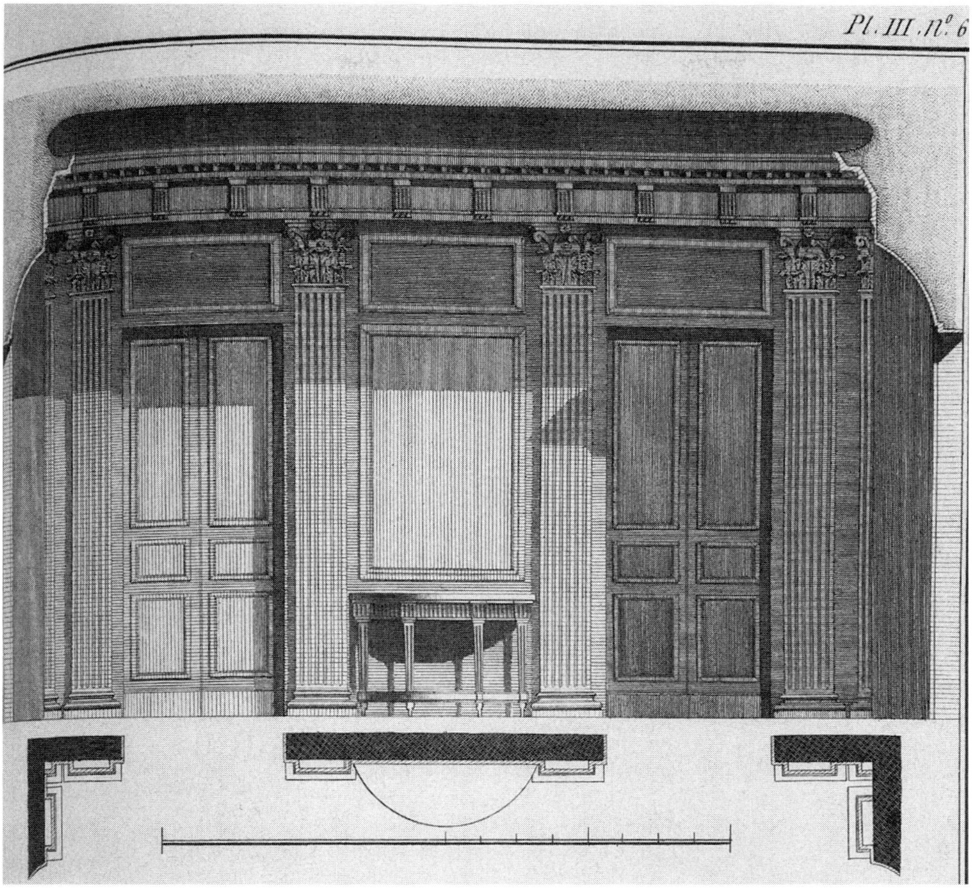

3.9 Benard, after J.-R. Lucotte, 'Menuisier', *Encyclopédie, ou Dictionnaire raisonné des sciences, des arts et des métiers*, Paris, 1751–1780, plate III, no. 6 from vol. 7. *Receuil de planches*. Engraving. London: The London Library.

Replacing the imitation of painting with modes of assembly shifts the emphasis from the finished object towards the worker and the manufacturing process; from evidence of output to evidence of means; attention to the object is now attention to the subject.

Secondly, Félibien distinguished mosaic, dependent art at the first level, from the dependent arts at the second level, marquetry and rocaille-work. He justified this distinction historically and conditionally. Thus he combined the diachronic with the structural, or degrees of imitation, and the corollary, according to which the further removed an art is from its model, the worse it is. Lucotte not only ignored the historical dimension, but also the spatial one: the degrees of removal from the original model. He moved the argument on by changing the criteria and by using binary oppositions to step up the scale of specificity. His two microsystems were a result of the logic of the lowest common denominator; he used categories of extension and comprehension, of genus and species. Whilst Félibien contented himself with an empirical organization, Lucotte constructed microsystems that were marked by a tendency to rationalize and abstract.

Thirdly, in the second microsystem, the position and function of mosaic and marquetry are inverted in relation to their earlier order. For Vasari and Félibien, mosaic constituted a genus of which marquetry was a little-valued species because it required no more than patience. For Lucotte, it is marquetry which becomes generic thanks to its redefinition as an 'art of neat and delicate assembly' (10:137), whereas mosaic, largely devalued, is no longer anything but a species. This inversion ignores notions of dependence – of the first as much as the second degree – and promotes marquetry as an art of sufficiently general scope to subsume particular arts, which were otherwise distinguished by their material.

Lucotte transformed marquetry's status. From an art which depended on painting yet failed to imitate it, marquetry emerged as a generic art in the formation of which painting no longer played any role other than that of a subordinate feature of a sub-species. Along with painting, the idea of dependence disappeared; thus was one of the conditions fulfilled that allowed some arts regarded as dependent to be re-viewed as autonomous. Lucotte's two microsystems threw the organization of the dependent arts into disarray. In these first, tentative steps towards autonomy the prolegomena to the idea of the decorative arts can be identified.

INTERIOR DECORATION

The plates for ARCHITECTURE that illustrate interior decoration show panelling and furniture (XXIX–XXXIV, plate 3.10), just furniture (XXXVI) or only panelling (XXXI–XXXII); as such they resemble those of joinery and cabinet-making, considered above. Do these representations of actual interiors lead to the conclusion that interior decoration was a category that prefigured the notion of the decorative arts? This would be as difficult to deny as to affirm, because the captions articulate two contradictory tendencies. On the one hand, interior decoration is conceived of as an entirely separate element of architecture; consequently, not only are the arts that it entails (for example, joinery and marquetry, as shown in the plates) judged dependent, but the properly architectural element appears indispensable: 'the form of the plans contributes essentially to the beauty of interior decoration,' clarifies the caption to plate XXXV.[37] On the other hand, the potential autonomy of the dependent arts is advanced; the explanation of plate XXXIII points out, for instance, that if ornament is shown, it has not been possible, by contrast, to render 'the beauties of the execution considered separately in each genre'.[38] If each object merits attention in itself, it is therefore possible to envisage certain arts as independent. However, the step from this point to thinking of the idea of the decorative arts is one that the *Encyclopédie* does not

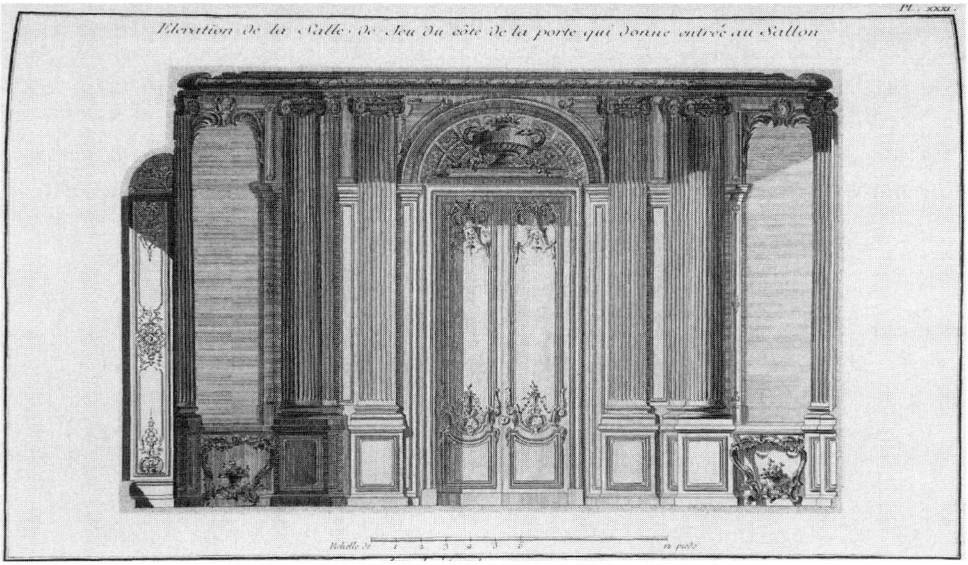

3.10 'Architecture', *Encyclopédie, ou Dictionnaire raisonné des sciences, des arts et des métiers*, Paris, 1751–1780, plate XXXI, vol. 1, *Receuil de planches*. Engraving. London: The London Library.

take. Is it by chance that, in joinery, Lucotte identifies the architect of the interior, as a 'decorator', whereas Blondel refrains from involvement in DÉCORATEUR?

As d'Alembert declared in the *Discours préliminaire*, there exist several systems of classification pertinent to knowledge but, ultimately, the editors selected only one. It is in the division 'uses of nature' in the branch of 'history' that the mechanical arts are lodged according to their materials. And yet, if Lucotte constructs his first microsystem by reference to this criterion (wood), in his second, he makes modes of production (neat and delicate assembly) play a primary role for the first time, and only after that does the material used come under consideration. His second microsystem could not be grafted onto the introductory encyclopedic tree because its logic is discordant; it constituted a branch of knowledge whose internal coherence prevents its integration into the general system. Thus, its autonomy implies contestation of the idea of the dependent arts and makes felt the absence of a branch reserved for those arts by the nineteenth century thought of as decorative.

Translated by Mia Jackson and Katie Scott

Notes

1 Denis Diderot and Jean le Rond d'Alembert, *Encyclopédie ou Dictionnaire raisonné des sciences, des arts et des metiers* (1751–1780), letterpress vols 1–17, Paris/Neufchatel, 1751–65, plate vols 1–11, Paris/Neufchatel, 1772–72, and supplement, 1780. Page references given in the text are to this edition.

2 The *Trésor de la langue française*, Paris, 1978 indicates that the adjective 'décoratif' is cited for the first time in the *Supplément du dictionnaire de l'académie* of 1836. É. Souriau, in *Vocabulaire d'esthétique*, Paris, 1990, dates the phrase 'art décoratif' from the 'final third of the nineteenth century' in the entry DÉCORATIF.

3 See I. Frank, ed., *The Theory of Decorative Art: An Anthology of European and American Writings 1740–1940*, trans. D. Britt, New Haven and London, 2000; P. Greenhalgh, *Quotations and Sources on Design and the Decorative Arts*, Manchester and New York, 1993; A. Loos, *Ornement et crime*, trans. S. Cornille and P. Ivernel, Paris, 2003.

4 For example 'Branch of the applied arts whose end is decoration' in *Trésor*, or 'discipline that aims at producing those elements proper to decoration' in *Grand Dictionnaire Encyclopédique*, Larousse, Paris, 1982.

5 Souriau, *Vocabulaire*, 1.

6 H. Osborne, ed., *The Oxford Companion to the Decorative Arts*, Oxford, 1975, v.

7 P. Rouaix, *Dictionnaire des arts décoratifs à l'usage des artisans, des artistes, des amateurs et des écoles*, Paris, 1890, listed : ameublement, armurerie, bijouterie, broderie, carrosserie, ciselure, costume, coutellerie, cristallerie, damasquinure, dentelles, émaillerie, faiences, horlogerie, joaillerie, miniature, mosaïque, niellure, orfèvrerie, porcelaine, poterie, sculpture sur bois, sculpture sur ivoire, serrurerie, tapisserie, tissu, verrerie, vitraux.

8 For example, the entries concerning painting are, for the most part, written by de Jaucourt, but Monnoye wrote PEINTURE À L'ENCAUSTIQUE. Those on print-making are generally by H. de Watelet, but J.-B.M. Papillon took care of GRAVURE EN BOIS, etc. See J.A. Calatrava Escobar, *La teoria de la arquitectura et de las bellas artes en la Encyclopédie de Diderot et d'Alembert*, Granada, 1992, 609–645. I would like to thank René Démoris for bringing this work to my attention and for lending me his copy.

9 See also on this entry Katie Scott, *The Rococo Interior*, London and New Haven, 1995, 24, and Calatrava, *La teoria*, 262–6.

10 On the gap between categories and practices, see Scott, *The Rococo Interior*, 28.

11 Emphasis here and in the following quotations is the author's.

12 D'Alembert, *Discours préliminaire*, in *Encyclopédie ou Dictionnaire raisonné des sciences, art et metiers (articles choisis)*, ed. Alain Pons, Paris, 3 vols, 1986, 1: 76.

13 Note the debt to Aristotle, *Nicomachean Ethics*, book 6: 86, 1139a, trans. T. Irwin, Indianapolis and Cambridge, 1999.

14 D'Alembert, *Discours*, 76.

15 D'Alembert, *Discours*, 105.

16 D'Alembert, *Discours*, 106.

17 D'Alembert, *Discours*, 108.

18 C. Batteux, *Les beaux-arts réduits à un même principe*, Paris, 1746, critical edition by J.-R. Mantion, Paris, 1989.

19 Diderot, 'Observations sur la division des sciences du Chancelier Bacon', 203, in *Encyclopédie*, ed. Pons, vol I, G, F.

20 Diderot, 'Observations sur la division', 204.

21 D'Alembert, *Discours*, 115.

22 D'Alembert, *Discours*, 115.

23 D'Alembert uses the phrase 'beaux-arts' in the *Discours préliminaire*, but Diderot uses it neither in 'Observations sur la division' nor in the 'Explication détaillée du système des connaissances humaines'; we know he had little time for Batteux.

24 Paul Oskar Kristeller, *Le système moderne des arts*, Nîmes, 1999, 65.

25 Kristeller, *Le système moderne*, 65.

26 Diderot, 'Explication détaillée', in *Encyclopédie*, ed. Pons, 1:200.

27 G. Vasari, *Le Vite dei più eccellenti pittori, scultori e architetti*, Roma, 2002, 73. Page references in the text are to this edition.

28 A. Félibien, *Des Principes de l'architecture, de la sculpture, de la peinture, et des autres arts qui en dépendent*, Paris, 1676. Page references in the text are to this edition.

29 D'Alembert, *Discours*, 104.

30 Diderot, 'Explication détaillée', 1:200.

31 The *Discours préliminaire* does not use this word but the phrase 'arts qui dépendent de', 176–83.

32 For the practice of joinery, see Scott, *The Rococo Interior*, 13–20.

33 Félibien, *Des Principes*, preface, n.p.

34 For example, DAMASQUINER [to damascene], quotes from *Des Principes*, and in so doing acknowledges its debt to Félibien and links damascening to drawing, in this following both Vasari and Félibien.

35 *Encyclopédie, Receuil de planches*, 8:1.

36 'Propreté' signifies neatness linked to ornament.

37 *Encyclopédie, Receuil de planches*, 1:35.

38 *Encyclopédie, Receuil de planches*, 1:33.

4

THE MARRIAGE OF ART AND COMMERCE: PHILIPPE DE LASALLE'S SUCCESS IN SILK

LESLEY ELLIS MILLER

> Oh Lyons . . . remember that it was within your walls that was born the celebrated Lasalle who has contributed so much to the glory and prosperity of your manufactures. This famous designer and manufacturer, truly worthy of the honours and advantages that the Sovereign poured on him . . . found a new route through the mixed colours and shades resulting from the multiplication of the lashes [on the drawloom]. Then, we saw on fabrics, something most astonishing, flowers and fruits imitating nature perfectly, peaches with all their velvety texture, grapes with their transparency, birds with all the richness and pomp of their colouring, charming landscapes in which the spaces were skilfully managed, they all created the most ravishing illusion. Up until him, no-one had ever executed these brilliant representations with that correctness, that lightness and that freshness in design that characterised him. From his manufactory came the vestments for the coronation of Louis XVI, the beautiful fabrics known by the name of 'The Renowned', 'The Gardener', 'The Flower-girl', etc., charming compositions; but for its effect and magnificence, nothing is comparable with the pheasant and peacock of China [plate 4.1]. This skilful businessman also had executed on the loom the portrait of Louis XV, that of the Empress of Russia, with an amazing verisimilitude. It was no longer the palette and the paintbrush that . . . represented the features of dear people, but the humble shuttle in the hands of . . . the most ignorant weaver . . .[1]

Thus wrote the abbé Bertolon, first apologist of Philippe Lasalle (1723–1804), in 1787, some forty years into Lasalle's prestigious career in silk manufacture in Lyons. Embedded in his praise was the notion that Lasalle's career epitomized the happy marriage of art and commerce, glory and prosperity attending the conversion of fine draughtsmanship into manufactured goods, artistic imitation into technical invention. At the time of Lasalle's death in 1804 an obituary in the national press echoed Bertolon's earlier summary portrait: *Le Moniteur Universel* lamented the loss of a man who combined two talents generally considered incompatible, 'that of an elegant designer (*dessinateur*), that of an ingenious and thoughtful tool-maker (*machiniste*)'.[2] The emphasis in the obituary lay on Lasalle's inventions, yet the writer was keen to define Lasalle's artistic credentials, gained from training in the workshop of the Lyonnais history painter Daniel Sarrabat (1666–1748) and a subsequent sojourn with no less a figure than the future first

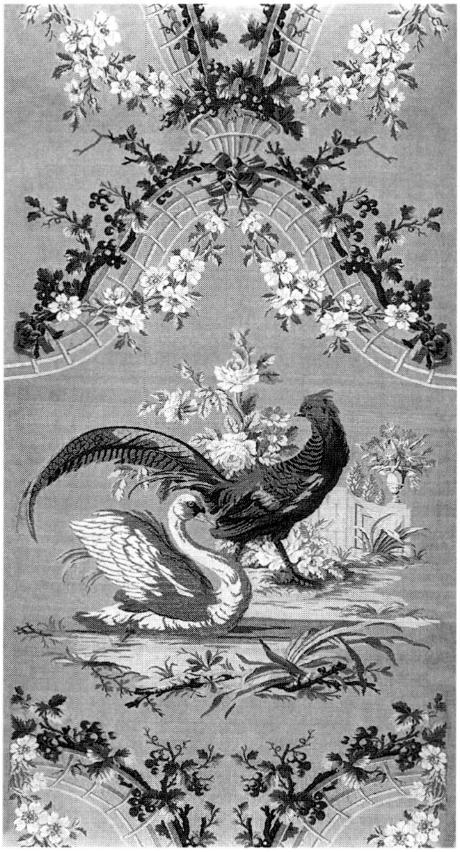

4.1 Philippe de Lasalle, panel of 'The Pheasant and Peacock of China' (single repeat), *c.* 1773. Silk, 192 × 79 cm. Photograph courtesy of Abegg-Stiftung, Riggisberg. Photo: Christoph von Viràg.

painter François Boucher (1703–1770).[3] These connections with academic art presumably bestowed some form of status on Lasalle.[4] Neither Bertolon nor the obituary exaggerated for Lasalle's skills and training had indeed transformed him from simple designer (*dessinateur*) in 1748, to businessman (*negociant*) and merchant manufacturer (*marchand fabriquant*) in 1751, to *chevalier de l'Ordre de St Michel* in 1776 and to *bourgeois* of Lyons, inventor (*inventeur*) and mechanic/loom-builder (*mécanicien*) after 1780.[5] Each additional descriptor used by the man himself – not just by contemporary observers – revealed his emergence as a successful Lyonnais with a national profile. Lasalle did not, however, follow the most common Lyonnais path to prominence, a path often determined by profitable and expert commercial practice in the coordination of the manufacture and marketing of woven silks, and inextricably allied to specific duties to the local community.[6] He did practise successfully as a merchant manufacturer, but only in 1780 did he begin to engage in overtly civic duties by becoming – remarkably – an administrator of the Lyonnais school of drawing (École gratuite de dessin), an institution based on a curriculum similar to that of the school of the Académie Royale in Paris.[7] After the Revolution, in 1801, he joined the intellectual community by becoming a member of the Lyonnais Académie des Beaux-Arts.

Lasalle's high profile in the late eighteenth and early nineteenth century has assured him a place in subsequent histories of the decorative arts, not least because relatively abundant written sources may be linked to surviving artefacts of his conception. Moreover, his existence and status are reinforced by extant likenesses of the man himself, as, unusually for an eighteenth-century Lyonnais designer–manufacturer, there exist two portraits. The first is presumed to be a self-portrait (plate 4.2); the second is a woven portrait (plate 4.3), inspired by an engraving of Lasalle by a near contemporary and fellow Lyonnais academician, Jean-Jacques de Boissieu (1736–1810). They convey different faces of the same man

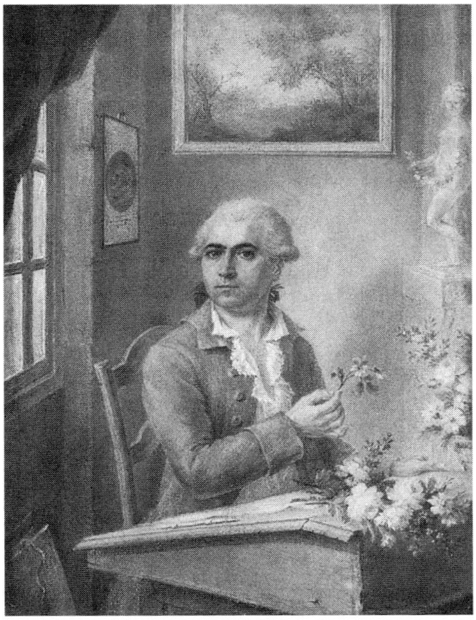

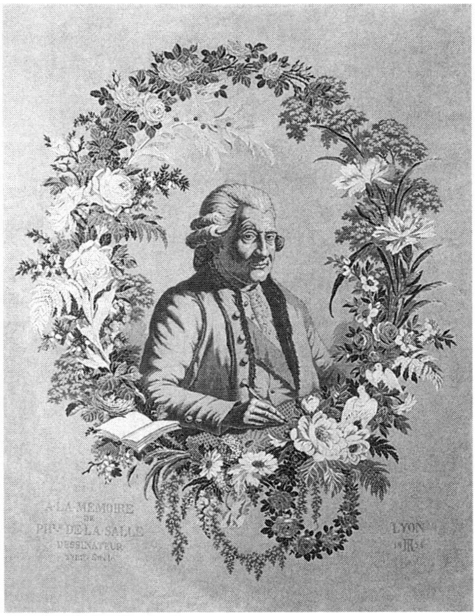

4.2 (left) Attributed to Philippe de Lasalle, *Self-Portrait*, *c.* 1770. Pastel on canvas, 36 × 29 cm. Lyons: Musée des arts décoratifs. Courtesy of the Musée des arts décoratifs, Lyons. Photo: Pierre Verrier.
4.3 (right) Portrait in silk of Philippe de Lasalle, after Jean-Jacques de Boissieu; design for garland by J. Reybaud; woven by J.-J. Ringard. 59 × 45 cm. Lyons: Musée des tissus. Courtesy of the Musée des tissus, Lyons. Photo: Pierre Verrier.

at different stages in his life: the pastel self-portrait is executed as a small-scale, intimate image of the artist at work at his desk in open-necked chemise and light blue informal coat (frock), hair powdered; the second is a formal tribute to the recipient of the *cordon de St Michel*, with neatly coiffed wig, tight cravat around his throat, and a formal coat worn over the waistcoat which displays with pride the ribbon of his honour across his chest. In both images artistic conventions tell something of Lasalle's occupation and preoccupations: he holds a drawing tool in his right hand, which is a reference to his design rather than to his manufacturing or technical skills. The nineteenth-century woven second portrait, made on a Jacquard loom some fifty years after Lasalle's death, set this bust in an oval medallion of flowers in which nestles a blank notebook. The portrait in silk is an appropriate salute to a man who was at once designer (implied by the rule paper) and manufacturer, and whose hand was credited with the execution of the first woven portraits in silk, virtuoso pieces of weaving that imitated painting and were framed with naturalistic ribbons and bouquets.

The richness and diversity of accessible documentation about Lasalle is rare for men of his trade in the eighteenth century. The discovery of elusive complementary archival references over the past two decades throws this public face into relief, making it possible now to achieve a clearer picture of Lasalle's trajectory and the strategies that he employed in gaining fame, remuneration and status beyond those of his contemporaries in Lyons. Following in the wake of a substantial literature on Lasalle devoted to one or other aspect of his reputation,[8] this article proposes that it was through the conscious marriage of art and commerce that Lasalle made his fortune and arrived at his technological inventions, that his efforts at turning painterly drawings into textiles acted as the springboard for his major commercial commissions and afforded him access to the taste leaders of eighteenth-century Europe. From these crowned heads he subsequently received major commissions which provided some of the necessary capital for his experimentation and consequently for his recognition as an inventor. Armed with a clear understanding of contemporary institutions and practices in academic art and textile manufacture, in particular the Académie Royale, the Manufacture Royale des Gobelins and the Grande Fabrique at Lyons, Lasalle drew fully on state incentives to expand upon and market ranges of French luxury goods. He is the example *par excellence* of the artisan–inventor who emerged in the second half of the eighteenth century demanding recognition in his own right, just as painters in academic circles did.[9] This proposal problematizes the existing views of Lasalle who has remained largely a local hero, nicely contextualized relative to Lyons and Lyonnais activities but somewhat underestimated relative to his manipulation of other worlds.[10] In focusing on the artistic component of his work, this essay pays only scant attention to his technological inventions which are currently the subject of investigation in France under the aegis of the history of technology.[11]

Detailed examination of Lasalle's known textile output from the time he formed his first partnership in 1751 until he fled from Lyons at the beginning of the French Revolution indicates that his output was rather more varied than most accounts suggest, historians having generally overlooked his more ephemeral and anonymous textiles. Lasalle's involvement in diverse ranges of products, however, lay at the heart of his manufacturing, marketing and inventing activities. Among these textiles a few stand out and their significance needs to be revisited and evaluated more thoroughly, not just as examples of superlative draughtsmanship and craftsmanship but also as commercial commodities. Here they will be analysed in terms not only of their material, aesthetic and technical composition but also as to how they furthered Lasalle's career through their roles as gifts or commodities, and how they embodied the silk weaving guild's strategies with regard to diversification. Between luxury and the everyday, between fashion and functionality, Lasalle's textiles grew from a particular branch of Lyonnais silk manufacture, so some examination of the historiographic treatment of textiles and especially the context for Lyonnais silk production must precede any analysis of Lasalle's practice. They reveal his immersion in a particular world of possibilities.

EIGHTEENTH-CENTURY FRENCH TEXTILES

The history of eighteenth-century textile production is complex precisely because textiles have a multitude of forms and functions from the prestigious to the mundane. The study of luxury furnishing textiles dominates most histories of the decorative arts in which a long tradition of connoisseurship has focused on artefacts that have survived the ravages of time, whose authorship is known or traceable, and whose provenance is available.[12] More recently, this data has benefited from socio-economic analysis which has uncovered the context and conditions of production and consumption, the diversity of the French luxury trades and their internal dynamic, the shifting relationship and changing discourses around the liberal and mechanical arts, and the impact of debates about state protection and free trade in an increasingly fashion-conscious market.[13] Textiles played a fundamental and much-admired role in eighteenth-century interiors,[14] at a time when the Académie Royale was championing the conceptual superiority of painting and sculpture in the public domain. Tapestries, figured silks and, after the 1770s, top-of-the-range plate-printed cottons were highly regarded possessions expressive of wealth and taste on a par with paintings or sculpture. They shared certain characteristics and life stories that differentiated them from their humbler, shorter-lived textile siblings. Intended for use in elite households as suites of furnishings that would last beyond the lives of their purchasers, they clothed walls, covered upholstered furniture, and hung at doors and windows (plate 4). Not necessarily unique one-off products, these pieces required raw materials (fibres and dyes) that were expensive and production methods that were greedy in terms of time and skill. Members of a skilled workforce rooted in a highly developed division of labour were responsible for different facets of the process: for example, skilled draughtsmen or academic artists created the decorative or narrative designs; skilled craftsmen wove them into cloth; and, in the case of cottons, skilled block-makers and printers applied the design. Guild officials (*syndics/maîtres-gardes*) evaluated their endeavours, affixing their mark of approval on the end product in an appropriate form.[15] These men and women were only the most prominent contributors to methods that relied on a host of semi-skilled and unskilled auxiliaries. Consequently, the end product was costly, appreciated by the cognoscenti but financially beyond the reach of the majority of the population.[16]

The involvement of artists, designers or draughtsmen in the conception and execution of these textiles made them stand apart from some of the cheaper ranges of furnishing and dress textiles, which were devoid of designs or whose designs were simpler. Ambitious to imitate nature closely, these artists created cartoons or designs that were for exact reproduction either through weaving or printing. They could be understood as pictures, flat canvases that in some cases combined narrative and decorative images, and drew on knowledge of the natural world in order to depict flora, fauna and sometimes the human figure. By the mid-eighteenth century tapestries had a particularly close relationship with the art establishment, the Manufacture Royale at the Gobelins and Beauvais being governed by one of the king's painters, a fully fledged member of the Académie Royale.[17] Silks and cottons did not have quite the same relationship with academic art practice, perhaps because their makers were geographically distant from Paris. In Lyons, there is no evidence that academic artists of this calibre supplied designs for silks although from the 1730s onwards some designers' first- or second-hand experience of the Gobelins, the Académie de St Luc and the Académie Royale informed silk design.[18] Bertolon's attribution of titles to some of Lasalle's figurative pieces is evidence of this link.[19] At Jouy, a similar practice was evident, for Oberkampf was happy to use academicians such as Jean-Baptiste Huet (1745–1811) to provide models for titled textiles, while his in-house designers worked for rather smaller remuneration on more modest motifs.[20]

Significantly, too, textiles of this type – or their preparatory drawings – were on public display, both while they were being made and afterwards, once they had found their home in an interior, or were resting. Classic itineraries of Paris throughout the eighteenth century broadcast the importance for tourists to the capital of a visit to the Gobelins and referred to Gobelins products in their descriptions of the interiors of the wealthy.[21] Some cartoons for tapestries were exhibited at the Salon prior to the weaving of the tapestry reproduction, and briefly, between 1763 and 1773, a handful of tapestries were hung at the Salon.[22] At a time when the Gobelins was facing difficulties because of the Crown's lack of funds, the marquis de Marigny, Directeur des Bâtiments du Roi, helped the Gobelins to reinvent itself as a more commercial enterprise by adapting the aesthetic of its output to the changing tastes of its clients. Evidently, that promotion included the said display of tapestries and their continued use as gifts for foreign dignitaries.[23] There were other venues where tapestries could be admired alongside other precious objects that made up royal interiors for, by the 1770s, the Gardemeuble opened a special store in place Louis XV in which prestigious items not currently in use in the royal palaces might be viewed.[24] In this setting, silks from Lyons might entice visitors to Lyons to tour the best silk-weaving workshops, should they be in the city, and Lyons was already a regular stopping-off place for tourists on their way to Italy.[25] Later, at Jouy, Oberkampf showed off his model print works, benefiting no doubt from their location between Paris and Versailles.

In contrast to these textiles, which were linked tenuously through their authorship to the art establishment, the textiles intended for dress and cheaper ranges of furnishings feature rarely in histories of the decorative arts. They do, however, play a prominent role in the works of social and economic historians who consider how the demand for such products stimulated supply, and how the fashion system began to function in the eighteenth century.[26] In some cases, such fabrics were quite heavily decorated, but the majority were plain, with no distinctive patterning. These ephemeral everyday items were made in batches, speculatively, and sold at accessible prices through retail and wholesale outlets, travelling salesmen and commissionaires.[27] Neither their manufacturers nor their designers can be traced with confidence, partly because of the anonymity of the sales process in which the silks passed from hand to hand.

The separation by historiography of spheres of production into luxury and the everyday, furnishings and dress does not reflect contemporary divisions of expertise for while it is true that some manufacturers drew attention to their particular strengths in textile types or techniques (e.g. velvet, gold and silver stuffs, etc.), they did not refer to end use in their categorization of themselves. They merely stated their calling as merchant manufacturers.[28] The dependence of different branches or specialisms on each other was surely part of the balancing act that manufacturers effected in their day-to-day commercial practices. In centres with a fine reputation for the most fashionable and luxurious products and an infrastructure of credit that facilitated their execution, a variety of simpler goods supported the luxury branches.[29] For example, the Grande Fabrique at Lyons and Oberkampf's enterprise at Jouy-en-Josas offered fashion leadership with their most painterly ranges, but maintained their solvency through the production of simpler ranges accessible at lower levels of the market. Within the Grande Fabrique, some wealthy and enterprising manufacturers could invest in their designs and long-winded weaving times while a goodly number of their confrères merely followed their lead, copying from their *produits-phares* or making simpler products. In a trade which was particularly sensitive to external circumstance, such as periods of war or mourning, manufacturers might also shift their allegiances, so that when demand for particular types of silks declined, they manufactured others. In the late eighteenth century some manufacturers qualified in the manufacture of figured silks shifted their allegiances to engage in the weaving of plain silks. There is every reason to believe that firms involved in the long-winded process of weaving furnishings used dress silks that were more quickly produced to sustain their enterprises and provide steady turnover as they awaited the completion of, and payment for, those furnishings.[30]

LASALLE AT LYONS

Lyons was the premier silk manufacturing centre in eighteenth-century France by the time that Lasalle first arrived in the city sometime before 1744. Located propitiously at the crossroads of trade between northern France, southern Europe and the Levant, the city had been a major commercial centre since the Middle Ages, hosting commercial and cultural exchanges that predated the implantation of silk manufacture and facilitated its development. The silk trade benefited to such an extent from Colbertian initiatives in the promotion of luxury manufactures in the 1660s that, by the 1680s, the members of the Grande Fabrique (silk-weaving guild) were in receipt of significant royal patronage, were gradually extending and perfecting their ranges of plain and figured silks, and were developing annual fashions in silk design.[31] The guild provided the infrastructure for silk weaving by policing a series of regulations (*règlements*), which controlled the nature and quality of the silks woven and the training of the operatives who made them. It also provided an important support network in times of need, petitioning municipal authorities and the king on behalf of its members. Far from being an inhibitor of change, the guild encouraged the dynamic development of skills and products, in particular rewarding individuals who extended the Lyonnais manufacturing repertoire by the acquisition and adaptation of aesthetic and technical innovations, whether in fabrics or in technology. They did so in a variety of ways: for example, by importing foreign artisans, imitating foreign techniques, and promoting the acquisition of drawing skills.[32] By the early years of the eighteenth century, Lyons was by far the biggest and most diverse silk-manufacturing centre in Europe, exporting figured and plain silks to all parts of the world.[33]

New regulations were published in 1744, the year that Lasalle signed up for his apprenticeship with the guild.[34] These were to remain in place with relatively little alteration right through his working life, in other words up until the French Revolution. They constituted an important landmark because they established beyond doubt the contested schism between merchant manufacturers (*marchands fabriquants*) and master weavers (*maîtres ouvriers*).[35] Both classes sat at the top of the manufacturing hierarchy having completed the ten-year apprenticeship necessary to set up a workshop containing four to five looms, take on an apprentice, employ journeymen and weave up silks without supervision. In practice, merchant manufacturers were much wealthier than master weavers, in a position not only to buy or rent looms but also to commission silks from a number of different workshops. Consequently, they tended not to involve themselves unduly in hands-on weaving, but rather deployed their capital in purchasing raw materials (including designs); employing master and journeymen weavers to weave up fabrics for piece rates; negotiating credit for their enterprises and markets for their silks. They needed their knowledge of weaving in order to evaluate the quality of workmanship produced by their workforce. Throughout the century, about four hundred merchant manufacturing firms were active at any one time, with about eighty functioning on a truly impressive international scale.[36] Over a lifetime, these men could amass modest fortunes that enabled them to retire from business and live in the same areas as Lyons's small but extremely wealthy nobility.[37] While this group was tight-knit, it did welcome certain outsiders.[38] The new recruits usually brought some particular talent or skill that the guild wished to utilize and they entered their first partnership having become merchant manufacturers by a special concession *(par ordonnance consulaire)* on the payment of the necessary registration fees. Drawing skill fell into this category and assured some of Lasalle's contemporaries who were not particularly interested in weaving of a remunerative career.[39] The successful prosecution of one partnership usually allowed such individuals to earn sufficient capital in order to invest it as well as their talents in their next enterprise.

Lasalle understood every detail of Lyonnais silk manufacturing and worked within guild guidelines from the time he decided to become a merchant manufacturer: he undertook an apprenticeship once guild regulations allowed men from the province of his birth to do so;[40] became a master by marrying a master's daughter;[41] and participated in a series of business partnerships which chose the best parts of town for the location of their premises.[42] He climbed the hierarchy of Lyonnais silk manufacturing firms quite rapidly; in 1758–59, only ten years after completing his apprenticeship, he was senior partner in a company that bore his name (Lasalle et cie.) and that firm enjoyed a comfortable position in the top thirty-two manufacturing businesses in Lyons.[43] In the 1770s and 1780s he was counted among the small number of manufacturers whose businesses were deemed worthy of visits from eminent figures on their way through Lyons,[44] and on the eve of the French Revolution, still manufacturing, his annual income was one of the highest in the city.[45] Overall he was extremely successful in his com-

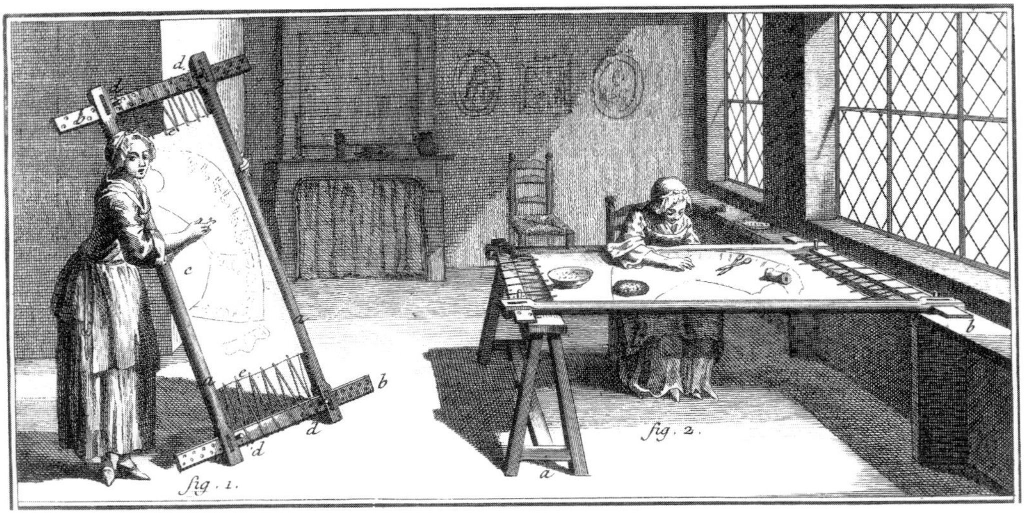

4.4 *Atelier de brodeur*, illustration of an embroidery workshop showing embroidresses copying designs on to men's coats directly from a paper model, from Denis Diderot and Jean le Rond d'Alembert, *Encyclopédie: Recueil de planches sur les sciences, les arts libéraux, et les arts mécaniques, avec leur replication*, Paris, 1772, vol. 2, *Brodeur*, pl. I. London: Victoria and Albert Museum. Courtesy of the Trustees of the Victoria and Albert Museum.

mercial ventures, but he was not averse to turning to the state for additional support when he experienced difficulties.[46] The innovations he sold to the state suggest that he had retained an interest in the raw materials and hardware of weaving, the loom and its tools, an interest that was not typical of all fellow manufacturers. His adaptations in this respect lead to major technological breakthroughs from the 1770s, all of which created economies in weaving, reducing the time or labour in a piece of fabric.[47]

Lasalle's technological inventions were to a great extent the expression of a spirit frustrated by the limitations of technology rather than by the constraints of guild regulations. While regulations defined certain silks, they did not preclude the execution of textiles that did not conform to their specifications as long as such 'illegal' textiles did not bear the seal of the Grande Fabrique when they left the city for the marketplace.[48] Changes to regulations between 1667 and 1744 suggest the incorporation of a range of new products over that period. By 1779, further diversification resulting in Letters Patent (1779) drew attention to the fact that these 'illegal' new silks might be incorporated into guild regulations, once they had received approval from consumers.[49] In essence these were official acknowledgement of the process of innovation and diversification that the guild's and state's one-off payments (*gratifications*) and pensions (*pensions*) already encouraged.

Diversification into new fabrics relied on experimentation both in woven techniques and in techniques applied to woven structures after weaving, and in Lasalle's case related to both the composition of fabrics (raw materials and their disposition) and the nature of the designs (colour, scale and method of incorporation). Weaving a pattern and painting or embroidering a pattern are very different processes. The brush and needle copy directly from the original design on to the surface of an already woven fabric using brushstrokes or stitches (plate 4.4). Weaving, however, requires other interventions because curved as well as rectilinear patterns must emerge out of threads that cross each other at right angles. Thus, between the original freehand drawing (*esquisse*) for a silk and the end product lay a long-winded, labour-intensive process of conversion: from paper to loom, from warp and weft into woven fabric. This process required the knowledge and skills of several different specialist artisans in succession: firstly, a designer or draughtsman had to translate the freehand sketch into a technical drawing or plan (*mise-en-carte*) on ruled paper (*papier réglé*); then the warper (*monteur de metier*) had to warp up the loom, while the reader of the design (*liseur de dessins*) and the lash-maker (*faiseur de lacs*) tied the simple (*semple*) which hung at its side and acted as the programme for the pattern; finally, the weaver (*maître ouvrier*) and drawgirls (*tireuses de cordes*) had to work in tandem to weave up the fabric. Basically, these last two operatives were involved in creating a background weave and the pattern which was incorporated during making. The drawloom (*métier à la tire*) catered for their needs through a dual method of control: the shafts (o in plate 4.5) controlled the warp threads of the ground fabric, and the lashes on the simple (r in plate 4.5) controlled the warp threads required to create the pattern. While the weaver worked the shafts by treadles (q in plate 4.5), the drawgirl operated the simple by standing at the side of the loom. When she pulled on the line of lashes, the correct warp threads lifted on the loom, permitting the patterning shuttles to pass through the space between the warps that had been raised and those that had not. The tying of the lashes was critical if the pattern was to work, so the designer's technical plan showed the pattern line by line in order that the conversion could be correctly calculated and executed.

The drawloom and the simple imposed certain restrictions on what could be woven or how it could be woven and resulted in certain costs. The loom and

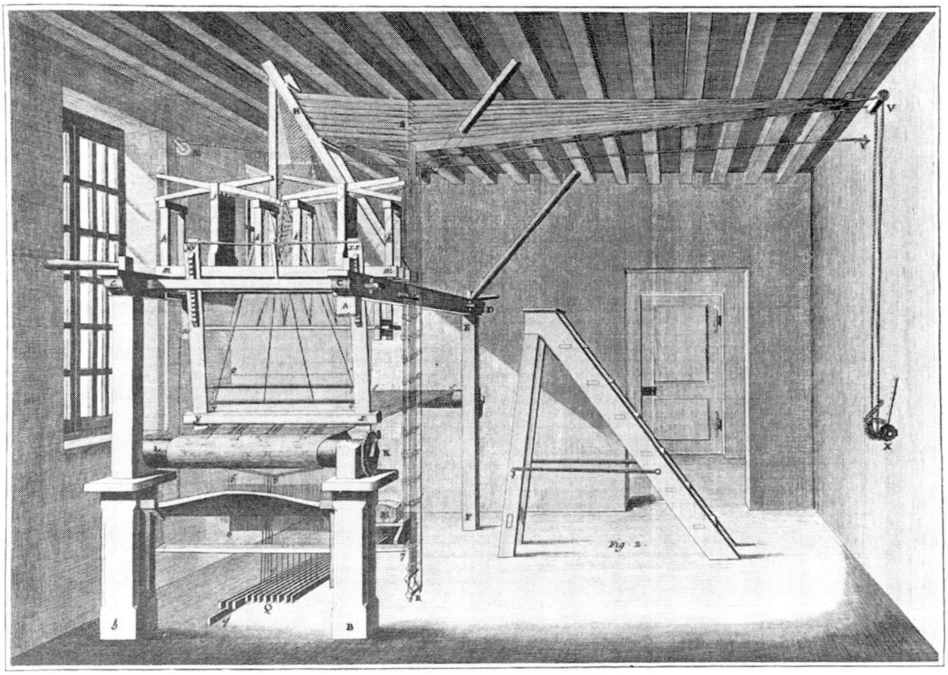

4.5 Illustration of Drawloom (*Metier à la grande tire*) from Denis Diderot and Jean le Rond d'Alembert, *Encyclopédie: Recueil de planches sur les sciences, les arts libéraux, et les arts mécaniques, avec leur replication*, Paris, 1772, vol. 11, pl. LX. London: British Library. Courtesy of the British Library.

weaving operation determined the width of the fabric, and the width of the fabric determined the calculations for the disposition of the pattern across the fabric; the simple which hung down the side of the loom defined the length of the repeat of the design up and down the fabric. Until the 1770s the simple could not be detached from the loom. Consequently, each time the weaver wanted to weave a new design,[50] he had to have the lashes on the simple untied and replaced by new lashes. In other words, the weaving had to stop for a period of time while the simple was retied. Certain lengths of design could therefore be woven up relatively economically as the design on the simple could be repeated over and over again, while other designs might suffer a delay during production because of the scale of their patterns. The interruption did not prevent the manufacture of long repeats but undoubtedly it slowed down the speed of their production, raised the costs of weaving for manufacturers and the price of the end product for consumers. Until the mid-1770s there was no way round this problem. Yet as, mid-century, seasonal fashions became established for dress silks, it seems likely that this drawback became particularly acute for manufacturers who wished to supply fashion-conscious consumers with up-to-the-minute goods within a three-month period. From the mid-1760s Lasalle thought through a solution to this design-driven issue. His experiments resulted in the invention of the detachable simple which could be tied, hooked on to the loom, removed after weaving, and reinstated if a repeat weave was required.[51] By the 1770s he was manufacturing complex patterns in widths greater than those laid down in guild regulations, and seeking ever more royal support for his endeavours.[52]

AN ORDINARY MERCHANT MANUFACTURING PRACTICE

Analysis of Lasalle's textiles confirms and throws into relief his strategy as a manufacturer who had to manufacture and promote his wares while coping with the constraints of the drawloom. The first twenty years of his business life (*c.* 1750–1770) were presumably crucial to the development of his insights into both the demands of fashion and of weaving and loom technology. They remain elusive because of the absence of surviving textiles. However, the fragmentary written record from commercial correspondence and from Lasalle's negotiations with the silk-weaving guild and the State does make possible an evaluation of what he was manufacturing, whether it differed radically from the output of his peers, how he innovated and how he sold. Importantly, it reveals that he was making both dress and furnishing silks and that little differentiated his workshop practice from that of fellow merchant manufacturers in *grands façonnés*. He dabbled in the kinds of minor interventions in textile construction that created the trade's novelties. Such innovations did not require major adaptations to existing technology but rather involved new combinations of materials or the assimilation of new techniques, such as introducing a linen warp where a silk warp would have been usual or painting patterns on to the silk rather than weaving them in it. There is no doubt that Lasalle was particularly active relative to his peers in this domain of experimentation.

Many of Lasalle's products were traditional and fitted the guild regulations perfectly well. As he belonged to the figured branch of the Grande Fabrique he would have expected to make the 'gown [length] of beautiful and good brocaded satin *trois lats*' that he promised to his landlord's daughter in 1751,[53] or the ten pieces of *étoffes en dorures* he made for Germany in 1754,[54] or the gown length of *fond argent* for Charles Nile Genory in Milan in 1756,[55] or the figured silks with chenille that he supplied via an agent to important silk mercers in Madrid in the early to mid-1760s,[56] and through other agents in Cadiz.[57] Even the 'tiger skin worked with a little art on a gold ground' that he claimed to have copied from nature in 1756 was exceptional only in that he was ahead of other manufacturers in choosing this particular source from nature (plate 4.6).[58] It was not exceptional from the point of view of copying closely from nature in order to produce a fabric that represented nature realistically. Even Lasalle's more controversial borders for men's coats made between the late 1750s and early 1760s followed the prevailing fashion of figured borders woven *à disposition* by broad silk weavers.[59]

Illusion was key to the motifs on these silks as they imitated nature in much the same way as tapestries did, via faithful representations of painting or drawing.

It was probably also the key to Lasalle's painted silks, which took up the challenge of the printed and painted cottons that could be manufactured legally in France from 1759.[60] Silk manufacturers had long feared the impact of such cottons, which had been imported from the East for well over a century, and there had been some attempt to copy them.[61] The attraction of painted/printed cottons lay in the vibrancy of their colours and the exoticism of their motifs, which contrasted with those of the conventional European idiom.[62] In the face of the new legitimacy of printed cottons, Lasalle applied himself to the development of fast, bright dyestuffs and designs that might be applied to plain silks, a timely impulse that suited his artistic training, his desire to educate, and his commercial interests. In Lyons his peers were happy to copy his lead and employ his trainees, although retailers in Paris were reticent about acquiring and selling these innovative goods, despite Madame de Pompadour's appetite for this commodity (plates 4.7 and 4.8).[63] Believing that he had pioneered a technique, Lasalle wrote to Jean-Charles-Philibert de Trudaine, the Intendant, with a view to gaining financial recognition for his recipes.[64]

This fragmentary evidence for Lasalle's early involvement in the manufacture of patterned silks demonstrates

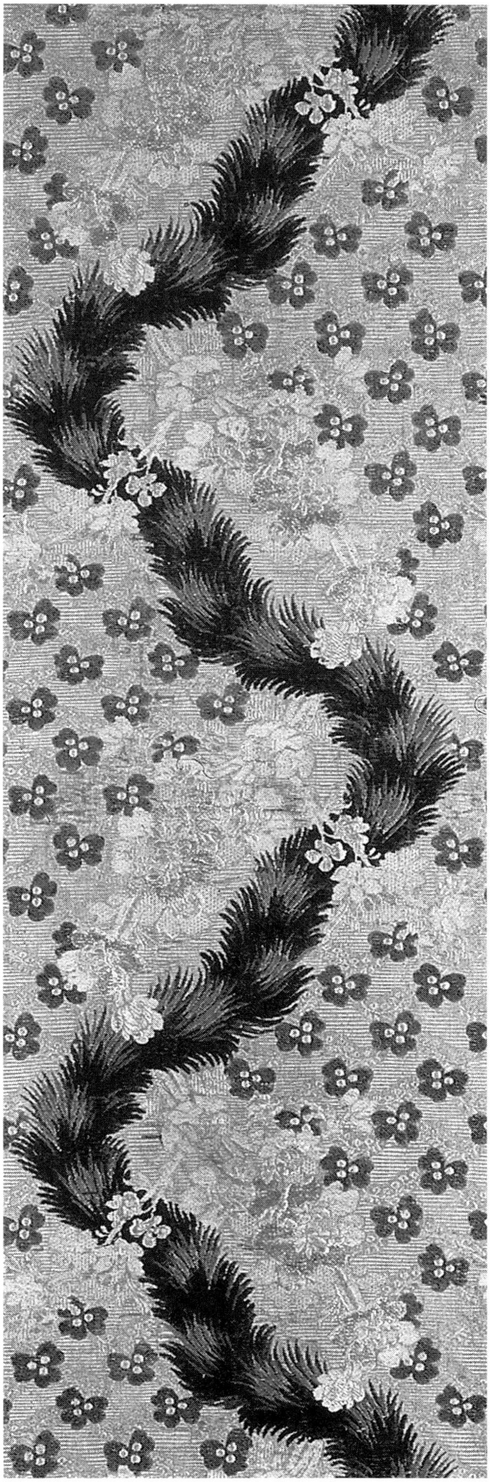

4.6 Unknown maker, three panels of silk with woven pattern incorporating fur and flowers. Silk, 105 × 66 cm. Lyons: Musée des tissus. Courtesy of Musée des tissus, Lyons. Photo: Pierre Verrier.

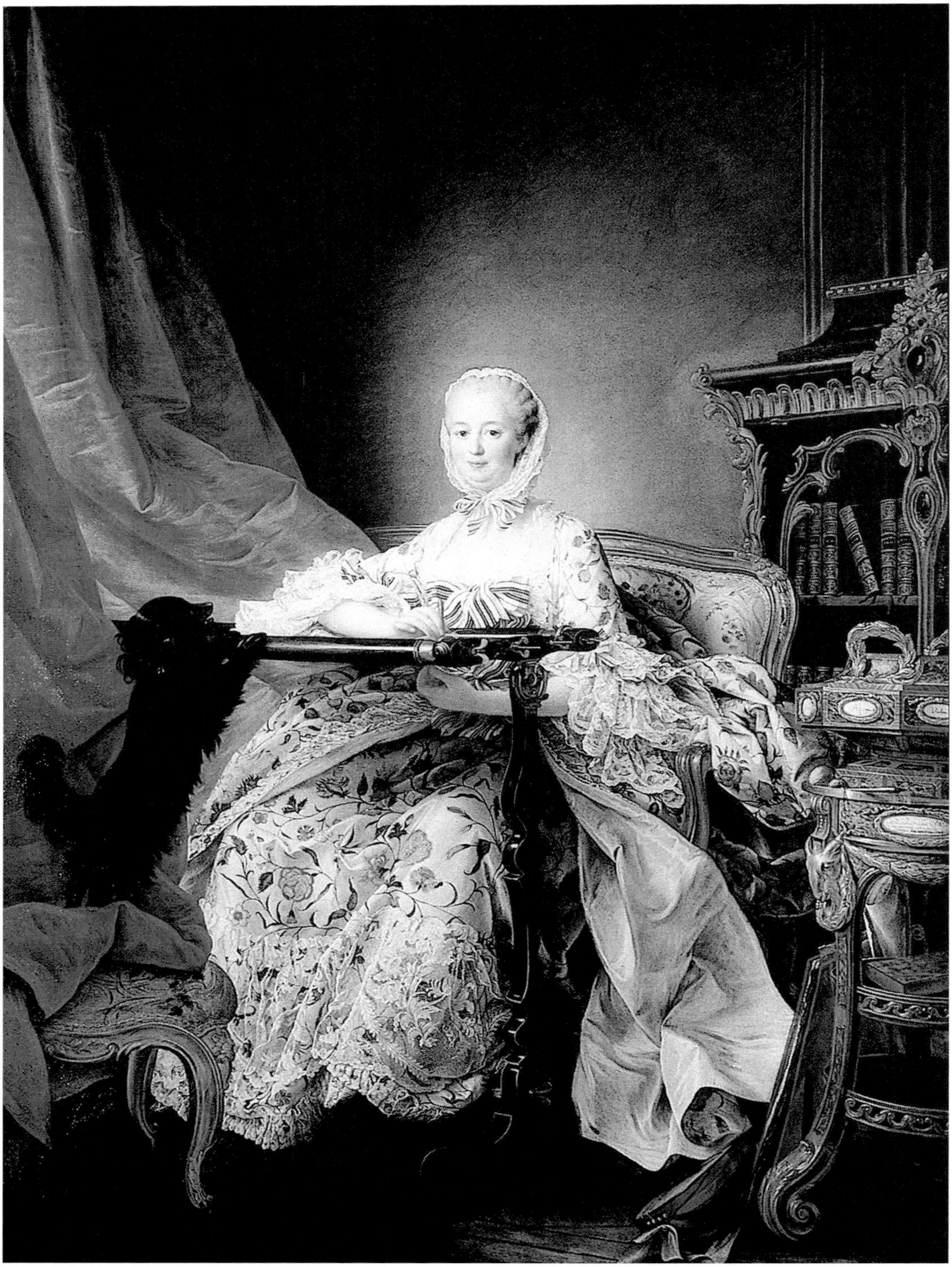

4.7 François-Hubert Drouais, *Madame de Pompadour*, 1763–4. Oil on canvas, 217 × 156.8 cm. London: National Gallery. Courtesy of the National Gallery, London.

his openness to experimentation, an intrinsic if regulated part of the silk trade in Lyons. What little is known of the destination of these silks suggests that Lasalle functioned like his peers, occasionally selling single gown lengths directly to individual merchants or clients but mostly selling substantial lengths through wholesalers and retailers based in different centres of distribution. His products were no more identifiable than those of his peers because when he wanted to claim pieces from the bankrupt stock of his agents, he had to send a sample of the fabric to match against the original.[65] In addition, he could boast international sales but his name was not attached to particularly elevated or noteworthy clients and he was in no way involved in supplying the most important of French customers, the Royal Household.[66] Against this backdrop, his outstanding pieces of weaving of 1771, the portraits in silk, emerge as extraordinary, both in terms of what they were and how he promoted them and himself through them.

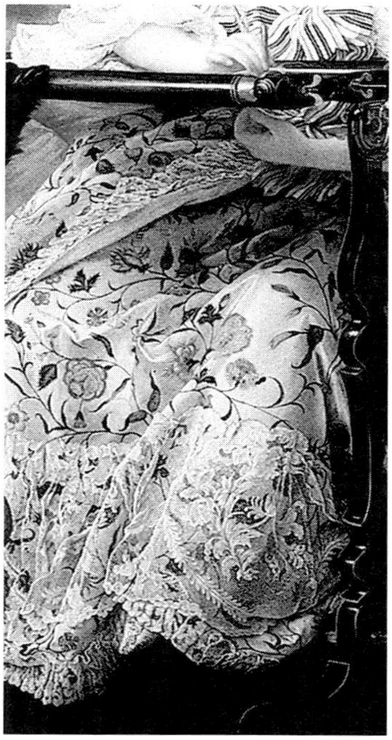

4.8 Detail of François-Hubert Drouais, *Madame de Pompadour*. London: National Gallery.

TURNING POINT

Lasalle's portraits in silk were mentioned in the national press in 1771, by the abbé Bertolon in 1787, and in his obituary in 1804.[67] These portraits – often seen as the culmination of his achievement in production on the basis both of their design and of their technical virtuosity – were significant because they intimated directly his close association with the crowned heads of Europe and his desire to stamp his own identity indelibly on certain textiles by signing them. This signature was a unique departure in and from eighteenth-century silk manufacturing practice.[68] In these portraits of Louis XV (plate 4.9), the comte de Provence and the comtesse de Provence, and Catherine the Great Lasalle delineated in profile monochrome busts reminiscent of cameos and surrounded them with an elaborate naturalistic floral garland topped with a magnificent bow. He probably also decided on the rectangular, gilded wooden framing of the silk in neoclassical style. The oval silk portrait and the silk with the garland were woven as separate pieces, the first in cream and grey silks on a white satin ground, the second in polychrome silks on a coloured taffeta ground. The oval was then inserted into the garland and secured there by embroidery. Lasalle's signature, LASALLE FECIT, was also embroidered on to the base fabric below or above the garland. The contrast of texture ensured that the light caught the fabric in different ways, emphasizing the virtuosity of the draughtsmanship. While the oval changed from portrait to portrait, the garland remained the same. Lasalle could therefore weave up a length of garlands in a single piece as a repeat pattern and then cut the length into short pieces of the appropriate dimensions. Consequently, Louis XV is surrounded by exactly the same flowers as the comtesse de Provence and Catherine of Russia. In theory the signature could have been woven into the ground silk at the same time as the garland, but instead Lasalle chose to insert the signature in embroidery after manufacture, thus making tangible the intervention of the artist and making possible the omission of the signature should he wish to use this base textile for a different purpose; indeed, he projected one such in a surviving point paper which contains a composition of birds within the same floral frame.[69] It is perhaps strange that he chose to capitalize his name rather than trace out his own signature, although, of course, capital letters are more legible from a distance and at a glance than 'joined-up' handwriting. In manufacturing terms this method of production was economical because the weaver did not have to dismantle and remount his loom each time that the central oval changed – an extremely costly process in the case of portraits, which Lasalle made up only in limited numbers.[70] This method of production was also used in some of his furnishing fabrics, where the economic implications were more serious because of the larger quantities of textiles required for palace walls. It is quite possible that the portrait project informed Lasalle's subsequent production of furnishings.

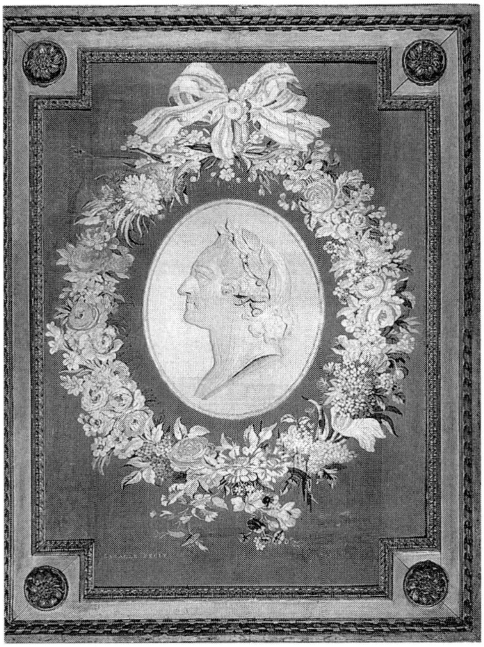

4.9 Philippe de Lasalle, *Woven Portrait of Louis XV*, 1771. Brocaded silk, 93 × 72 cm. Lyons: Musée des tissus. Courtesy of Musée des tissus, Lyons. Photo: Pierre Verrier.

There is no evidence that Lasalle sold his woven portraits commercially or made any up purely speculatively.[71] Nor is there any indication that Lasalle intended to give each portrait to its subject. The known owners or recipients of the portraits were, however, significant players in French cultural or manufacturing life. Catherine of Russia's portrait, possibly the first woven, graced the home of Voltaire at Ferney, and thus came to the attention of his visitors and Catherine herself; this and a second allegorical portrait of Catherine as Minerva as commemoration of the Battle of Chesma were sent to Catherine;[72] Lasalle presented the portrait of Louis XV to the comtesse de Provence in May 1771, to his friend and fellow designer/manufacturer Pierre-Toussaint Déchazelle in the same month, and to the Bureau de la Grande Fabrique (headquarters of the silk weaving guild) of Lyons in November 1772;[73] madame du Barry, the king's mistress, and de Trudaine, Intendant Général des Finances, kept a copy of the portrait of the King.[74] This evidence suggests the existence of some of these artefacts in relatively public locations where they might act as advertisements of the skill of their author whose name was there for all to see. How the portraits arrived in these locations is rather more elusive. Only Lasalle's dealings with the comtesse de Provence are reported, and, in her case, Lasalle's largesse was assertive and public: he gave her the portraits of her future father-in-law and husband as a gift when she visited his workshop in Lyons en route to marriage in Paris; and six months later he travelled to Versailles to present her with her own portrait on 27 November 1771. In other words, their first encounter was probably in the presence of his workforce, her entourage and representatives of the Lyonnais municipal hierarchy, while the second was at court, in the presence of an elite whose impressions of the manufacturer's skill might result in commissions. This second encounter reached a wider public two days after its occurrence through a report in the *Gazette de France*.[75] This was apparently the first time that Lasalle had penetrated the French Royal Household, and, significantly, it preceded later invitations to design ornaments for the coronation of Louis XVI in 1775 and to redesign the robes of the Order of the Saint-Esprit in 1777.[76] It also preceded Lasalle's receipt of his letters of nobility in 1776.

While the novelty value or originality of Lasalle's portraits and the mark of their author are noteworthy in the context of silk manufacture, their form and composition were not unprecedented in the decorative arts as the king and other less exalted consumers would have been aware. Certain elements of their composition dated back to Flemish paintings of the fifteenth century and had been carried into tapestry portraits, which were made at the Manufacture Royale des Gobelins from the 1750s onwards, especially in the workshop of Cozette.[77] By the second half of the eighteenth century portraits in silhouette were becoming popular in a variety of media: in pottery, porcelain, precious stones and paper.[78] The tapestries are particularly important relative to the launch of Lasalle's portraits, not only because their status was validated in the Parisian art world in the decade immediately preceding Lasalle's efforts, but also because of Lasalle's purported relationship with Boucher, the artistic director at the Gobelins. Equally important is the similarity in technique between the construction of those tapestries and his silk portraits and the similarity of viewers' response to the pieces.

Arguably, Lasalle was well aware of what was going on at the Gobelins and of the inclusion of Gobelins portraits in the biennial exhibitions of the Académie Royale between 1763 and 1773. Although pictures intended for conversion into tapestries had hung in the Salon prior to 1763, it was in this year that, for the first time, an actual tapestry from the workshops of the Gobelins appeared on display and thus merited a short description in the *livret* of the Salon. That description followed the long list and fulsome descriptions of numerous paintings, sculptures and engravings by Royal Academicians, and was clearly situated at the bottom of the artistic hierarchy in terms of precedence.[79] The verisimilitude of these tapestries was remarkable and art critics revelled in the fact that these tapestries were so skilfully woven that they could not be distinguished from the original painting.[80] Moreover, Diderot's commentary praised exactly the same qualities in the tapestries as Bertolon did twenty years later when faced with Lasalle's silk portraits.[81]

The size and subject matter of these tapestries in comparison with most of the suites produced at the Gobelins surely appealed to the new art 'publics' that attended the Salons and who increasingly had the buying power to consume 'luxury' goods of all sorts.[82] Portraiture was an accessible form of art and middling consumers often owned engravings of royalty or commissioned their own likenesses in pastels or oils.[83] The tapestry busts of prestigious sitters and Van Loo's evocation of *Painting* exhibited between 1765, 1769 and 1773 were more accessible to such publics, and were evidently exhibited just like the academicians' paintings in wooden frames.[84] The dimensions conformed to art practice with regard to standard portrait sizes: 91 × 76 cm for a bust, more or less the same as Lasalle's portraits in silk. His portrait of Louis XV measures 105 × 74.5 cm.[85] There is also evidence of other tapestry portraits that were not exhibited at the Salon but which, like Lasalle's portraits, were made specifically for members of the Royal Family and presented as gifts. Cozette, for example, wished to offer portraits to the king, the queen and the comtesse d'Artois in 1774.[86]

The relevance of this consideration of Lasalle's portraits and their relationship to Gobelins tapestries may be summarized as follows. The author had a firm grasp of drawing and could execute not only naturalistic flowers and ornament but also convincing renderings of the human figure after models by other artists. He did so in a manner reminiscent of Boucher, but in a distinctive medium and context, and he chose different subjects (with the exception of the king). In Lasalle's environment, while good draughtsmanship and weaving were highly regarded, neither artist nor weaver identified himself on the piece of fabric. In contrast, the artists who worked for the Gobelins had academic status, and the workshop heads, Lasalle's equivalent,[87] gained kudos through the marks they wove into their tapestries and, in the 1760s, from the endorsement of the academy exhibitions. Lasalle was undoubtedly aware of what was being exhibited in the 1760s and of the benefits of exhibiting, but was not in a position to submit work to the Salons because he was not an academician. He could gain access to the Crown and potential clients among the elite by making similar, yet exceptional items and could exploit the fortunate timing of the royal marriage in 1771 to make contact with his targets.

While it would be unwise to attribute too much to Lasalle's portraits, there is no doubt that they had an impact both abroad and at home. The impact on Catherine of Russia is well documented because from this date onwards she acquired a number of furnishing fabrics in substantial quantities for her palaces. They were delivered between 1771 and the 1780s via different agents. Indeed, Tatiana Voltchkova is convinced that without the patronage of Catherine of Russia between 1771 and 1773, Lasalle would not have been able to continue his experiments in technology.[88] Closer to home, Lasalle achieved a less quantifiable success. He gained access to the Royal Household but this access did not result in major orders for furnishing fabrics, the kinds of orders that would have provided revenue for experimentation. They may, however, have led indirectly to the commissions for ceremonial dress textiles that he received in the mid-1770s. Ironically, these textiles required designs for embroidery, not weaving. Their translation, therefore, would not have needed the technical expertise that Lasalle promoted through his portraits. Nevertheless, the prestige attached to creating anything for the coronation and for knightly ceremonial robes that were to last well into the nineteenth century in the same form should not be underestimated, even if it is not clear what financial benefit their maker achieved. Moreover, even if Lasalle did not suddenly become a supplier of furnishings to the palace, he did receive furnishing commissions from members of the court. The prince de Condé had made orders for the Palais Bourbon from June 1769 and continued to do so until 1773, choosing one of the patterns that Catherine of Russia was to use at Peterhof, a 'blue *cannelé* decorated with red partridges'. He later supplied Lasalle with a reference for one of his petitions.[89]

STATE INTERIORS AND FASHIONABLE DRESS

Lasalle had made silks for furnishings and dress before 1770 and continued to do so thereafter, although in these later decades there was a great contrast between the resilient furnishing silks that remained *in situ* for decades and the flimsy silk gauzes that wore out and disappeared because of their intrinsically delicate nature and their function as fashion fabrics. Both types of product were in their own way pioneering and commercially astute and importantly demonstrate Lasalle's engagement in a variety of products, not just those that seem most salient today.

Lasalle's furnishings display both conservative and progressive trends in their design and manufacture. Some of those executed in the 1770s and 1780s exploited the well-established idiom of scrolling 'rococo' patterns made up predominantly of flowers and birds while the others fit firmly into a neoclassical aesthetic with dominant rows of medallions surrounded by garlands or foliage or other simpler framing motifs. Both types of fabric were evidently intended for similar use: they were stretched and hung flat across the surface of large expanses of wall, framed by ornamental, gilded wooden fillets. Several widths of the textile were needed for each expanse so that, when joined, the panels formed a repeat pattern not only vertically but also horizontally (see plate 4). Consequently, the flow of the pattern across the walls was important to the overall effect. These textiles were also used to upholster chairs and make curtains. The methods of production utilized

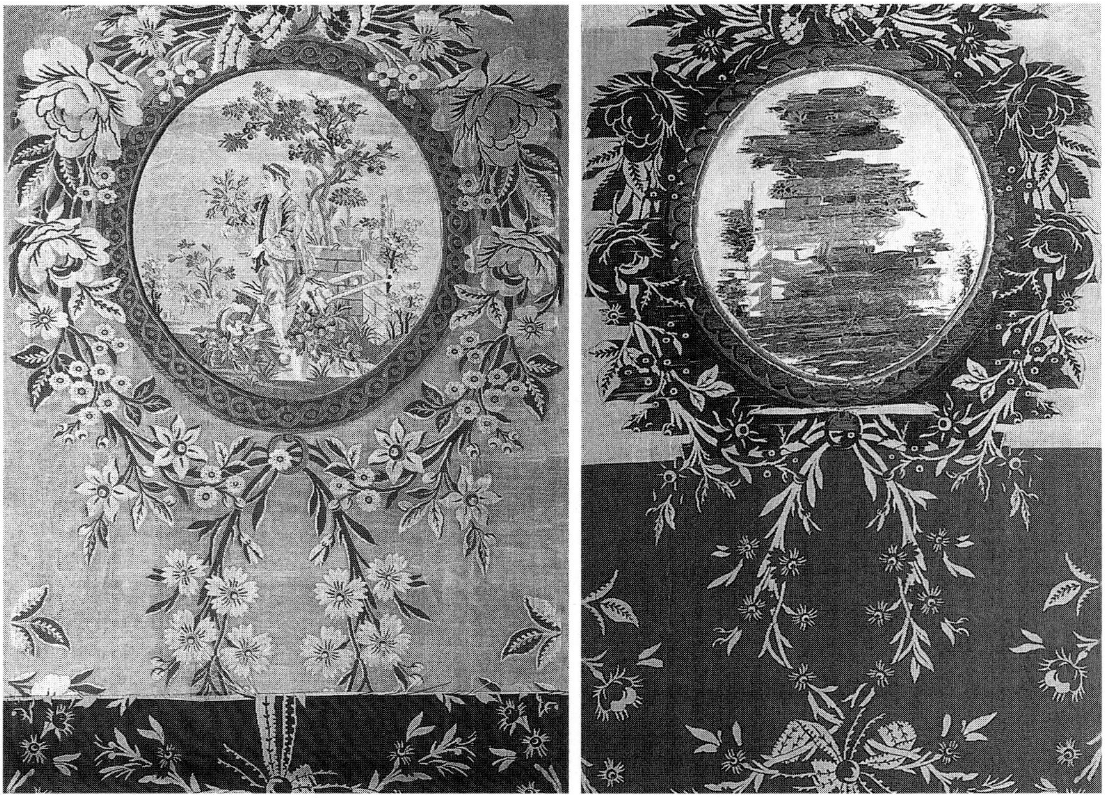

4.10 Attributed to Philippe de Lasalle, panel of 'The Gardener' (recto left and verso right), early 1770s. Brocaded silk, 92 × 54 cm. Toronto: Royal Ontario Museum. Courtesy of the Royal Ontario Museum, Toronto.

in each case seem to have been different: those that fitted firmly within the tradition of grand Lyonnais silks were made in a repeating pattern that required two panels of silk to complete one repeat of the pattern width-wise, each panel of which was made in one piece, with repeats of over a metre. They were, therefore, costly in terms of time and labour, and Lasalle, who sought economies in production whenever possible, would have been driven to contemplate the restrictions of the simple and thus devise his detachable version. Typical of this variety are the five silks traced in the Russian archives to Catherine II's enthusiasm for Lasalle's work.[90] While their compositions were more naturalistic, more painterly than many of the preceding furnishing silks, they demonstrate precisely the same fascination with imitating nature as the 'tiger skin' (see plate 4.6) that Lasalle had so proudly claimed as his own in the late 1750s, and their patterns meander in a similar way.

In contrast, the silks in the newer neoclassical idiom bear a remarkable resemblance to Lasalle's portraits and to some of the products of the Gobelins. The economical method involved in their production echoes practices at the Gobelins.[91] As the portraits had been, the medallions were woven on satin grounds and then inserted into the space left for them in a contrasting textile framework. The insertion was achieved through embroidery. The framing textile in these cases did not need to be as complex in composition as that chosen for the portraits and a 'mix-and-match' process might take place, so that the same medallion occurred in a different ground, interspersed with other medallions. Thus, for example, 'The Flower Girl' ('*La Bouquetière*') and 'The Gardener' ('*Le Jardinier*') (plate 4.10), mentioned by Bertolon in 1787, have survived in different manifestations and fit right into the idiom favoured by Boucher in the *Les Enfants* series.[92] Samples in the Royal Ontario Museum show how they were adapted for furnishings. In both pieces, the base into which the medallion was inserted is a yellow and red lampas; the colours match perfectly, but the motif is different. The wall-hanging encircles the boy in an elaborate scrolling pattern, while the stool cover encompasses the girl in a simple red pocket-watch shape. Other framings of these figures exist – in different colour ways and complexities of motif, and a version of the comte de Provence in the same framing as 'The Gardener' also exists in Lyons.[93] They allowed flexibility for both manufacturer and client at a late stage in the making-up process, and the insertion of the medallions by embroidery (probably by a poorly paid female workforce) was swifter than the dismantling and retying of the simple. Given the scale on which large quantities of furnishings silks had to be delivered and the speed expected, this method offered useful possibilities already deduced at the Gobelins and in other media. In other words, for the manufacturer, they were probably much more economical than the more traditional form of furnishings because cheap female labour (embroidery) was used for part of the process rather than expensive male labour (weaving).[94]

Lasalle did not limit himself to these prestigious furnishings during the final decades of his manufacturing activity. He also took on the new fashion for simple dress silks that, from the 1760s, had increasingly replaced heavily figured silks. By the 1770s the new trend was for extremely lightweight open-weave silk gauze both for trimmings and for garments. It was transparent and came plain, with stripes or small spots.[95] Elisabeth Vigée-Lebrun's famously scandalous portrait of the queen in 1783 included a sash of such silk, an echo of a large wardrobe that revealed a preference for plain silks, closely followed by striped items, including gauze.[96] Lasalle was clearly well aware of this shift in taste and by the late 1770s was working on improvements that would allow much wider widths of gauze to be woven.[97] While a little is known of the technological side of this venture, it is not clear whether Lasalle actually intended to manufacture gauze as a commercial proposition or merely to devote himself to improving the looms on which his fellow manufacturers worked.

This analysis of Lasalle's manufacturing output has revealed the benefits of marrying texts with textiles and looking beyond the conventional framework of histories of technology and the decorative arts. In the scheme of Lyonnais silk manufacture Lasalle's textiles tended towards the luxurious and fashionable rather than the everyday, although their author remained involved in quotidian workshop practice. However, he also looked for stimuli beyond his locality, in particular to tapestry production, which was inextricably linked to academic art practice and its elite audiences in the capital. Not only was he conversant with developments in design at the Manufacture des Gobelins – the shift from rococo to neoclassicism and the move to the exact reproduction of images by academic artists – he was also aware of the methods by which heads of the tapestry workshops made economies in production, adapted to court taste, and brought their works to the king's attention. Based at Lyons, such direct contact with the court was less easy to achieve. However, when the opportunity arose, as it did in 1771 with the passage of the future comtesse de Provence through Lyons, Lasalle grasped it with both hands, and benefited thereafter from royal patronage and nationwide publicity. Self-promotion and the promotion of luxury goods went hand in hand: Lasalle invested in special pieces on the expectation of no immediate financial return but in order to gain long-term attention for his firm. In this approach to business Lasalle may be compared with other entrepreneurial spirits of his age who sought to benefit from new methods in manufacturing and advertising.[98]

The marriage of art and commerce in Lasalle's case supports the view that his knowledge of draughtsmanship was learned in the studio of good masters who valued figure drawing. Throughout his life Lasalle was happy to participate in debates about the training of designers, in the 1760s advocating that they limit their learning to flower painting and technical drawing, precisely the view propounded to the Lyonnais by experts at the Gobelins.[99] Later, he presumably subscribed to the notion that an academic training was appropriate, accepting a post as administrator of the Lyonnais École de Dessin. But by this time he had explored the potential of the human figure in silk design and had proved his own excellence in drawing and making, and in exploiting the market. He had harnessed the draw-loom to the service of designer and manufacturer, enabling the humble shuttle to execute the creations that so impressed Bertolon and his contemporaries.

Notes

This article has taken shape under Katie Scott's generous editorship. I record my gratitude for her helpful references, inspiring ideas and incisive comments. I am also grateful to colleagues in a number of institutions for their help in securing appropriate images: in Bern, the Abegg-Stiftung; in Lyons, the Musée des Tissus; in London, the National Gallery and the Victoria and Albert Museum. For additional support and information, my thanks go to Tom Campbell of the Metropolitan Museum of Art, New York, Anna Jolly of the Abegg-Stiftung and Tatiana Lekhovich of the Hermitage, St Petersburg.

Abbreviations have been employed in the notes:
ADR – Archives départementales du Rhône; AML – Archives municipales de Lyon; AN – Archives nationales de France; BML – Bibliothèque municipale de Lyon; MT – Musée des tissus, Lyons.

1 P.N. Bertolon, *Du commerce et des manufactures distinctives de la ville de Lyon*, Montpellier, 1787, 195.

2 *Le Moniteur universel*, 2 avril 1804, 877.

3 Both his masters had received the approval of the Académie Royale, although only Boucher actually became an academician. *The Grove Dictionary of Art*, London, 2000; *François Boucher*, exhib. cat., New York: Metropolitan Museum of Art, 1986.

4 The accuracy of the claims about that relationship awaits confirmation. It is to be assumed that the information in the obituary came from Lasalle's widow or his one surviving daughter.

5 AML St Pierre et St Saturnin 1748, no. 409 *Mariage Lasalle/Charrier*; St Pierre et St Saturnin 1751, no. 139, f. 30 *Baptême de Marie Elisabeth Lasalle*; BB345 *Lettres de noblesse*, 1776.

6 Lesley Ellis Miller, 'Manufactures and the Man', *Textile History*, 29:1, Spring 1998, 19–40. From as early as 1758 he was receiving a state pension of 600 livres. It rose to 1,200 livres in 1760, and by 1775 that annual pension had reached 6,000 livres; in 1776 the Crown granted him letters of nobility; and three years later he was awarded a gold medal for his contribution to French national manufactures and the economy. AN F12 1444A, folders 26–8, 27 décembre 1758 and 1772–75, *Pièces relatives aux gratifications accordées au Sieur de Lasalle*; AML BB446 *Bourgeoisie nommée*, f. 30, 20 avril 1780.

7 Marie-Félicie Perez, 'Soufflot et la création de l'école de dessin de Lyon, 1751–1780', in *Soufflot et l'architecture des lumières*, Paris, 1980, 108–113.

8 Henri Algoud, 'Un maître du décor de la soie: Philippe de Lasalle', *Gazette des beaux-arts*, December 1911; Belle Borland, *Philippe de Lasalle*, Chicago, 1930; Raymond Cox, *Philippe de Lasalle, son œuvre au musée historique des tissus*, Lyons, 1906; Jacques Coquillat, 'La vie et les œuvres de Philippe de Lasalle', *La soierie de Lyon*, 1930, 326–38; M.-T.Schmitter & François Guicherd, *Philippe de Lasalle, exposition de tentures à l'occasion de l'inauguration d'un medaillon le 11 mars 1939*, Lyons, 1939; Daryl Hafter, 'Philippe de Lasalle. From Mise-en-Carte to Industrial Design: Philippe Lasalle', *Wintherthur Portfolio*, 12 January 1977, 139–64; Marie-Jo de Chaignon, 'Philippe de Lasalle, dessinateur et fabricant d'étoffes de soie à Lyon au XVIIIe siècle', *Le Monde alpin et rhodanien*, 2e-3e trimestres 1991, 65–84.

9 Guy Richard, *La noblesse d'affaires au XVIIIe siècle*, Paris, 1997, 115–30; Liliane Hilaire-Perez, *L'invention technique au siècle des lumières*, Paris, 2000, 143–88.

10 The most balanced account of Lasalle and his achievement to date still falls into this trap, contextualizing nicely the diversity of his engagement in a variety of activities but ignoring the broader implications, pointing out the deficiencies in the factual base of previous accounts but perpetrating similar misjudgements. De Chaignon, 'Philippe de Lasalle, dessinateur et fabricant d'étoffes'. Chantal Coural provides the documented factual base for Lasalle's wider context relative to the Royal Household in *Soieries de Lyon*, Lyons, 1988, 57–61.

11 The current work of Liliane Hilaire-Perez promises to revise views of his profile as an inventor.

12 For example, Coural, *Soieries de Lyon*.

13 For example, Michael Sonenscher, *Work and Wages. Natural law, politics and the eighteenth-century French trades*, Cambridge, 1989; Katie Scott, *The Rococo Interior*, New Haven and London, 1995; Philippe Minard, *La Fortune du Colbertisme*, Paris, 2001; Mary Schoeser, *French Textiles from 1760 to the Present*, London, 1991.

14 Schoeser, *French Textiles*, 18–55.

15 Names and symbols woven into tapestry borders, lead seals attached to ends of pieces of silk, or the name of the firm printed on to the end of pieces of cotton.

16 Daniel Roche, *The People of Paris*, Oxford, 1987, 150–2; Annik Pardailhé-Galabrun, *La naissance de l'intime. 3,000 foyers parisiens XVIIe–XVIII siècles*, Paris, 1988, 366–76.

17 Edith Standen and Jennifer Wearden, 'Early Modern Tapestries and Carpets', *The Cambridge History of Western Textiles*, ed. David Jenkins, Cambridge, 2003, vol. 1, 597–630.

18 See Lesley E. Miller, 'Jean Revel: fine artist, designer or entrepreneur?', *Journal of Design History*, 8:2, 1995, 79–96; Miller, 'Manufactures and the Man', 19–40.

19 Alistair Laing, 'Madame de Pompadour et "les Enfants de Boucher"', in *Madame de Pompadour et les arts*, ed. Xavier Salmon, Paris, 2002, 40–9.

20 Melanie Riffel, Sophie Rouart and Marc Walter, *Toile de Jouy. Printed Textiles in the Classic French Style*, London, 2003, 16. The same was true for wallpaper. See Christine Velut, 'Between Invention and Production: The Role of Design in the Manufacture of Wallpaper in France and England at the Turn of the Nineteenth Century', *Journal of Design History*, 17:1, 2004, 61–4.

21 Etienne Jollet, 'L'accessibilité de l'œuvre d'art: les beaux-arts de Paris au XVIIIe siècle', in Gilles Chabaud, Evelyne Cohen, Natacha Coquery & Jérôme Penez, eds, *Les guides imprimés du XVIe au XXe siècle. Villes, paysages, voyages*, Paris, 2000, 167–77; Maurice Fenaille, *Etat général de tapisseries de la manufacture des Gobelins depuis son origine jusqu'à nos jours, 1600–1900*, Paris, 1907, vol. 4, 320, citing Thiéry, *Le guide des amateurs et des étrangers voyageurs à Paris*, Paris, 1787, vol. 1, 82; Nicolas Joubert de l'Hiberderie, *Le dessinateur pour les étoffes d'or, d'argent et de soie*, Paris, 1765, 92.

22 Fenaille, *Etat général des tapisseries*, vol. 4, chap. 14.

23 'Lettre addressée aux auteurs du journal encylopédique au sujet des ouvrages exposés au Salon du Louvre en 1769', *Journal Enclyclopédique*, 1 décembre 1769. It identified his motivation as 'pour encourager les personnes qui travaillent avec supériorité à la Manufacture des Gobelins'. Fenaille, *Etat général des tapisseries*, vol. 4, especially chap. 14.

24 Coural, *Soieries de Lyon*.

25 Jeremy Black, *The British Abroad. The Grand Tour in the Eighteenth Century*, Stroud, 1997, 29–30; Coural, *Soieries de Lyon*, 102.

26 For example, Carlo Poni, 'Fashion as flexible production: the strategies of the Lyon silk merchants in the eighteenth century', in C.F. Sabel and J. Zeitlin, eds, *World of Possibilities: Flexibility and Mass Production in Western Industrialization*, Cambridge, 1997, 37–74; Beverly Lemire, *Fashion's Favourite: The Cotton Trade and the Consumer in Britain, 1660–1800*, Oxford, 1992.

27 Carolyn Sargentson, *Merchants and Luxury Markets. The Marchands Merciers of Eighteenth-Century Paris*, London, 1996, 97–112; G. Vrignaud, *Vêture et parure en France au dix-huitième siècle*, Paris, 1995; Lesley Ellis Miller, 'Paris-Lyons-Paris: Dialogue in the Design and Distribution of Patterned Silks in the Eighteenth Century', in Robert Fox and Anthony Turner, eds, *Luxury Trades and Consumerism in Ancien Régime Paris: Studies in the History of the Skilled Workforce*, Aldershot, 1998, 139–67. Some of the cheaper silks were even accessible for purchase to skilled artisans by the end of the century. Roche, *The People of Paris*, 160–96.

28 *Almanach général des marchands, des négocians, armateurs et fabricans de la France et de l' Europe et autres parties du monde*, Paris, various edns: 1774, 1778, 1779, 1786, 1788.

29 Poni, 'Fashion as flexible production'.

30 BML Fonds ancien ms. 1923, Grognard to Pernon, 1787.

31 See Justin Godart, *L'ouvrier en soie*, Geneva, 1976 (reprint of 1899 publication); Peter K. Thornton, *Baroque and Rococo Silks*, London, 1965; Coural, *Soieries de Lyon*.

32 Lesley Ellis Miller, 'Education and the Silk Designer: A Model for Success?', in *Disentangling Textiles*, eds Christine Boydell & Mary Schoeser, London, 2003, 185–94.

33 Thornton, *Baroque and Rococo Silks*; Poni, 'Fashion as flexible production'; Lesley Ellis Miller, 'Innovation and Industrial Espionage in Eighteenth-Century France: an Investigation of the Selling of Silks through Samples', *Journal of Design History*, 12:3, 1999, 271–92.

34 *Statuts et règlements*, Lyons, 1744.

35 Maurice Garden, *Lyon et les lyonnais au dix-huitième siècle*, Lille, 1970, 572–81.

36 BN ms. Fr. 11855, *Mémoire général sur la manufacture d'étoffes de soye, or, et argent qui se fabriquent dans la ville de Lyon écrit en janvier 1731*; AML CC178 Rolle de capitation, Grande Fabrique, 1758–9; *Almanach général des marchands*. These firms comprised two to six partners who invested between 10,000 to 60,000 livres each for a period of three to six years; shared the profits at the dissolution of the agreement; and usually reinvested in new partnerships thereafter. Jean Peyrot, 'Capitalisme commercial et fabriques dans la France du sud-est au XVIIIe siècle', in *Négoce et industrie en France aux XVIIIe et XIXe siècles*, eds L.M. Cullen & P. Butel, CNRS, Paris, 1980, 76–84.

37 Garden, *Lyon et les lyonnais*, 243ff.

38 Outsiders because they had either not been born in the provinces immediately surrounding the city or did not have the requisite training or capital to join their number.

39 Miller, 'Manufactures and the Man'; 'Representing Silk Design: Nicolas Joubert de l'Hiberderie and *Le dessinateur pour les étoffes d'or, d'argent et de soie* (Paris, 1765)', *Journal of Design History*, 17:1, 2004, 29–53. 'Designers in the Lyon Silk Industry, 1712–1787', chap. 6.

40 Lasalle began at the age of twenty-one, not the usual fourteen. ADR 3E7888 Saulnier (Lyons): 29 juillet 1744 Aprentissage Lasalle avec Mazancieu.

41 AML St Pierre et St Saturnin 1748, no. 409 *Mariage Lasalle/Charrier*; ADR 3E3578 Chazotte (Lyons): 24 avril 1748, *Mariage Lasalle/Charrier*; AML HH589 Registre des compagnons, f. 119; HH579 Registre des maîtres, f. 137; HH621 Registre des marchands, no. 273.

42 ADR B Dissolutions de sociétés, 19.12.1756 Dissolution Lasalle, Bouchet, Charrier et Charrier; 3E6913 Patrin (Lyons): 3 octobre 1751 Bail à loyer Tanliat/Lasalle.

43 AML CC178 Rolle de capitation 1758–9, f. 149; ADR 3E6913B Patrin (Lyons): 21 janvier 1751, Bail à loyer Tanliat/Lasalle; 3E1496 F, Delabat (Brignais): 21 septembre 1780, Bail Reverdy/Lasalle; 3E8500 Geors (Oullins): 17 avril 1783; 3E6075 Lecourt (Lyons): 12 et 23 décembre 1788, Cautionnement Lasalle/les intéressés des salins de Cette; *Indicateur alphabétique*, Lyons, 1788.

44 *Journal de Lyon*, 4 juin 1784, 190, cited in Coural, *Soieries de Lyon*, 102.

45 *Tableau des declarations pour la contribution patriotique*, Lyons, 1789, 75.

46 AN F12 2199, no. 8926 Lasalle to Intendant, 6 décembre 1760.

47 Hafter, 'Philippe de Lasalle'.

48 Anna Jolly, *Seidengewebe des 18. Jahrhunderts II. Naturalismus*, Abegg-Stiftung, Riggisberg, 2002, 388–90.

49 *Lettres patentes du roi concernant les manufacture. Données à Marli, Le 5 Mai 1779*, Paris, 1779, 3.
50 Or even just extend a design beyond the length of what was already on the simple. For a description of increase in length of designs, see AN F12 2201 Examen signé DeMontigny, 25 avril 1778, f.2.
51 Hafter, 'Philippe de Lasalle', 151–3.
52 The furnishing silks attributed to him are wider than the stipulated 54 cm. Those made in the 1770s range from between 70 cm and 82 cm wide. Coural, *Soieries de Lyon*, 113–14.
53 ADR 3E6913 Patrin (Lyon), 3 octobre 1751, Bail à loyer Tanliat/Lasalle.
54 AML HH135 Registre des permissions accordées, no. 42, 9 juillet 1754.
55 ADR 3E3214B Cabaret (Lyon): 22 juillet 1756, Procuration Lasalle.
56 ADR 8B1173 Irruegas y Gil to Rey Magneval y Dumas, Madrid, 29 noviembre de 1762 and 20 diciembre de 1762.
57 AML HH135 Registre des permissions, f. 5, 19 juin 1765.
58 AN F^{12} 2199 Letter dated Lyons, 3 octobre 1760.
59 AML Inventaire Chappe, Grande Fabrique, HHII, Art 3, titre 4, no. 62F, 14 mai 1758 note of the 'Signification ... rendu a la requeste des passementiers contre Lasalle'; HH 135 Petition dated 6 mars 1761; HH 135 Registre des permissions accordées à differents fabriquants, 14 octobre 1762.
60 Josette Brédif, *Classic Printed Textiles*, London, 1989, 21; Stanley D. Chapman and Serge Chassagne, *European Textile Printers in the Eighteenth Century*, London, 1981, 103–110.
61 Note that Benoît Mangean, a fellow designer in Lyons, had been championing painted silks from the 1740s. Coural, *Soieries de Lyon*, 113; Lesley Ellis Miller, 'Designers in the Lyons Silk Industry 1712–1787', unpublished PhD thesis, Brighton Polytechnic, 1988, vol. 2, 108–109.
62 Printed or painted cottons tended to be a decorative medium rather than a medium for portraiture or complex figurative or narrative compositions until the advent of copper-plate printing in the 1770s.
63 *Peints* has been translated in different articles as 'printed' rather than 'painted'. It is unlikely that it will be possible to clarify beyond doubt which is correct, but I veer towards 'painted' on the grounds of the gender of maker because we know that *peintresses* in other cities did 'paint', usually on top of printed patterns.
64 ADR 1C201 Demande de Lasalle, 28 janvier 1765, 19 mars 1765; AML HH552 *pièces* 36–7, 15 janvier 1766 (Guild's view of his colours); Archives de la chambre de commerce et d'industrie de Lyon, déliberations, 22 février 1762, ff. 53v–54 (Chamber of Commerce view).
65 AML HH135 Registre des permissions, f. 5, 19 juin 1765.
66 Coural notes that at no point did Lasalle supply the Royal Household directly. The mercers she identifies with Lasalle are unlikely to be related. See *Soieries de Lyon*.
67 *Gazette de France*, 29 novembre 1771, cited in Pierre Arizzoli-Clementel, 'Philippe de Lasalle (1723–1804): Les portraits tissés de Louis XV 'et de la Comtesse de Provence au musée des Tissus de Lyon', *Revue du Louvre*, 1992, no. 3, 53; Bertolon, *Du commerce et des* manufactures, 195.
68 Arrizoli-Clementel, 'Philippe de Lasalle (1723–1804)', 47–55.
69 Arrizoli-Clementel, 'Philippe de Lasalle (1723–1804)', 52, pl. 10.
70 De Chaignon, 'Philippe de Lasalle, dessinateur et fabricant', 72; Arrizoli-Clementel, 'Philippe de Lasalle (1723–1804)', 52.
71 Cozette, his equivalent at the Gobelins, did not do so either although he did petition the subject in the hope that he would commission portraits that the client would pay for and present as gifts. Fenaille, *Etat general des tapisseries*, vol. 4, chap. 14.
72 The Russian State collections have a copy of the portrait and of the oval of Catherine as Minerva. Tatiana Voltchkova, 'The Russian Commissions of Philippe de Lasalle', *Bulletin du CIETA*, 1999, vol. 76, 114–18.
73 Coural, *Soieries de Lyon*, 59–60.
74 Arrizoli-Clementel, 'Philippe de Lasalle (1723–1804)', 53.
75 Coural, *Soieries de Lyon*, 59; Arrizoli-Clementel, 'Philippe de Lasalle (1723–1804)', 51.
76 Lasalle was present on 20 May 1775 when the vestments were presented and on 21 May 1777 when the new uniform of the Order of the Saint-Esprit was presented. Coural, *Soieries de Lyon*, 57.
77 Arrizoli-Clementel, 'Philippe de Lasalle (1723–1804)', 47; Fenaille, *Etat general des tapisseries*, vol. 4, chap. 14.
78 Examples of the different media are well represented in Salmon, ed., *Madame de Pompadour et les arts*.
79 For example, in 1753 Boucher exhibited *Le Lever du Soleil* and the *Le Coucher du Soleil*, both of which were destined for tapestry production. Paris, Salons, *Collections de Livrets*, 1753, 15–16.
80 Diderot wrote in 1765, 'Deux morceaux en tapisserie; le portrait de *Pâris de Montmartel*, d'après le pastel de La Tour; c'est à s'y tromper. C'est le tableau. Un médaillon de la *Peinture*, d'après Vanloo. Ma foi, si quelqu'un discerne à quatre pas le tableau du morceau de tapisserie, je les lui donne tous deux'. Seyznec, ed., *Diderot, Salon 1765*, 234.
81 Bertolon, *Du commerce et des manufactures*, 195.

82 On art publics, see Matthew Craske, *Art in Europe 1700–1830*, Oxford, 1997, 13.

83 Pardailhé-Galabrun, *La naissance de l'intime*, 386–7.

84 Mathon de la Cour fils, *Quatrième lettre à M. sur les peintures, sculptures et gravures*, 1765 (Deloyne, VIII, 111).

85 MT Inv. 45.306. Note that eight versions of tapestry busts of Louis XV were woven between 1769 and 1778, three of Marie Lezcinska between 1769 and 1778, one of the Dauphin (future Louis XVI) and three of the Dauphine (Marie-Antoinette) between 1769 and 1774, one of Louis XVI, one of each of Marie-Antoinette's parents between 1773 and 1784. Fenaille, *Etat general des tapisseries*, vol. 4, 326.

86 AN, F12 636B Letter from Cozette to Marigny, 5 novembre 1774.

87 Workshop heads, weavers such as Audran and Cozette.

88 Voltchkova, 'The Russian Commissions', 118.

89 Between 1769 and 1773, Coural, *Soieries de Lyon*, 60, citing Gustave Macon, *Les Arts dans la Maison de Condé*, Paris, 1903; Voltchkova, 'The Russian Commissions', 119. Surviving samples of the partridges design at the Abegg-Stiftung near Bern (Inv. no. 2581), The Hermitage in St Petersburg (Inv. no. T12212) and the archives of Tassinari et Chatel in Paris reveal different colour ways, as do samples in recent Parisian auctions. Caution is required as they may be nineteenth-century re-weaves, which underlines the longevity and popularity of this design. I am grateful to Anna Jolly for supplying this information.

90 Voltchkova, 'The Russian Commissions', 117–23.

91 Note the tapestry series by Boucher still hanging at Osterley Park, Twickenham, London.

92 Salmon, ed., *Madame de Pompadour et les arts*.

93 Arrizoli-Clementel, 'Philippe de Lasalle (1723–1804)', 55, pl. 15. A much cheaper framing than that of his wife.

94 On the use of cheap embroidresses outside city walls, see Archives de la chambre de commerce et d'industrie, déliberations, 10 décembre 1785, f.45ff.

95 Anne Kraatz, 'La "Gazette des atours" de Marie Antoinette' and Françoise Tétart-Vittu, 'La garde-robe de Marie Antoinette: le regard des historiens' in Michelle Bimbenet-Privat, ed., *Art et Commerce au service de Marie-Antoinette. Les Atours de la Reine*, Paris, 2001, 25–44. *Galerie des Modes* (1778 and 1787) demonstrates the range of gauzes. Stella Blum, ed., *Eighteenth-Century French Fashions in Full Color*, New York, 1982, 1, 7, 12, 16, 25, 26, 27, 28.

96 Kraatz, 'La "Gazette des atours" de Marie Antoinette', 27; Mary Sheriff, *The Exceptional Woman. Elisabeth Vigée-Lebrun and the Cultural Politics of Art*, Chicago and London, 1996, 143–7.

97 Hafter, 'Philippe de Lasalle', 154.

98 Such as Josiah Wedgwood in Britain.

99 AN F12 2199 First petition requesting *gratification* to teach design, 25 décembre 1759; ADR 1C201 Letter proposing classes in design and appropriate remuneration, signed by Lasalle, 18 mars 1765; *Almanach de Lyon*, Lyons, 1780.

5

REGENERATION THROUGH THE EVERYDAY? CLOTHING, ARCHITECTURE AND FURNITURE IN REVOLUTIONARY PARIS

LEORA AUSLANDER

The French Revolution is renowned for its attempts radically to transform everyday life.[1] Participants argued that the Revolution could not be made only on the street, in political tracts, in public meetings, or on the battlefield; it also had to occur when the ordinary citizen listened to music, got dressed, walked the streets of the locality, ate supper, spoke, sat down, or watched a play. Moreover, the Revolution could not be the work of a few; it needed to be lived by all. Contemporaries justified the rather counter-intuitive idea that a change in the political ordering of society required changes in clothing, language, calendars, weights and measures, theatre and street names, by arguing for the extraordinary power of signs and symbols. As one contemporary, Gastin, put it in 1799: 'The language of signs has always had a powerful effect on the spirit and the heart. Signs have a magical quality, which has, in all times, ruled men, leading them either into bondage or freedom.'[2] While political discourse reached the mind, another, Armand-Guy Kersaint, argued that signs and material things reached the heart: 'If I were to speak to men chosen at random and in need of education ... I would focus on ... the need to strike the spirit of the multitude with the help of buildings and monuments, at the same time as I attempted to convince them by reason.'[3]

Signs were understood, then, to have a powerful pedagogic effect, one that could be harnessed to the cause of the revolutionary transformation of society and state. Properly conceived and used they could, as one scholar has recently put it, 'win more people to independence than will battles'.[4] Signs could either freeze the world in the old ways of subservience to the king, or convince people of the validity of the new principles of rationality, liberty, fraternity and equality. Once people were engaged in the revolutionary effort, signs could be used actually to regenerate the nation. The old styles that '[u]nder the empire of despots, the useless class of unemployed rich people had determined ... blindly follow[ing] the vicissitudes of fashion' would, according to the *Société populaire et républicaine des arts*, be replaced by a style 'dictated by reason and approved by good taste'. Not only would a rational aesthetic form replace the foolish 'caprices of rich people's imagination' but also differences in 'rank and fortune' would no longer be marked by style.[5] Later in the revolutionary decade they promised to fill the void left by the death of the king. The people, now that it was no longer united under its royal father, needed a new means of bonding with the abstraction called 'France'. A sense of national belonging was to be created by 'a common and distinctive sign of the French'.[6] A unified national clothing style, for example, would enable people to feel truly French. It was thought that '[a] national costume will accomplish the goal, a goal which is so important to a free people, to announce, or to be reminded of oneself everywhere and at all moments.' Given the novelty of the experience of freedom and democratic representation, without this reminder they feared that a person might 'forget' him/herself as a free citizen. It was not only domestic pedagogy that was at stake, however, but perception of the French abroad. 'French citizens will no longer be confused with those of nations still languishing in the irons of slavery . . . .'[7] Thus the pedagogic power of signs could have a range of effects: it could trap people in old ways, reinforcing the evils of monarchism and social differentiation; it could draw people into the revolutionary cause; it could, once they were engaged in the Revolution, help to rid them of the last vestiges of their old ideas; and, finally, it could help to consolidate the French nation.

These ideas did not remain abstract but were, rather, implemented through law and practice. Within the space of a few years, French citizens saw many aspects of their everyday lives radically changed. They were to speak a different language; to hear and sing new kinds of music; to wear clothing of an altered style. French people no longer went to church; their roads and towns had unfamiliar names; the boundaries of their *départements* were newly demarcated; their weeks had ten days; their months bore a novel nomenclature; their food was weighed in new units; and new forms of architecture were hotly debated. Neither the discussions about appropriate forms for republican style, nor actual transformations of aesthetic, linguistic and ritual form reached all domains, however. Most notably, revolutionary pamphlets and legislative debate are oddly silent on the issue of a new style for life at home. No laws were passed, no restrictions imposed, and no calls were made for new visions of domestic interiors during the revolutionary years.

It is, therefore, in some sense, not surprising that there is almost complete consensus among art historians specializing in the history of furniture that there was no Revolutionary style in furniture or the other decorative arts.[8] Many chronologies of furniture styles leap directly from Louis XVI to Empire, and even those that do pause at the turn of the century at most identify Directory and Consulate styles lying between the two styles named for two authoritarian regimes. A few disparaging sentences are generally offered concerning the relatively few extant pieces of furniture decorated with revolutionary symbols or texts. Have scholars missed something, or was the revolutionaries' stance towards furniture and the decorative arts indeed different from their position on other domains of everyday aesthetics? And what were producers' and consumers' aesthetic practices during these years?

The revolutionaries' securely documented preoccupations with clothing style on the one hand and architecture on the other render this question particularly intriguing. Why attempt to change clothing and the built environment but not furniture and the other arts of the home? Clothing and furniture are commodities with great symbolic potential; both were, in fact, used by crown and court in the *ancien régime* to augment their power. And historians have been arguing for fifteen years that the onset of a consumer society in France should be dated to the mid-eighteenth century at the latest.[9] If France was indeed a consumer society – that is, one in which social and political identities were constituted as much (or more) by the acquisition of goods as by other means – then the revolutionaries ought to have been concerned with all domains of the everyday aesthetic repertoire. Their relative silence on the subject of interior decoration – for revolutionaries were quiet not just about furniture, but also about domestic architecture, china, silverware and tapestries – was not simply a result of the brevity of the revolutionary period or the destruction of the court system, as many have suggested. It was also a symptom of the limits of a nascent consumer society and of the revolutionaries' understanding of the relation between the public and the private.

As a silence can only be understood when juxtaposed to speech, before both sketching what happened in furniture design (with a few comparative examples from the other decorative arts) and offering an explanation for its particular fate during the Revolution, I shall start with the two examples – clothing and architecture – by way of contrast.

CLOTHING

When the Third Estate reconvened as the National Assembly in June 1790, one of its first acts was to reject the official costumes that had been prescribed for each of the three orders – Nobility, Clergy and Third Estate – of which the Estates General had been composed.[10] That early preoccupation with clothing was to continue throughout the revolutionary decade, shifting from an initial refusal of *ancien régime* restrictions to an elaboration of republican style. During the three years following the taking of the Bastille, therefore, not only did legislators claim the freedom not to dress according to their estate; some of their fellow citizens took to wearing the red-heeled shoes that had been reserved by law for the king and the aristocracy until the fall of the monarchy, while others used clothing even more explicitly to mark their political positions, adopting, for instance, an extreme austerity of style (plate 5.1). Many of those who were opposed to the upheaval took to wearing black as a sign of mourning, while those in favour wore military uniforms even when not on duty (or not even in the military), and still others marked their position by an absence, giving their silver and gold shoe buckles for the revolutionary cause.[11]

As the Revolution became more radical during the summer of 1792 the politicization of clothing intensified and moves were made to enforce national homogeneity and an obligation to demonstrate one's adherence to the nation through one's clothing. On 5 July, for example, a law was passed requiring all adult men to wear the tricoloured cockade (this obligation was extended to women the following April). Later that year a recommendation (inspired by Plutarch's *Life of Lycurgus*) was made that '[t]he form of dress worn by all citizens, their arms, their exercises, their festival paraphernalia and all things of common concern should likewise be determined by the legislature.'[12] That suggestion was not translated into law at that time, but it did plant a seed. In the spring of 1793, the *Société populaire et républicaine des arts* invited *all* French citizens to submit ideas for republican dress. This was one of many contests held encouraging collective participation in the construction of a new national – republican – everyday. None of the designs submitted was considered adequate, however, and the Committee of Public Safety had to resort to expertise and invited the painter Jacques-Louis David to present 'his views and suggestions on the means of improving national costume and of rendering it more appropriate to republican morals and to the character of the Revolution'.[13] David's designs, too, were laid aside. Imposing an entire clothing style, even at this more radical moment in the Revolution, was judged to represent too great a limit on citizens' liberty, even as it was thought positively to reinforce the two other elements – equality and fraternity – of the revolutionary call to arms. It was not, therefore, doubt concerning clothing's pedagogic and communicative capacities that caused the revolutionaries to allow a degree of freedom, but rather a weighing up of the relative importance of liberty, equality and fraternity.[14]

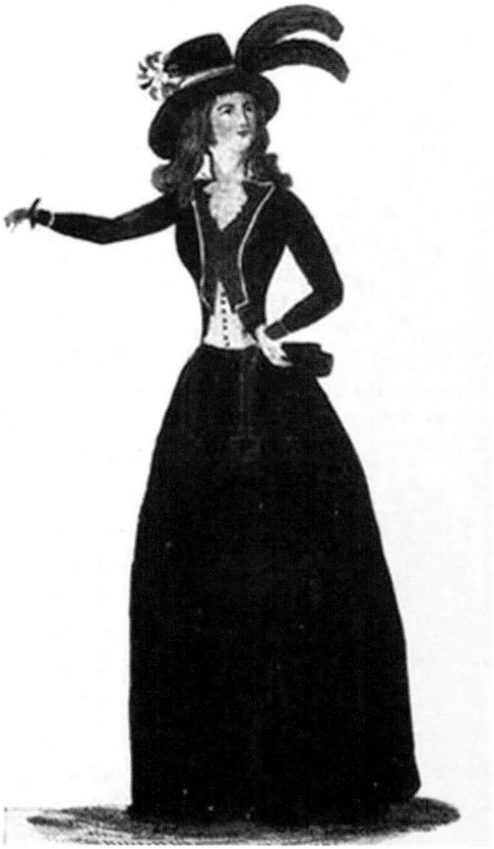

5.1 *Women's Clothing*, c. 1790. Hand-coloured print.

In matters of style, the commitment to personal freedom on the one hand, and a sense of their importance as pedagogical and representational political strategy on the other may be seen in the failure to pass legislation imposing a complete uniform, and the labelling of one of the Revolution's most important groups by their style of clothing. Thus, freedom of attire was, admittedly after much heated discussion, deemed a right by the Convention in the Autumn of 1793 (9 Brumaire, Year II).[15] And the nomenclature of a critically important political group in the early years of the Revolution, the sans-culottes, came from their clothing style. Their name was derived from their choice to wear the long pants characteristic of popular urban dress rather than the breeches – culottes – of the elite. The sans-culottes further adopted the Phrygian cap (or *bonnet rouge*), originally worn in Rome by those recently freed from slavery, as a sign of their political position.[16]

Finally, in September 1795 (Vendemaire, Year IV), the celebrated abbé Grégoire published a report arguing that the wearing of uniforms specific to office would enhance the dignity of the office at the same time that it would remind the office holders that their social recognition depended entirely on their social utility (rather than birth or wealth).[17] Unlike many of his predecessors, however, abbé Grégoire suggested that it would not be possible to regulate the clothing or behaviour of all, but that the people would have to be relied upon to seek to emulate the officials. Grégoire's arguments were apparently convincing and one of the last acts of the Convention in October was to pass a law prescribing clothing for officials but not returning to a model of obligatory dress for ordinary inhabitants. The wisdom (and realism) of this choice may be seen in the very extravagant fashions adopted a few years later under the Directory.[18]

This focus on clothing as a political domain was not new with the Revolution; clothing had long been intensely politicized in France.[19] From the medieval into the early modern period clothing was, in theory at least, supposed to indicate the wearer's social and political position. Dress was not a matter of individual choice, but rather of collective identification. That this system was already breaking down – in the face of an expanding market – may be seen by the sumptuary legislation promulgated from the Renaissance to the mid-eighteenth century.[20] These laws were repeated efforts to ensure that people dressed according to who they were, as opposed to who they aspired (or chose to pretend) to be.[21] A particular justification of these laws was proposed: because 'the excess usage of silk has been observed on the part of a large number of bourgeois women, who thereby transformed themselves into ladies from one day to the next, we have prohibited and again prohibit, these women to change estate, if their husbands are not gentlemen.'[22] Clothing enabled its wearers literally to alter their social and political position. Not only was this deception dangerous to the political order, it risked damaging the private, family worlds upon which that order depended. A law of 1649 noted, 'There is a no more certain cause of the ruin of state than the excess of unregulated luxury, which by the subversion of individual families, necessarily brings about the ruin of the public ... .'[23] The advent of new fabric at lower prices on a relatively open market had thus, from the mid-eighteenth century, long before the Revolution, made clothing a good subject to frequent replacement, a good subject to fashion, among urban elites (and perhaps not so elite).[24] This commodification of clothing enabled French men and women to use clothing to express social desires and contest the political order. The sartorial commemoration of significant political events – such as the American Revolution – clearly demonstrates this transformation in the use of clothing in the pre-Revolutionary period.

Revolutionaries' efforts to regulate or at least influence the clothing styles worn in France can thus be understood to be building on an inherited tradition and practice, and also to be intervening where intervention was possible. Clothing design was relatively easy, its production relatively quick, and the cloth, thread and findings (including ribbons and buttons) of which it was made required no seasoning period before use. Revolutionaries thus built on the old and the new, the discursive and the material, in their efforts to turn monarchists into republicans through dress. The idea of legislating on clothing they drew from the days when the crown (and church) could impose style; the idea of changing clothing quickly they drew from the much newer world of fashion; and they relied on the organization of production actually to produce the clothing. Revolutionary legislators discovered, however, that they could not reach consensus even among themselves concerning a new 'sumptuary' system. They, therefore, limited their regulatory efforts to accoutrements (like the cockade) for all, or whole uniforms for official representatives of the state. While there were considerable political constraints on efforts to create a new republican style of dress, there were few material constraints; if the legislators could have reached consensus and persuaded the public, the clothing industry could have rapidly produced and distributed the clothing.[25] The extensive debate concerning dress, therefore, seems to make sense. Another domain of intervention, architecture, poses a different set of questions.

ARCHITECTURE

Architecture lies at the other pole – in both temporal and material terms – from clothing. Designing new buildings is a lengthy process, their actual construction even more so, and requires massive capital investment. 'Revolutionary' architectural forms built on and modified earlier designs and, in fact, the oeuvres of many of the most celebrated architects of the Revolution are characterized by considerable continuity between their royal and republican projects. Architecture also, of course, had a very different relation to the market. While guild artisans theoretically had a monopoly on clothing production and distribution before the Revolution abolished the corporations, they had, in fact, been competing with 'free' labour for a least a century. Architecture, even for private use, had been much more successfully policed (even if the labour in the building trades, too, was less so). When revolutionary legislators and theorists turned their attention to the pedagogic and representational potential of the built environment, therefore, they saw different possibilities and constraints to those presented by dress. The state's power was far less disputed, but so too was its capacity. And, in fact, the Revolution's impact on French cityscapes was generally negative rather than positive. That is, the Revolution succeeded in destroying a great many ecclesiastical, monastic, royal and noble sculptures, edifices and monuments. The Revolution constructed very little and certainly did not create a republican built environment.

Despite the failure actually to erect structures, however, a great deal of energy and thought went into imagining what they should look like. Architecture was

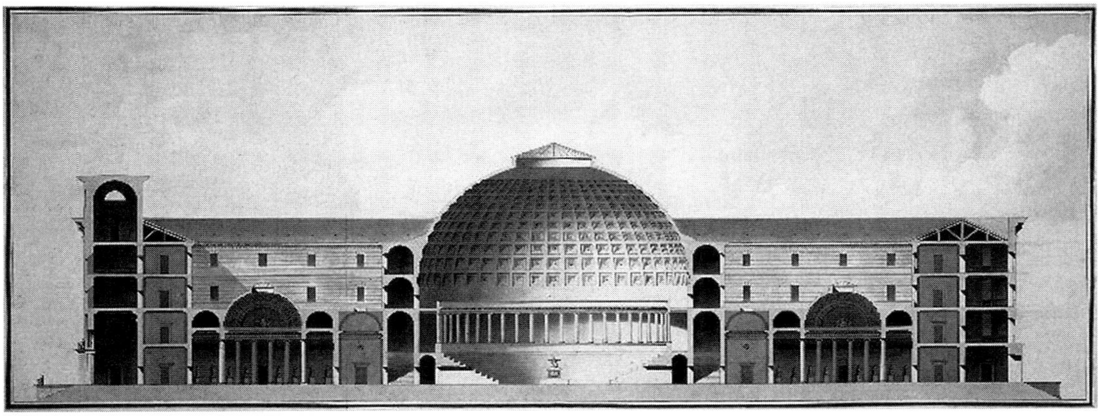

5.2 Etienne-Louis Boullée, *Design no. 3 for the Palais national*, 1792. Paris: Bibliothèque national de France.

understood as a means of public education; buildings and monuments were to promote virtue. Their materiality and scale were understood to give them particular powers. As the architect Étienne-Louis Boullée put it, 'The images that they [buildings] offer to our senses should arouse in us feelings analogous to the use to which the building is put.'[26] The built environment had the capacity, therefore, to change how people felt; a properly built law court would inspire sentiments of justice or a school a desire for learning. Revolutionary leaders were eager, therefore, to encourage reflection on republican architecture. In Years II and III of the Revolutionary epoch alone, the government sponsored at least fourteen architectural or monumental competitions that were designed either to generate designs for the commemoration of important events, the renovation of buildings, or to provide space for activities considered important.[27] These *concours* attracted a great deal of attention from lay people and architects alike.

Three architects dominated the architectonic vision of the new revolutionary everyday – Étienne-Louis Boullée (1728–1799), Claude-Nicolas Ledoux (1736–1796) and Jean-Jacques Lequeu (1757–1824).[28] Although the three had quite distinct visions, they all show a marked influence of the Greek and Roman worlds, but at the same time a desire to adapt those aesthetic norms rather than simply to reproduce them. Their hundreds of drawings were also almost all characterized by utopianism, as if they had known, which they may well have, that these projects would only ever exist on paper. Two examples of projects, Boullée's design of 1792 for the Palais national and Lequeu's 'Temple de l'égalité' of Year II (1794/1795), demonstrate efforts to embody the political principles of the Revolution in architecture.

Boullée's design (see plate 5.2) was most probably drawn up in response to a call from the Academy of Architecture in August 1790 for designs for a building to house the National Assemblies. The building was characterized by sharply drawn geometric forms, embellished and softened with revolutionary emblems and texts. Its basic shape was delineated by a cube, at the centre of which stood a sphere forming an amphitheatre in which the deputies would meet. The façade was unbroken by windows, but relieved by a massive inscription of the Declaration of the Rights of Man and Citizen. The Palais national thus melded symmetrical two- and three-dimensional geometric forms – squares and spheres – representing the principle of the equality of all representatives of the nation, the pedagogic literalness of revolutionary text, and the allegories of republican virtues.[29] While full of references to the classical world, the design is wholly forward-looking and original: a new building for a new form of government.

A sphere is also the central form of Lequeu's 'Temple de l'égalité', but in this case it is encircled more lightly in a portico of Doric columns (plate 5.3). Lequeu chose, furthermore, triply to underscore the theme. Not only was the sphere contained within the circular portico, but he inscribed a smaller sphere within the sphere. As visitors penetrated the temple, they would find themselves before a small figure, *Egalité*, balancing precariously on the contained sphere, gazing out at walls ornamented with classical motifs. The unrelenting roundness – even the round columns are deprived of their conventional square bases and capitals – is destabilizing, perhaps as destabilizing as entering into a political and social system based on equality from a society of orders. The exterior of the globe is, however, both nationalized and rendered less abstract by a parade of tri-coloured flags set into the top of the portico. The flags humanize the temple, bringing it back to earth, and grounding it in the French nation.

While it would be a radical oversimplification of a massive production of diverse projects during the revolutionary decade (and particularly during Years II and III) to claim a status of 'typical' for either Boullée's Palais national or Lequeu's 'Temple de l'égalité', many of the projects produced in response to the government's calls for designs did share some fundamental characteristics with these two buildings: classical form, proportion and decorative elements were borrowed from the classical world, but altered to create something new; austere geometric form was combined with allegory, a melding of universalist and national tropes; and an effort was systematically made to evoke nature and nature's beauty. Equally important was their very public nature. With one exception – a competition to design the ideal rural building – all the government's calls were for

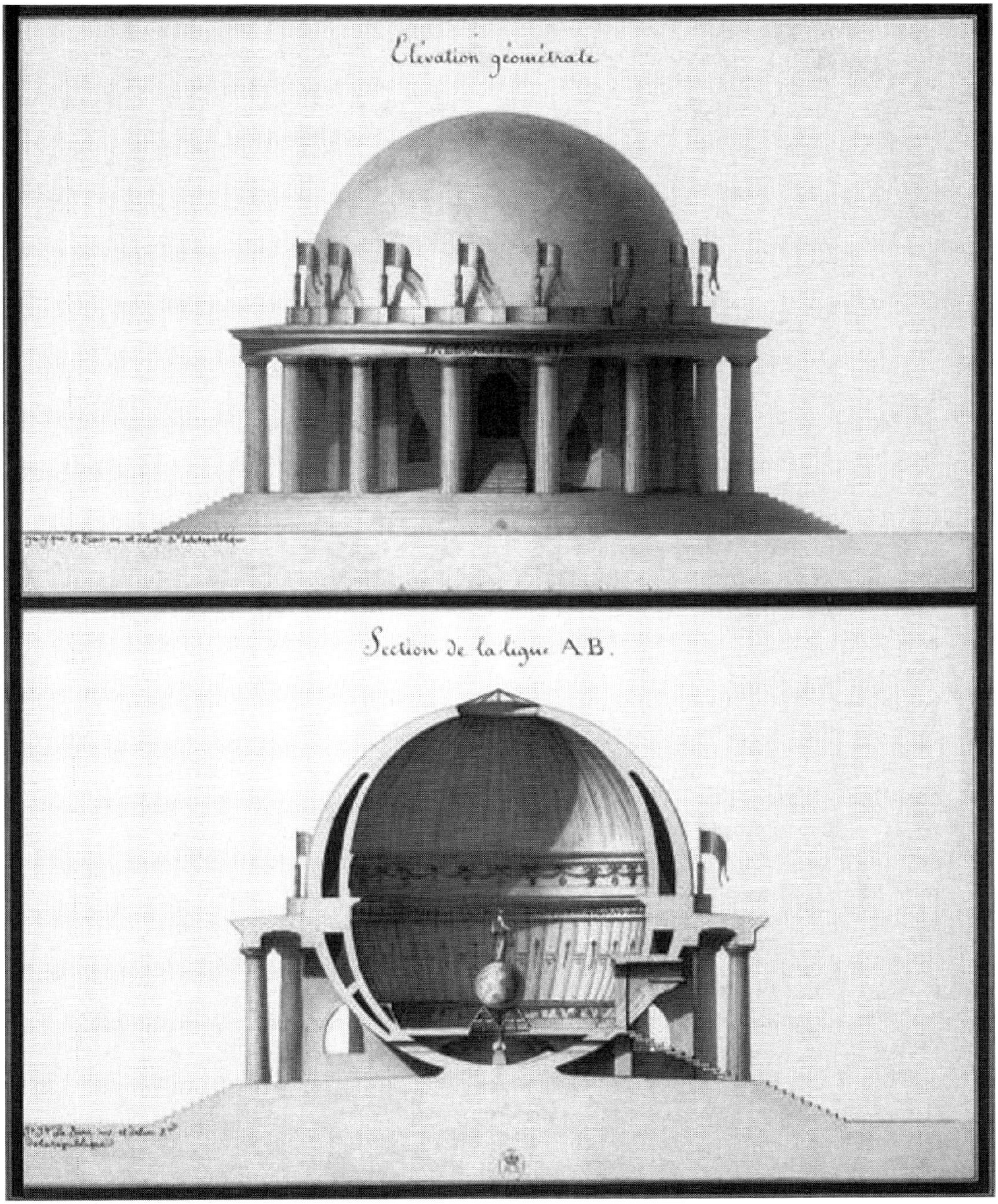

5.3 Jean-Jacques Lequeu, *Temple of Equality, elevation and section*, *c*. 1793–4. Pen, ink, wash and watercolour, 40.2 × 28.1 cm. Paris: Bibliothèque national de France.

buildings or monuments either to represent fundamental republican principles (like Lequeu's temple), to provide appropriate space for a crucial political or cultural function (like Boullée's palace), or to commemorate a hero or a crucial revolutionary victory. Although the vast majority of the architects active during the Revolution had extensive experience in domestic architecture, pamphleteers or legislators who were far more preoccupied with the pedagogic possibilities of the public than those of the private sphere did not call upon that expertise.

Having briefly explored revolutionaries' investments in, and producers' and consumers' use of, two domains of republican transformation of everyday material culture, I shall turn to one that lies for me between the two: furniture.

FURNITURE

The revolutionary decade and a half were marked, then, by several temporalities in the domain of goods of style, with clothing, whose design and production could both happen quickly, occupying one extreme and architecture, in which both processes took much longer, at the other. Furniture occupied a position in the middle of this spectrum. High-quality furniture required wood seasoned over years, the collaboration of many artisans and workshops, and thousands of hours of labour. Radical changes in furniture's structure necessitated extensive reflection and experimentation. Thus, while changes in clothing practices could happen from one month to the next and architectural innovations were matters of decades and great capital investment, alterations in furniture were a matter of years. At the time when the Bastille was taken on 14 July 1789, Parisian furniture-makers were engaged in work that would take months (and in some cases far longer) to finish and had a backlog of orders from the crown, the court and urban elites. One of the ironies, therefore, of French furniture history, as noted by Pierre Arizzioli-Clémentel, is that some of the finest representations of Louis XVI style furniture were finished during the revolutionary period.[30] Georges Jacob, Bernard Molitor, Adam Weisweiler and other celebrated furniture-makers continued delivering pieces to Marie Antoinette, Louis XVI, Monsieur, comte de Provence and others until 1792.[31] This royal and noble clientele even commissioned some new pieces in this period.

While some of this furniture retained the ornateness and ostentatious luxury of court furniture, much of it, like the architecture of the time, even when made for noble or royal clients, embodied a seemingly austere form of neoclassicism. Neoclassicism was not, of course, a novelty at the end of the eighteenth century, but rather had been gradually gaining influence since the discoveries of Pompeii and Herculaneum in the mid-century.[32] But while most of the furnishings inspired by neoclassicism earlier in the century had combined angularity with rich ormolu mounts and even Japanese lacquer, by the 1790s the ormolu had been reduced to a minimum (if present at all) and large surfaces were covered with single sheets of veneer.[33] As Ulrich Leben points out, given the expense of mahogany veneer, such pieces could cost easily as much as their most ornate

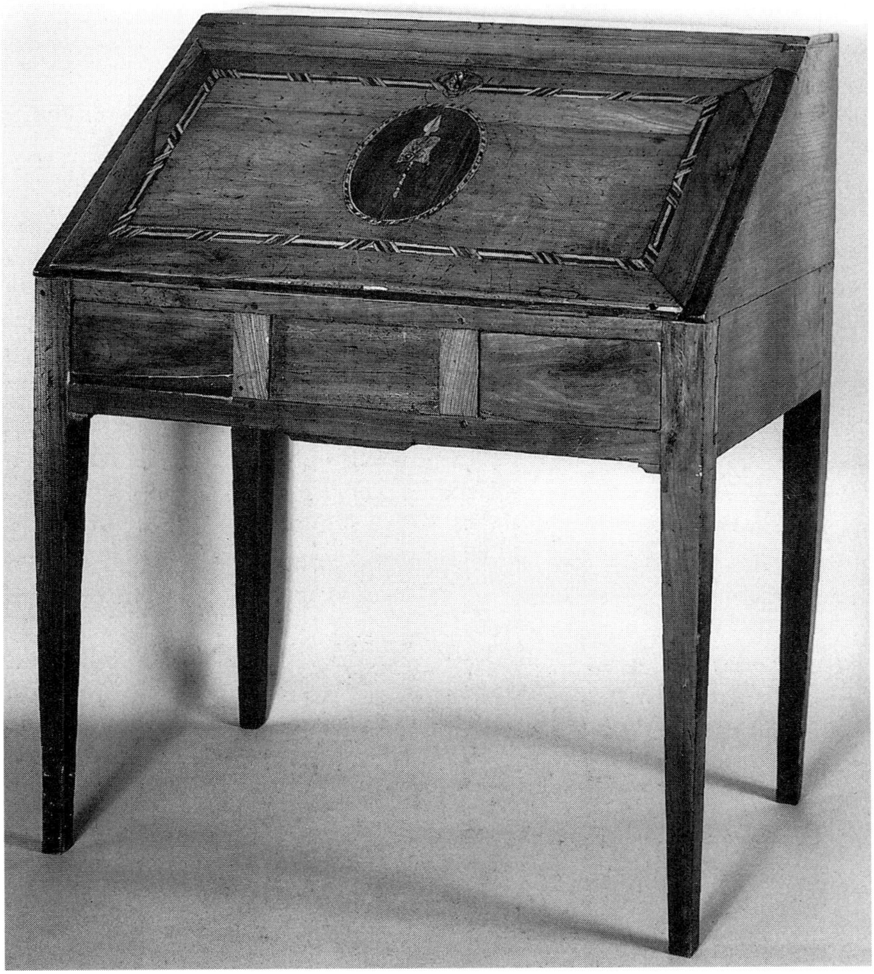

5.4 Writing desk, *c.* 1795. Walnut. Paris: Musée Carnavalet.

competition. At stake was not economy, but rather the representation of sobriety and seriousness (and, some would argue, republican masculinity).

During the period of the first Republic (from 1792 to 1795) some of those same artisans, most notably Georges Jacob, started working on official republican furniture because new forms of political organization required new furniture.[34] When plans were made to convene the National Convention in 1792, it was realized that the legislative body would not be able to do its work without chairs in which to sit and tables at which to write. The architects Charles Percier and Pierre-François-Léonard Fontaine were asked in 1792 to design the furnishings for the National Convention. While David did a sketch for the armchair of the president, Percier and Fontaine provided Georges Jacob with the rest of the drawings.[35]

These pieces followed the already established model of luxurious simplicity but with more explicit references to the Roman Republics. Thus, two winged griffons supported the president's desk,[36] and the front legs of the representatives' chairs took the form of winged lions (carved out of mahogany).[37]

Although new furnishings were commissioned for the new republican political space, the problem of furnishing the new representative political body did not provoke anything like as much interest as the problem of clothing the literal bodies of the Republic's citizens. Neither in 1792 nor the years following was there any discussion of mandating appropriate furnishings for the homes of French citizens. A parallel may be seen in another decorative art – porcelain. During the Revolution the director of the Sèvres porcelain manufactory, Antoine Régnier, was ordered to destroy the *ancien régime* moulds and drawings, but not given a positive programme to follow.[38] No national competitions were held for styles or forms of furniture, ceramics, or tapestry appropriate to the Republic, nor was there debate on the topic. Once the National Convention was furnished, the issue seems to have faded from official concern, never to reappear. Further reducing the incentive for stylistic innovation was the economic crisis. This period saw a rise in unemployment and corresponding destitution in Paris. By the winter of Year IV, some two thirds of the Parisian population was receiving some aid from the government and the situation in the luxury trades was worse than elsewhere.[39]

Given the lack of official engagement and the crisis in the decorative arts trades from Year IV of the Revolution onwards, it is remarkable that any innovation occurred at all, but some did. 'Republican' furniture was made of natural, solid wood (rather than being veneered) and of indigenous and relatively inexpensive materials (instead of exotic woods, precious stones and metals); moreover, it sported marquetry inlays of Phrygian caps, pikes and revolutionary texts (see plates 5.4 to 5.8). In these pieces not only did indigenous wood replace imported kinds, but it was also often left in close to its natural state. While this was in part no doubt due to the constraints posed by wartime austerity, it was coherent with the revolutionaries' valorization of nature. Even if the inlay of gemstones or exotic woods or bronzes was both too closely associated with court and crown and too costly for the period, the nakedness and humbleness of the wood could have been hidden under paint or coloured varnish – neither of them expensive techniques. In parallel, while carved and turned elements

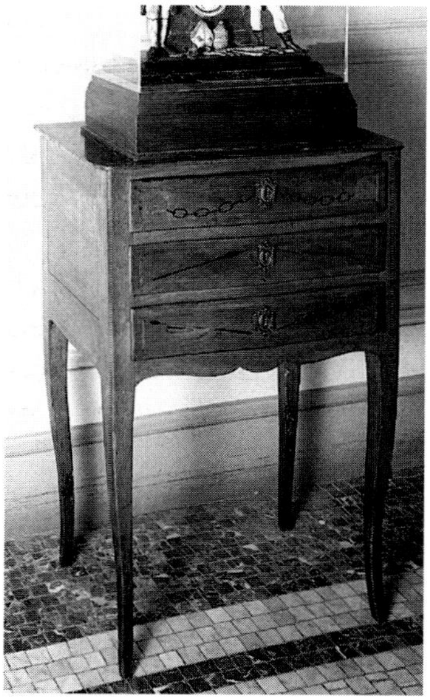

5.5 Bedside table with three drawers, *c.* 1795. Walnut. Paris: Musée Carnavalet.

became relatively rare, the surfaces of many desks, armoires and tables were ornamented with marquetry depicting revolutionary scenes and emblems, and reproducing revolutionary texts.

The desk by an unknown maker in plate 5.4 appears to have been constructed from indigenous walnut finished with no more than wax polish. Its legs are sawn and devoid of ornamental detail. Aside from a minimalist softening of the bottom edge, the desk's only departure from radical austerity is a simple marquetry motif on the front: a pike overlaid with a Phrygian cap in an oval medallion, framed by a rectangle in fine baguettes. Almost equally plain is a small three-drawer side-table (plate 5.5), also most probably in French walnut (but it could even be pine), ornamented with marquetry muskets, pikes, Phrygian caps and chains. It is a slightly more complex piece of furniture: the legs bear the gentle curves characteristic of the period between Louis XV and Louis XVI and there is an elegant bronze lock on each of the drawers. Acquired by the Musée Carnavalet – the museum of the history of Paris – both pieces doubtless owe the honour of their home to their historical, rather than artistic, interest. In neither case would the design or the quality of the craftsmanship earn them a place in a decorative arts (as opposed to historical) museum. But their very simplicity contributes to their interest and importance. Modest people would not have commissioned new furniture – however simple – during these difficult and uncertain times. The austerity of these pieces must, therefore, have been intentional, an austerity that expressed in the most thorough manner possible the republican sentiments of their owners.

Two further pieces at the Musée Carnavalet, a wardrobe and a dressing table, underscore that argument. The *meuble à deux corps* (plate 5.6) is ostentatiously revolutionary in its motifs. Each of its six figures includes a text with a revolutionary theme, surrounded by revolutionary and patriotic symbols ranging from the cock (*le coq gaullois*) to pikes and flags, while an overseeing eye of reason coifs the entire piece. Unlike the other two objects, however, this chest is entirely covered with an elegant veneer, the marquetry is quite elaborate, and the piece is very carefully finished. The materials remain modest – it is made of French wood and uses no precious metal – but the craftsmanship is relatively complex. Thus, although the detail (plate 5.7) demonstrates that the marquetry was cruder than that worked on court pieces earlier in the century, it remained nevertheless an expensive and luxurious piece of furniture. Likewise, the top of a dressing table (plate 5.8), though crafted of unrefined solid wood, conveys its revolutionary message in carefully and quite intricately sculpted bas-relief. The range of furniture inscribed with revolutionary images or texts or bearing republican motifs was very wide and included beds, bedside tables, *coiffeuses* (dressing tables), desks and *armoires* (wardrobes). They could, therefore, have been found in most rooms of the dwelling, indicating that those who chose to purchase them were not merely concerned with appearing republican in the most public rooms of the private sphere (the dining room and *salon*), nor in simply reflecting their

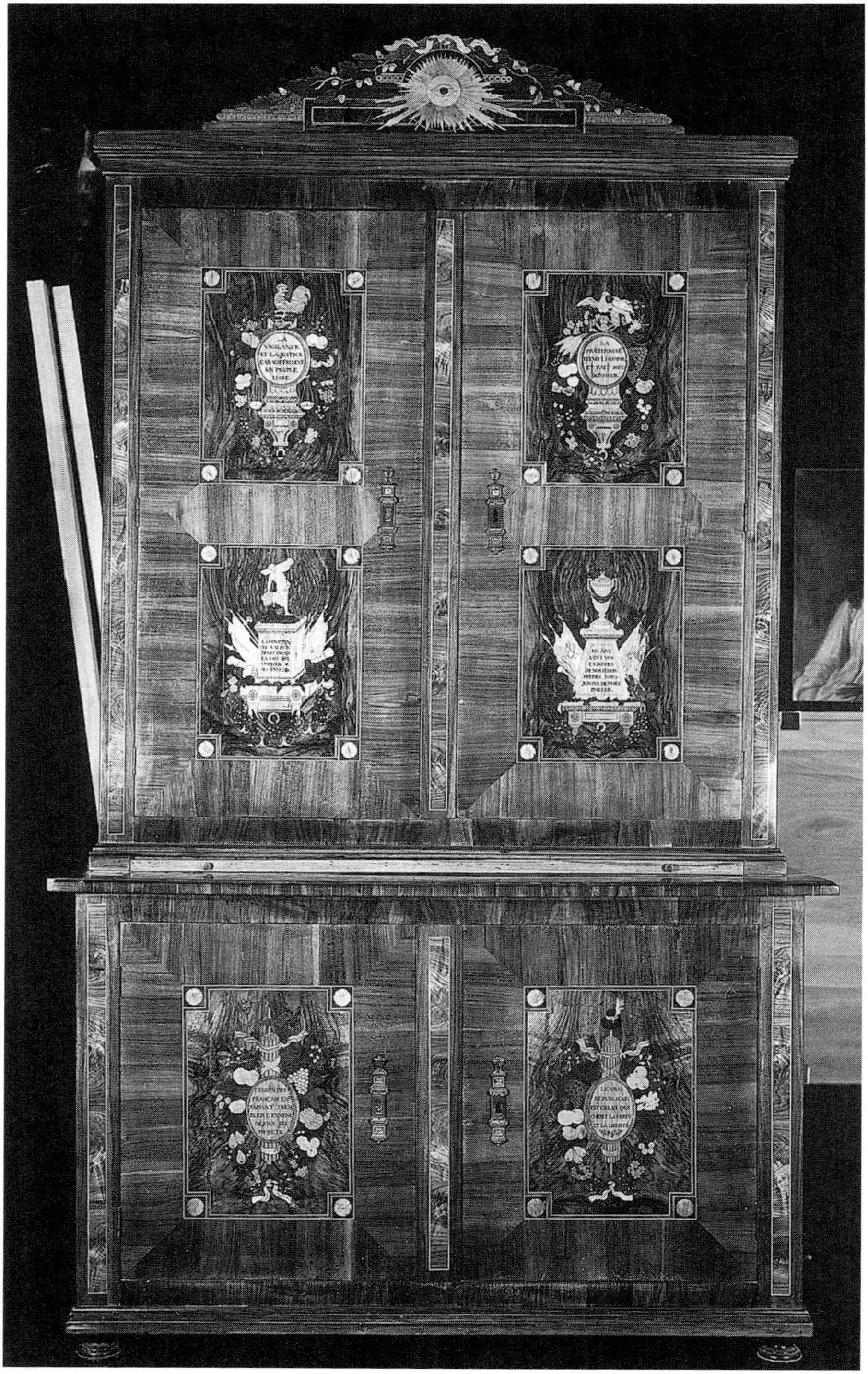

5.6 Two-tier armoire, *c.* 1795. Paris: Musée Carnavalet.

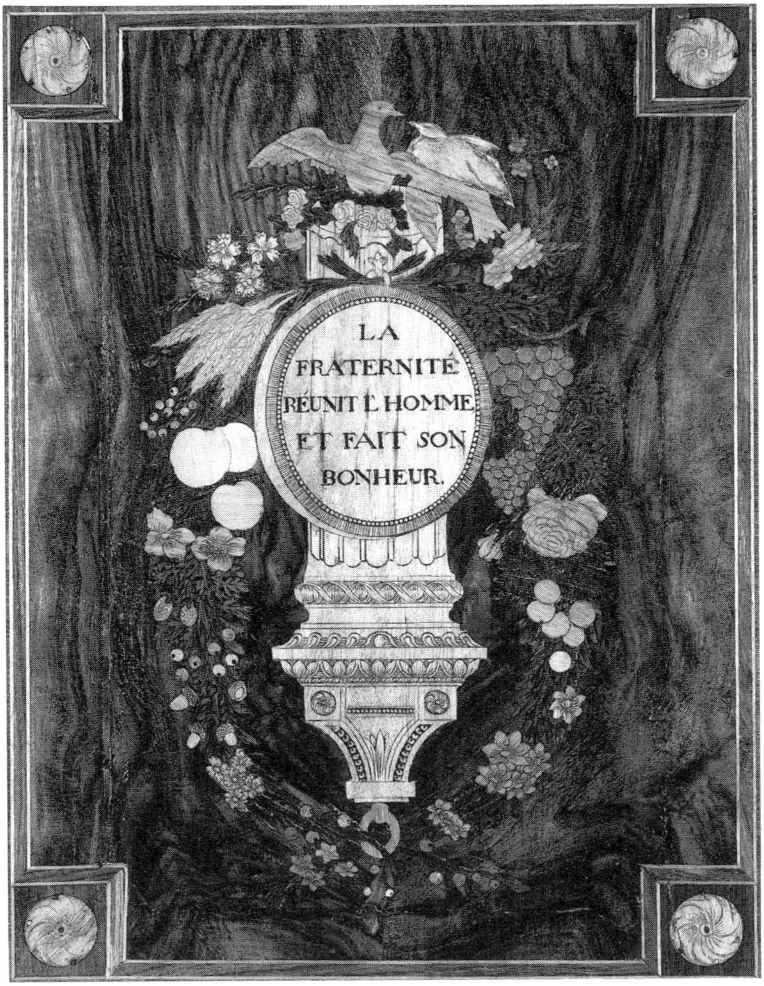

5.7 Detail of upper front panel 'La Fraternité réunit l'Homme et fait son Bonheur', of two-tier armoire (see plate 5.6) Paris: Musée Carnavalet.

political sentiments back to themselves in the most intimate space of the bedroom.

A parallel set of changes occurred in the other decorative arts, ones that accompanied furniture: from a porcelain teapot decorated with a Phrygian cap[40] or a more plebeian ceramic plate showing a cock standing on a cannon under the legend, 'Je veille pour la nation',[41] items for setting upon desks and tables, to wallpaper depicting Liberty and Equality in the guise of young women in classical dress,[42] for creating an environment for furniture. The vocabulary of decorative elements was drawn in all instances from the repertoire of revolutionary symbols, events and texts. These goods are somewhat puzzling. As noted above, there was no requirement, or even explicit encouragement for their consumption or

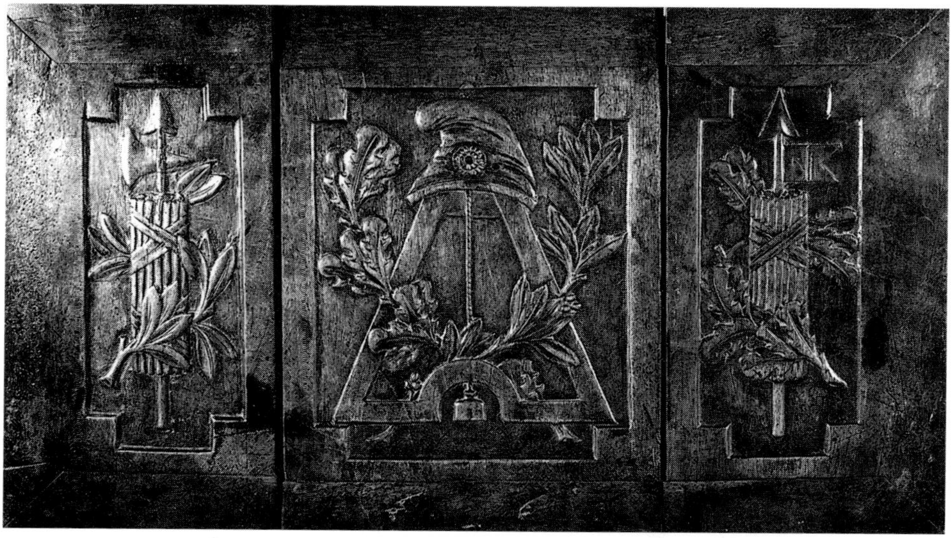

5.8 Detail of top of dressing table, *c.* 1795. Wood. Paris: Musée Carnavalet.

production by revolutionary governments or pamphleteers. In the absence of such exhortation, and given their cost, who would have made or bought them and why? The motivation for their production – generally anonymous – is difficult to establish with certainty. It is certainly likely, however, given the very high rates of revolutionary participation by artisans in the decorative arts industries, that many of these objects reflect the convictions of their makers. They did not necessarily have the time or the resources to engage in a thorough redesign of their goods, but wanted, nonetheless, to make them conform to republican principles. One of the styles they had mastered in the last years of the *ancien régime*, the more austere form of neoclassicism, was, in its references to the Roman republics and Greek democracies, perfectly compatible with current political views. When those forms were inscribed with revolutionary emblems they became even more appropriate for politically active producers. Artisans would not, however, have made these goods if no one wanted to buy them. But who would want such things? The purchase of such durable and encumbering, yet fragile, items in the middle of revolutionary upheaval, although far less luxurious than furnishings and decorative items from the late *ancien régime* or the Directoire, suggests both means and a very powerful commitment to republican principles. One would imagine that some of those who had been buying the more sober neoclassical furniture and other decorative goods in the late *ancien régime* were now buying explicitly revolutionary-style items. Although detailed evidence is lacking, it would seem likely that the clientele for furnishings ornamented with Phrygian caps and pikes would be non-noble elites who sought to display, affirm, or be reminded of their republican rights and obligations.

Styles changed with the Directoire (November 1795–November 1799). That period was characterized by a return of both ostentatious luxury and a new version of neoclassicism marked by Napoleon's Egyptian campaign of 1798. A daybed (plate 5.9) produced by François H.G. Desmalter (1770–1841) and Georges II Jacob (1786–1803) sometime between 1795 and 1803 shows the change very clearly. This piece is crafted of solid mahogany, mahogany veneered on beech wood, and gilt bronze. And while the style is reminiscent of the neoclassicism of Louis XVI, the armrests are composed of two winged sphinx-like creatures, and the feet are protected with bronze castings resembling palm leaves. The object itself – a daybed, which became popular in this period in part because of its reference to Roman forms – was indicative of the return to a melding of luxury and neoclassicism (albeit an expanded classical world). Thus, just as flowing dresses made of transparent fabric were favoured by the *jeunesse dorée* in these years, their elders commissioned exotic and sensual versions of neoclassicism to signal a transformation in the revolutionary dynamic, a transformation presaging the return of court culture under the First Empire.

Furniture and the other decorative arts did, therefore, change under the Revolution. The chronologies of French furniture styles that leap from Louis XVI to the Directoire are missing something. And yet, they are also not entirely wrong. Revolutionary changes in the decorative arts were generally improvised and left to the initiative of producers and consumers. There was no public debate, no mandate and no articulation of what a revolutionary home should look like. Even when décor was clearly a matter of state – as was the case with the outfitting of

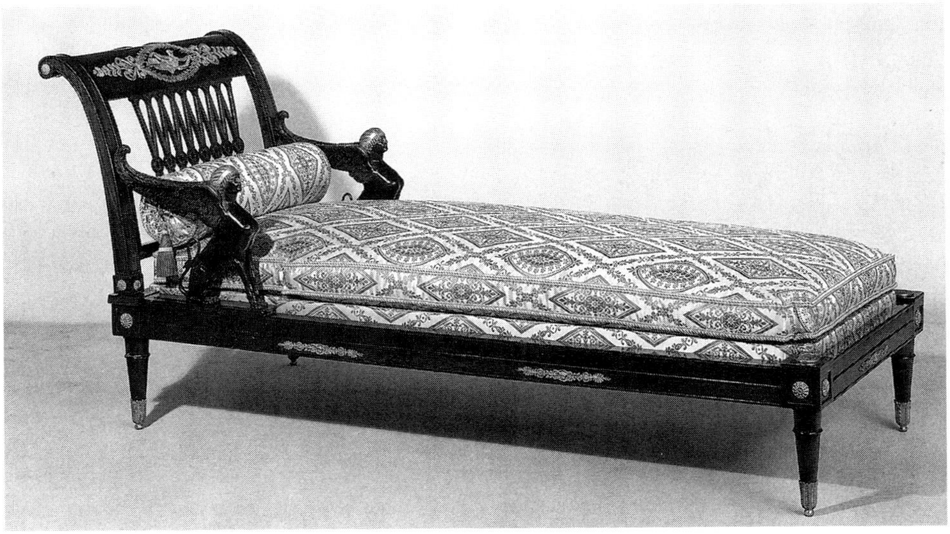

5.9 François H.G. Desmalter and Georges II Jacob, known as Jacob Frères, Daybed, between 1785 and 1803. Mahogany, mahogany veneered on beech wood, gilt bronze mounts. New York: the Metropolitan Museum of Art, Gift of Mr and Mrs Charles Wrightsman, 1971.

the National Convention, it seems to have attracted little attention. This essay will conclude with an attempt to explain that gap.

CONCLUSION

Production rhythms and the loss of market may go a long way to explain both the continued construction of monarchical-style furniture and limits in how much republican furniture was made in this period, but it does little to explain the absence of discourse on the subject. At first glance one might think that the explanation for the revolutionaries' unusual silence lies in the material conditions of the trade: why waste time discussing something one cannot change? The massive debate on architecture, particularly monumental architecture, however, belies that hypothesis. Examples are not limited to architecture either; revolutionary legislators, journalists and pamphleteers were voluble on a fantastic array of topics concerning republican design and everyday life, whether practicable or not.

I would like to suggest that the lack of engagement with domestic interiors by thinkers and legislators who were obsessed by the minutiae of everyday life may be explained by the conjuncture of four phenomena. First of all, while more people did indeed have access to more consumer goods in eighteenth-century France than before, the dominant domains in which that change significantly affected any more than a very small elite were clothing and small decorative objects, or *bibelots* and mirrors.[43] The precocity of the commercialization of clothing may be seen in the very early advent of fashion magazines. The earliest periodicals devoted to *la mode* date from the last third of the eighteenth century, whereas decorative arts journals only start to appear in the nineteenth century. And, while some of those magazines, most notably the *Journal de la mode et du goût*, do mention furnishings, they are backdrops to the main subject of interest. In parallel, while furniture-makers and distributors did start advertising their wares in the *ancien régime*, those advertisements are far less elaborate than those for other – less costly – items.[44]

Secondly (and related), it was only in the second half of the nineteenth century that the domestic space of ordinary citizens (as opposed to elites in the *ancien régime*) would take on political meaning.[45] While Jules Michelet and his fellow nineteenth-century republicans wrote extensively about the implications of domestic style for political identity and position, their eighteenth-century forebears did not. Part of that change was to do with the market for by the end of the nineteenth century more people could make more choices about the appearance of their home; and part of it was to do with changing understandings of both republicanism and the nation.

Thirdly, a shared characteristic of all the topics of intensive revolutionary debate was that they could be understood primarily to concern the *public* world, the world outside the home. Clothing, of course, moves between the private and the public, and architectural innovation will change the lives people live inside as well as what they perceive from the outside. In the revolutionary era in discussions of these two critical elements of everyday life, however, it was their public meaning that was of greatest concern. Discourses on republican clothing had very little to say about how it might influence familial relations, either between wives and husbands or parents and children. And, unlike feminist dress-reform efforts of the next century, there was no interest expressed in an increase in individual freedom of movement or practicality. Clothing was to be republicanized in the interests of promoting – at different moments of the Revolution – liberty of choice or collective identification or political values.

Revolutionary-era architectural projects were, in parallel, unless they concerned buildings to which the public would have access, largely preoccupied with the façades, and the exteriors more generally. Texts do not discuss, again as later ones would, how living in a dwelling in which space was differently allocated, or with a different relation to the outside world, might help to form republican subjects or inculcate a sense of national belonging. This is not only a textual omission; in the thousands of extant architectural drawings, little attention is paid to conveying a detailed and powerful sense of the experience of dwelling in a building. The built environment, like clothing, largely mattered in so far as it shaped people's public, collective experience.

It is, therefore, no accident that the only furnishings actually commissioned by the revolutionary government were for public buildings, ranging from legislative bodies, to schools, city halls and libraries. The furnishing of citizens' everyday life was of little concern both because of the liberal separation between a public sphere of state intervention and a private sphere of individual liberty, and because it was not understood to matter politically. In so far as a consumer society existed in eighteenth-century France, it was still limited in its reach. The vast majority of urban dwellers lived in extremely cramped quarters and made do with whatever furnishings would be most useful while occupying the smallest possible space. They did not select their furnishings to construct a social or political identity in the same way as some were already choosing their clothing for that purpose. The elaboration of a model of a solidaristic public polity resting on a culturally unified private nation would happen gradually over the course of the nineteenth century. The grandchild of the Revolution – the Third Republic – would therefore come to take a great interest in the political and social signification of all of its inhabitants' dwellings.

And yet, as has been seen, furniture inscribed with revolutionary emblems, and furniture seeking to embody a republican aesthetic form, was made, sold and purchased during these years, making it clear that neither all French artisans nor all French consumers of furniture shared the legislators' and pamphleteers' disinterest in domestic interiors. This production and consumption of, at least a few, politically marked furnishings indicates that the idea of fashion – of timely goods – had extended beyond the domain of clothing and *bibelots* and that the revolutionaries' message of the need to regenerate and republicanize everyday life had been persuasive. The differences in the rhetoric and practice in the domains of clothing, architecture and furniture also suggest, however, that generalizations concerning the onset of consumer society or the meaning of things must be approached cautiously. The materiality of objects means that each is constrained and enabled by unique conditions of production, distribution and consumption. Given those conditions, objects impose their own temporalities, their own constraints, their own possibilities on their makers and users who, in their turn, work to transform those conditions so that the objects can serve them.

Notes

1 Serge Bianchi, *La Révolution culturelle de l'an II: Elites et peuples (1789–1799)*, Paris, 1982; Lynn Hunt, 'Symbolic Forms of Political Practice', in her *Politics, Culture and Class in the French Revolution*, Berkeley, 1986, 52–86; Leora Auslander, *Revolutionary Taste: Everyday Life and Politics in England, Colonial America, and France*, in preparation.

2 Gastin, *Sur le projet de résolution relatif à la cocarde nationale* (29 Floréal, year 7–18 mai, 1799), 6.

3 Quoted in Daniela del Pesco, 'Entre projet et utopie: les écrits et la théorie architecturale, 1789–1799', in *Les architectes de la liberté, 1789–1799*, Ministère de la culture et de la communication des grands travaux et du bicentenaire, Paris, 1989, 329–33.

4 Del Pesco, 'Entre projet et utopie'.

5 *Considérations sur les avantages de changer le costume français; par la société populaire et républicaine des arts*, Paris, n.d., 2.

6 D'Eschasseriaux, le jeune, *Sur le projet de résolution relatif à la cocarde nationale* (3 Floréal, Year VII), n.l. 179, 5, 7.

7 *Considérations sur les avantages de changer le costume français*, 3.

8 The one exception is Paul Avril, *L'ameublement parisien avant, pendant, et après la révolution*, Paris, 1929, but Avril is unable to bring much evidence to bear for his argument.

9 See, for example, Jennifer Jones, '*Coquettes* and *Grisettes*: Women Buying and Selling in Ancien Régime Paris', in *The Sex of Things: Gender and Consumption in Historical Perspective*, eds Victoria de Grazia and Ellen Furlough, Berkeley, 1996, 25–53; Cissie Fairchilds, 'The Production and Marketing of Populuxe Goods in eighteenth-century Paris', in *Consumption and the World of Goods*, eds John Brewer and Roy Porter, London and New York, 1993, 228–42.

10 Aileen Ribeiro, *Fashion in the French Revolution*, New York, 1988, 101.

11 Annemarie Kleinert, 'La Mode – miroir de la révolution française', *Francia*, 11:2, 1989, 91, 78, 79, 81.

12 J. Guillaume, ed., *Procès-verbaux du comité d'instruction publique de la convention nationale*, 5 vols, Paris, 1891, vol. 1: *Projet d'éducation nationale, par P.-P. Rabaut, deputé de l'Aude, du 21 décembre, 1792, l'an 1 de la république*, 233–5, cited in Jennifer Harris, 'The Red Cap of Liberty: A Study of Dress Worn by French Revolutionary Partisans, 1789–95', *Eighteenth-Century French Studies*, 14:3, 1981, 302.

13 Harris, 'The Red Cap of Liberty', 299.

14 On this, see Lynn Hunt, 'Freedom of Dress in Revolutionary France', in *From the Royal to the Republican Body*, eds Sara E. Melzer and Kathryn Norberg, Berkeley, 1998, 224–50.

15 On 29 October 1793 (9 Brumaire, Year II).

16 Harris, 'The Red Cap of Liberty'. A classic (and more detailed text) on this is Jules Renouvier, *Histoire de l'art pendant la révolution, 1789–1804*, Geneva, 1996, original edn, Paris, 1863, 463–80 and Richard Wrigley's authoritive, *The Politics of Appearances: Representations of Dress in Revolutionary France*, Oxford and New York, 2002, chap. 5.

17 Grégoire, *Rapport et projet de décret sur les costumes des législateurs et des autres fonctionnaires publics* (28 Fructidor, Year III) in Bernard Deloche and Jean-Michel Leniaud, eds, *La culture des sans culottes*, Paris, 1989, 295–303.

18 Ribeiro, *Fashion in the French Revolution*, 124–9.

19 Daniel Roche, *La culture des apparences*, Paris, 1989. See also on royal and courtly dress, Madeleien Delpierre, *Se vêtir au XVIIIe siècle*, Paris, 1996, 107–130.

20 Alan Hunt, *Governance of the Consuming Passions: A History of Sumptuary Law*, New York, 1996, particularly chap. 3.

21 *Edit sur la réforme des habits (1)*, Paris, 12 juillet 1549, in *Recueil générale des anciennes lois françaises*, vol. 13, Paris, 1828, 102.

22 *Edit sur la réforme des habits (1)*, 104.

23 *Déclaration portant règlement pour les habits, et défenses de porter aucuns passemens d'or et d'argent*, Paris, 31 mai 1644. *Recueil générale des anciennes lois françaises*, vol. 17, Paris, 1829, 41.

24 Daniel Roche, *The People of Paris*, trans. Marie Evans, Berkeley, 1987, 162.

25 On conditions of production, see Claire Crowston, *Fabricating women: The seamstresses of Old Regime France, 1675–1791*, Durham, 2001.

26 Cited in del Pesco, 'Entre projet et utopie' 334.

27 See Verhelst, *Plan allégorique d'un jardin de la révolution française et des vertus républicaines*, Paris, 16 prairial, year II; Jean-Pierre-Louis-Laurent Houël, *Projet d'un monument public*, Paris, an VIII (1799–1800); Antoine Voinier, *Projet d'un monument triomphal en l'honneur des quatorze armées de la république*, Paris, 1794; Nicolas Letemple Goulet, *Le temple des lois et de la liberté: projet présenté au comité d'instruction publique de la convention nationale, par le citoyen Goulet, architecte expert du département pour l'estimation des domaines nationaux*, Paris, n.d.; François-Antoine Davy de Chavigné, *Projet d'un monument sur l'emplacement de la Bastille*, Paris, 1789; Auguste Hubert, *Rapport sur l'embellissement du palais et du jardin national, du pont et de la place de la révolution; présenté au comité de salut public par Hubert, architecte*, Paris, 1794; A-R Chevalier de Mopinot de la Chapotte, *Proposition d'un monument à élever dans la capitale de la France, pour transmettre aux races futures l'époque de l'heureuse révolution qui l'a revivifiée sous le règne de Louis XIV*, Paris, 1790. The most helpful secondary texts on this issue are James A. Leith, *Space and Revolution: Projects for Monuments, Squares and Public Buildings in France 1789–1799*, Montreal, 1991, and Werner Szambien, *Les projets de l'an II: concours d'architecture de la période révolutionnaire*, Paris, 1986.

28 Staatliche Kunsthalle Baden-Baden, *Revolutionsarchitektur: Boullée, Ledoux, Lequeu*, Stuttgart-Bad Cannstatt, 1970. Although, as Leith points out, they were not themselves necessarily convinced republicans. Leith, *Space and Revolution*, 34.

29 On this building, see Leith, *Space and Revolution*, 79–85; Philippe Madec, *Boullée*, Paris, 1986, 64–71.

30 Pierre Arizzoli-Clémentel, 'Les Arts du décor', in *Aux armes et aux arts! Les arts de la révolution, 1789–1799*, eds Philippe Bordes and Régis Michel, Paris, 1988, 283.

31 For a complete listing of Georges Jacob's revolutionary era production, see Hector Lefuel, *Georges Jacob: ébéniste du XVIIIe siècle*, Paris, 1923. For Bernard Molitor, see Ulrich Leben, *Molitor: ébéniste from the Ancien Régime to the Bourbon Restoration*, trans. William Wheeler, London, 1992; and for Adam Weisweiler, see Patricia Lemonnier, *Weisweiler*, Paris, 1983.

32 Ronald Paulson, *Representations of Revolution (1789–1820)*, New Haven, 1983, chap. 1; Guillaume Janneau, *Les ateliers parisiens d'ébénistes et de menuisiers aux XVIIe et XVIIIe siècles*, Paris, 1975, 41.

33 On this see particularly, Leben, *Molitor*, 125ff.

34 Lefuel, *Georges Jacob*.

35 Arizzoli-Clémentel, 'Les Arts du décor', 299.

36 Lefuel, *Georges Jacob*, 144ff, and Michel Beurdeley, *Georges Jacob (1739–1814) et son temps*, Paris, 2002, chap. 10.

37 Marie-Noelle De Grandry, *Le mobilier français: directoire, consulat, empire*, Paris, 1996, 32.

38 Laurie Dahlberg, 'France between the Revolutions, 1789–1848', in *The Sèvres Porcelain Manufactory: Alexandre Brongniart and the Triumph of Art and Industry, 1800–1847*, ed. Tamara Préaud, New York, 1997, 16.

39 Raymonde Monnier, *Le faubourg Saint-Antoine, 1789–1815*, Paris, 1981, 81ff.

40 Manufacture de Sèvres, about 1795, currently held in the Division of Ceramics and Glass, National Museum of American History, Smithsonian Institution, Washington, DC Alfred Duane Pell Collection. Figure 2 in *L'art de vivre: Decorative Arts and Design in France, 1789–1989*, ed. Catherine Arminjon, et al., London, 1989.

41 Bordeaux, Musée des arts décoratifs, inv. 5376. Plate 93 in *La vie en France autour de 1789: Images et représentation 1785–1795*, exhib. cat., Paris, 1989.

42 Musée Gadagne, Lyon. Plate 96 in Michel Beurdeley, *La France à l'encan 1789–1799: exode des objets d'art sous la revolution*, Paris, 1981, 91.

43 See, for example, Roche, *The People of Paris*, chap. 6, esp. 151–2 and 194.

44 Contrast, for example, the advertisements for medical items analysed by Colin Jones in 'The Great Chain of Buying: Medical Advertisements, the Bourgeois Public Sphere and the Origins of the French Revolution', *American Historical Review*, 101:1, 1996, 13–41, and those for furniture housed in the advertising collection of the Bibliothèque historique de la ville de Paris.

45 For a fuller elaboration of this argument, see Leora Auslander *Taste and Power: Furnishing Modern France*, Berkeley, 1996.

6

FRAMING AMBITION: THE INTERIOR POLITICS OF MME DE POMPADOUR

KATIE SCOTT

In the history of classical architecture in France, the eighteenth century is characterized as a period during which the treatment of interior space gradually assumed an importance equal to the handling of exterior form, and one marked by abrupt transformations in decorative style: from rococo to neoclassicism. These shifting priorities and changing tastes seemingly found a common cause in the rejection of the socially sanctioned formalities, or decorum, of the baroque. A longing for privacy, comfort and individuality was articulated spatially by the proliferation of small, intimate rooms – chambers, *cabinets*, boudoirs, bathrooms, etc. – and in decoration by the customization of the vocabulary of classical ornament. According to Michael Dennis, in the second half of the eighteenth century architects 'found fresh inspiration in the personalities of their clients', which led to 'great diversity' in the format of the later classical *hôtel*.[1] More recently Alice Friedman and Tannis Hinchcliffe have argued for the significant role played by *women* in the evolution towards the modern house, notwithstanding the legal and financial constraints that significantly limited the early modern woman's capacity to engender 'works' of her own.[2] Was Jeanne-Antoinette Poisson (1721–1764), marquise de Pompadour and official mistress of Louis XV from 1745 until her death, such a woman?

Recent scholarship has focused particularly on Pompadour's strategies of self-fashioning, especially in relation to portraiture but also as a patron of the fine and decorative arts.[3] Although Pompadour occupied, bought, built and leased an astonishing array of accommodation during her twenty years at court, her architectural patronage has perhaps attracted rather less attention, certainly of the kind that is alert to issues of gender and aims to make sense of her cultural role in relation to the transgressive nature of her position, of her place outside the law. The aim of the present essay is twofold: to give a straightforward, factual account of some of the apartments, châteaux and town houses decorated for Mme de Pompadour and, more speculatively, to interpret her choices of distribution and decoration as strategies by which to survive at a court which, within two years of her instauration, eagerly anticipated, where it did not actively connive at, her

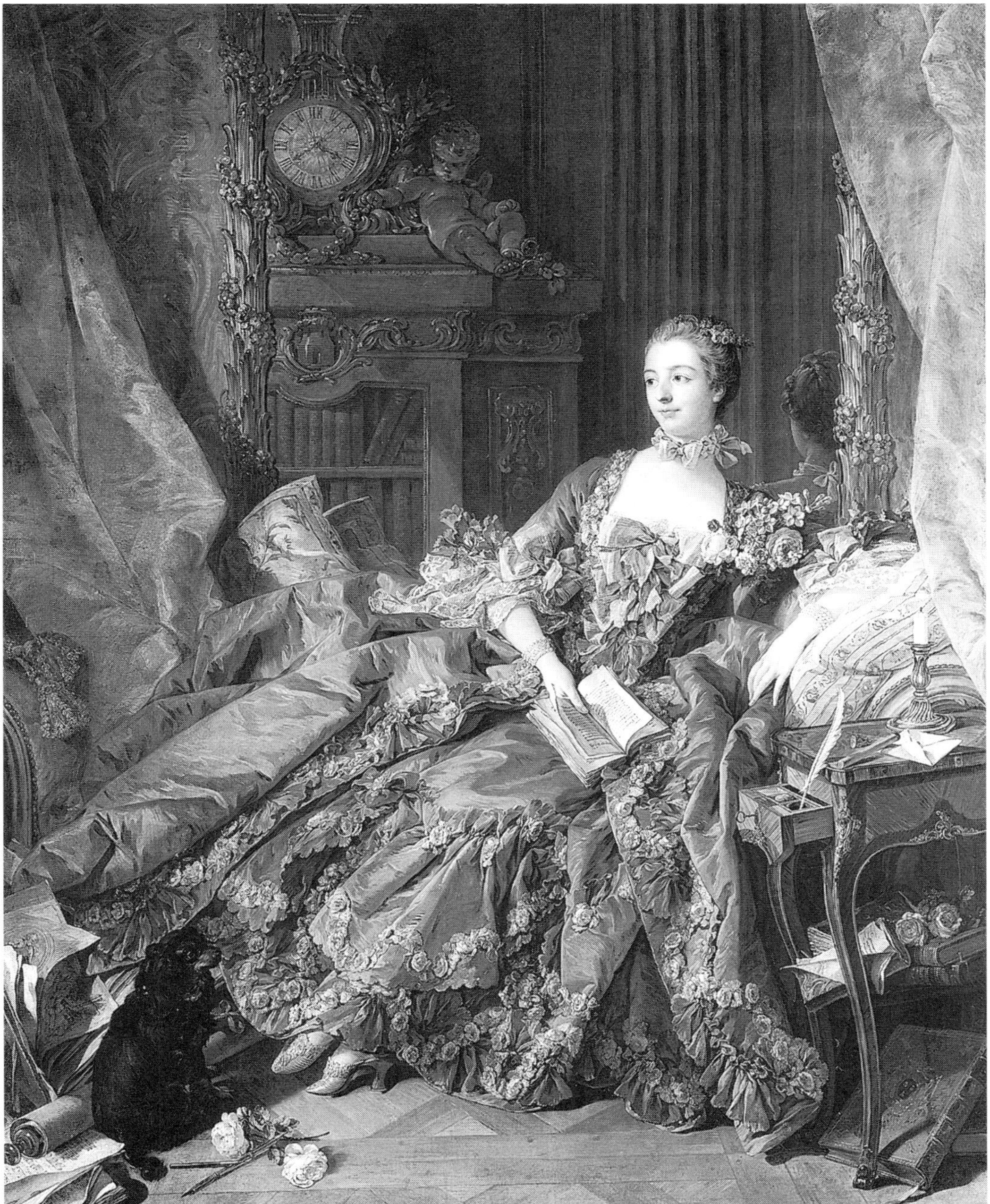

6.1 François Boucher, *Portrait of Mme de Pompadour*, 1756. Oil on canvas, 201 × 157 cm. Munich: Alte Pinakothek. Copyright: Alte Pinakothek. Photo: Staatsgemaldesämmlungen.

downfall. The first of these stories is, of course, a familiar one;[4] novelty arises here merely from consideration of the interplay between her apartments at Versailles, her château de Bellevue (located on a straight line between Versailles and Paris) and the hôtel d'Evreux, her residence in the capital, situated on the rue saint Honoré near the royal palaces of the Louvre and the Tuileries.

The surviving visual evidence of the excessive luxury of which she stood accused by many of her contemporaries with respect to these examples is disappointingly meagre: a handful of architectural drawings (plans and elevations), some fragments of oak panelling, a fraction of the original furnishings and a somewhat better showing of paintings and sculpture, though all of these have now been torn from their original settings. By way of compensation, the textual record of her occupation and dominion of these spaces is rich, owing to the closeness with which her behaviour was observed and appraised by court diarists. The diaries of the ducs de Cröy and de Luynes and of the marquis d'Argenson tend, of course, to evoke the social rather than the material culture of the court, and were, moreover, thoroughly prejudiced, but the descriptions or portraits they contain of Pompadour constitute an unrivalled record of the ways in which her cultural performance was apprehended and misapprehended in her own day. In particular, they expose an obsessive anxiety with architectural 'communication', that is, with the manner in which the distribution of space eases or frustrates social encounters, and the way decoration narrates not only a typology of built forms but a gendered and socially ordered subject. Another source, the painted portraits of Pompadour indoors, is similarly turned to account. While depicting generic if not outright fictional places, her portraits have the merit of not only articulating the interaction of mistress and world, but of doing so from the sitter's point of view. Theirs was an authorized elaboration of a room about the subject, a sanctioned projection of the sitter's self into the decorated and thing-filled space of the interior – a good place to start.

PORTRAIT OF AN INTERIOR

Painted to celebrate the formalization of Pompadour's relation to another (her appointment as supernumerary lady-in-waiting to the queen, Maria Leszczynska, in February 1756), paradoxically, François Boucher's Munich portrait (plate 6.1) captures her alone, relaxing upon a chaise longue in a room often described by scholars as a *cabinet* which, in eighteenth-century terms, is to say the most interior of interior spaces, one to which a person might withdraw for solitude, or to enjoy the closest intimacy with the company kept. The sense of the space as intimately and exclusively hers is conveyed both by her capacity to fill and dominate it, and by the further empire of her things: pieces that are marked as her personal possessions either literally, by the coat of arms (the towers) that appears upon them – the red leather-bound book in the right foreground and the carved bookcase with clock, 'behind' her (plate 6.2) – or by her evident use of them: the book she holds, fingers loosely interleaved; the ones she has held, the paperback below the desk visibly thumbed, warm; the prints and drawings she has organized, or rather disorganized, in the portfolio to the left; the letter she has read, and the pen, ink, sealing wax and candle that stand on the open van Risenburgh desk ready to serve her in reply. Others have noted Boucher's allusion to Pompadour as herself an author, a 'maker of images', by the inclusion of some of her etchings among the prints and drawings.[5] Less obviously, Boucher draws attention to her craft of the interior by her taste in things and by the care she has seemingly had worked upon them: the waxed glow of wood, the dusted lustre of damask; satin's lighter, plumped-up radiance and gold and silver's shine in use. The interior is defined by its shining contents rather than by its geometrical space.[6] To follow Gaston Bachelard, it appears rebuilt from within.[7]

6.2 Detail of Boucher, *Portrait of Mme de Pompadour*. Munich: Alte Pinakothek.

Of the disarming openness with which Pompadour is portrayed in her corner of the world, the golden drapery to left and right of her speak eloquently, for if, at one level, it represents actual curtains, on another, it stands as a metaphor for revelation – the veil of formality momentarily drawn aside, seemingly to give the viewer privileged understanding of the subject. However, this conventional conceit of truthfulness in portraiture prompts, by its artifice, a review of the place. On reflection, the interior appears contradictory. The treatment of the wall behind the marquise and that reflected in the mirror do not correspond: the first is clothed in yellow stuff, the second articulated by a giant classical order, in the form of a stone-coloured, deep-fluted pilaster. The only space so divided between an enclosed, upholstered realm and an open, formal stage in the eighteenth-century dwelling was, of course, the *chambre de parade*, or premium reception room, in the formal or state apartments, where the courtly rituals of the *lever* and *coucher* were pompously performed. This is not to say that a mistake has been made about the place of the portrait. Such would be to misunderstand the status of Boucher's depicted interior. It represents not a real place – although it does resemble apartments at Versailles, where it received its finishing touches[8] – but a discursive one, within which contradiction was meaningful. The likeness to a *cabinet*, combined with the gesture of revelation, tells the viewer that Pompadour's interest in the arts was more than conventional, more than a formality: in fact, a warm and sincere personal attachment. Meanwhile the discrete references to a ceremonial *chambre* (by means of the classical order in the looking glass, the

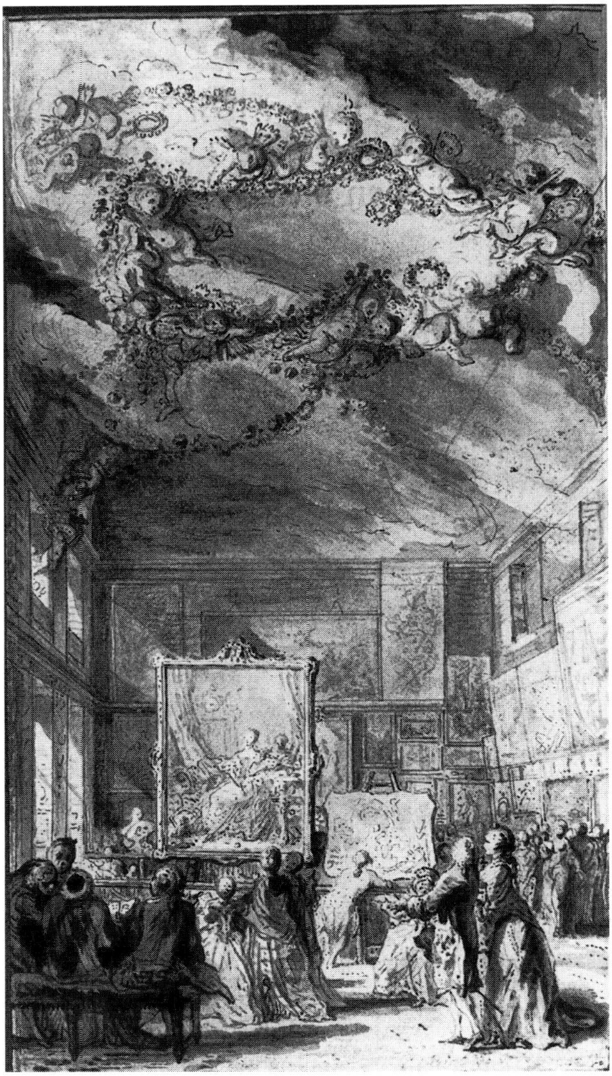

6.3 Gabriel de Saint Aubin, *Salon of 1757*, 1757. Pen and ink, wash and watercolour, 20 × 12.5 cm. Buckinghamshire: Waddesdon Manor. Copyright: The National Trust.

recumbent pose, and the curtains, potentially those of a bed), together with the scale, the sheer mass of the work, indicate that this personal taste was of public consequence, that it framed a political ambition. Pompadour's image, public *and* private, personal *and* conventional was, in short, constructed from an interpenetration or compression of spaces of distinct character.

Spatial representations like Boucher's were, of course, themselves the product of the social space of the *ancien régime*, of the particular figuration of social relations and ideology 'secreted' by court society.[9] Pompadour's relation of dependence on Louis xv, as a woman and as a mistress, is registered in the portrait by the way that the 'tower' of her blazon shelters under the Apollonian lyre in the hierarchy of ornament distributed upon the bookcase (plate 6.2). The marquisate of Pompadour was given to her by her royal lover in 1745; the tower became her new identity. In July of that year, the duc de Luynes had recorded in his diary that the purchase of her property was proceeding and that Louis, in anticipation of completion, was writing daily letters to Mme d'Étiolles addressed 'to Mme la marquise de Pompadour', and sealing them with 'gallant device' encircled by the words 'Discret et Fidèle'.[10] It is tempting to suppose that the tower of Pompadour's coat of arms was the device in question, made gallant in chivalric discourse by the woman within, who waits quietly, faithfully, and by the man without, who storms the castle of love.[11] At a later date Louis gave Pompadour a jewelled tablet that combined his spiked monogram with her rounded towers.[12] However, in the portrait the language of lyres and towers lends itself to another interpretation. Gabriel de Saint-Aubin's depiction of the portrait at the Salon of 1757 (plate 6.3) records the original frame, at the centre of the top rail of which presided a solitary tower. Circumscribed, ultimately then, as her place, Pompadour sits in her castle daydreaming about her desire for status and autonomy in terms of a different tower, the philosopher's tower which, according to Michel de Montaigne's famous characterization, offered pure dominion over a small, intellectual corner of the world.[13] In this corner, Pompadour herself as 'femme savante' wielded the lyre; set the arts to sing; and, in so doing, apparently laid claim to a royal and a masculine prerogative.[14]

Actual interiors are not, of course, eloquent in this way; the necessary control of the realm of representation is beyond the reach of three dimensions. But, the idea that the interior could function *pictorially*, as a sign of identity and an emblem of intent, suggests a wider horizon of possible interpretations of the eighteenth-century interior than is usually proposed. Eighteenth-century writers on architecture made more than conventional reference to the sister arts, deriving by analogy to painting and poetry an architectural notion of character with which this essay will be concerned later. The openness of eighteenth-century minds to thinking about the expressiveness of façades and faces in analogous terms of composition, justifies, for the present, the licence of taking a lesson from the frame, because the frame presents the spectator with an element that belongs both to the realm of imitation and to the 'real' world of the built environment. Boucher's Munich portrait is, for instance, not only framed and thus an object in space, on the wall; it also incorporates framing into the formal arrangement of its composition. On the vertical axis Pompadour is confined by a 'nest' of parallel lines that, starting with the actual frame, via the depicted curtains, mirror and painted grooves of the pilaster, progressively encroach upon her person, finally determining, or fixing the tilt of her head. Moreover, along the horizontal axis, Boucher extends, with a lighter touch, the line of the lintel of the bookcase to skim the top of Pompadour's head and tucks her feet and dress within the symmetries of the parquetry floor. The frame serves by its repeated lines of confinement to concentrate the sitter's identity and to impose unity, order and coherence on the disorderly array of tastes, interests and roles that fell to

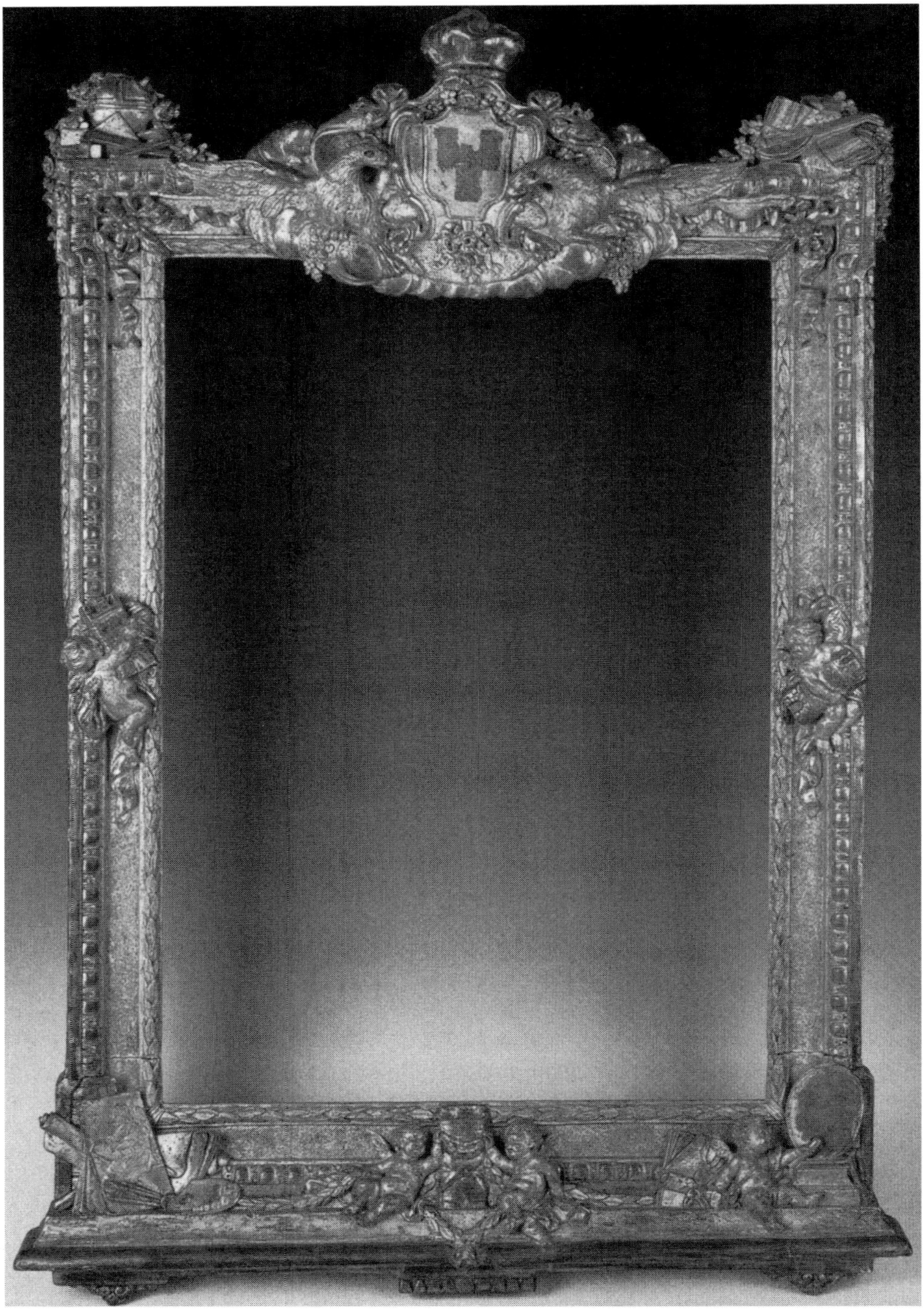

6.4 Frame with the arms of Madame de Pompadour, *c.* 1755. Wood gilded in two colours of gold, 69 × 46.4 cm. Paris: Private collection.

Pompadour's lot and are manifest in the mess of detail. It is not difficult here to recognize the monumentalizing and immortalizing function of the frame; it encloses, stills and raises up the real to the order of the aesthetic.

The sculpted and gilded decoration of an actual frame (plate 6.4) that belonged to Pompadour acknowledges these functions of aestheticization and memorialization in its deployment of genii, variously armed with her arms or playfully at work painting and carving.[15] Moreover, the fact that the frame has the means to stand as well as to hang, makes explicit its relation to the interior: the genii assume the function of doorkeepers, the frame that of a threshold. In short, this frame draws attention to the continuities between the frameworks operating inside picture frames and those many outside that variously worked to constitute the eighteenth-century domestic interior: window frames, mirror frames, door frames, sequences of perfectly aligned door frames, known in French planning as *enfilades*, and, finally, whole rooms. The mirror, of course, most closely resembles the work of art because it not only encloses a scene, it also reproduces it, a reality acknowledged by Boucher in his record of the reflection of the mirror's frame along the length of its right-hand edge. The partial repetition of the frame, read confusedly almost as a loss of focus, establishes, however, the limits of the frame's authority within the interior. Decorative investment in frameworks notwithstanding, mirrors, windows, doors and rooms framed accidentally a more-or-less random content only momentarily captured within their sights.[16] Indiscriminately, the elect and their servants moved in and out of these frames, some no doubt composing themselves for a scene – an entrance, an exit – others merely going about their daily business.[17] Thus, while such frames were capable of conferring order and creating significant relationships, they were not able consistently to impose their own design.

6.5 Detail of Boucher, *Portrait of Mme de Pompadour*, Munich: Alte Pinakothek.

A last reflection on the portrait: the mirror that silvers its painted pool upon the wall not only reflects, assigning the 'real' Pompadour a phantom attendant (plate 6.5), it also 'looks'. It forms its own opinion. When the picture appeared at the Salon it prompted a satirical response from Thomas-Germain de Saint-Aubin that he recorded in his pocketbook (plate 6.6). A satyr perches on a volume entitled *Mœurs* (or *Morality*) the better to scrutinize the likeness. He is, in a sense, the personification of the mirror held up to the world as arbiter of truth. We do not

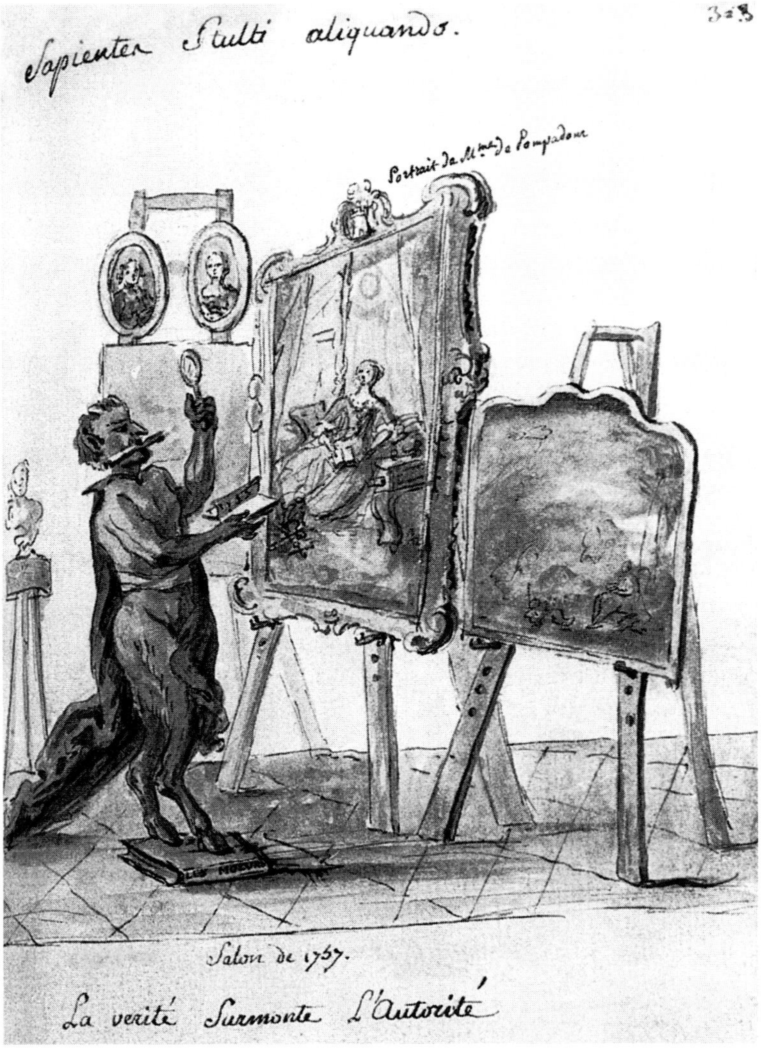

6.6 Thomas-Germain de Saint Aubin, *Satyr at the Salon of 1757*, 1757. Pen, ink and watercolour, 19 × 13.5 cm. Buckinghamshire: Waddesdon Manor. Copyright: The National Trust.

see what he sees but the inscription 'Truth overcomes Authority' indicates that a veil of pretension has been stripped away and the would-be queen – her portrait displayed on an easel, freestanding in the exhibition space, a distinction customarily reserved for portraits of royalty – has been revealed as the low-born mistress. The frame, of the portrait, mirror or room, and the status to which it lays claim, is thus seemingly inseparable from the critique to which it also gives rise. Pompadour's patronage was (it will be made clear) as much the history of contemporary reactions to it as a record of the possessions she ordered.

MEMOIRS FROM THE INTERIOR

Boucher's portrait was painted from Pompadour's second apartment on the ground floor of the château de Versailles, directly below the *grands appartements* (plate 6.7), a set of rooms to which she acceded in 1751.[18] High ceilinged, with full-length windows and doors arranged symmetrically *en enfilade*, the rooms comprised an apartment of two antechambers, a bedchamber and two *cabinets* with attendant service spaces, and was much sought after. A prestige location vacated by the king's cousin and his wife the duc and duchesse de Penthièvre, Pompadour had had to compete with Louis's own daughters for possession of it.[19] In contrast to this triumphant removal, Pompadour's arrival at Versailles in 1745 had been a much more discrete and modest affair. In March of that year Emmanuel, duc de

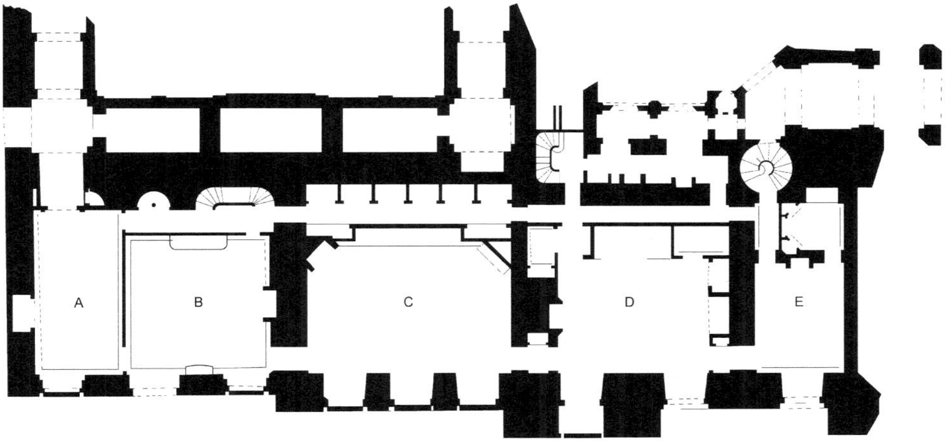

6.7 Plan of the ground-floor apartment of Mme de Pompadour: A first antechamber; B second antechamber; C cabinet; D bedchamber; E cabinet.

Cröy (1718–1782) recorded in his journal that the king's new mistress was receiving at court and was said almost to have preferment at her command; he had thought to present himself but had not found the time.[20] Charles Philippe d'Albert, duc de Luynes (1694–1757) had in the same month confidently predicted that Pompadour was no more than a royal 'galanterie', certainly not a mistress,[21] a statement he revised shortly thereafter. In April he acknowledged her presence at court though he was unable to locate her precisely in the palace.[22]

Cröy's and Luynes's early blindness to the reality of Pompadour's presence, like the compressed perspective of Boucher's later portrait, belies the fact that above all she was manifest spatially at Versailles, that is, in terms of the plan. Only on 14 September 1745, two days after Pompadour's official audience with the queen, did Luynes register that she 'inhabits the apartment of Mme de Châteauroux', to which he noted only 'some alterations' had been made and the furnishings left as they were.[23] Of the same apartment, situated in the attics, above the *grands appartements* (plate 6.8) and occupying some eleven rooms, including two *cabinets*, a bedchamber and two antechambers, arranged *en enfilade*, Cröy was similarly reticent. Only in November 1746 did he first attend her *toilette*, and notice some unspecified further embellishment.[24] In fact, up until 1748 little work seems to have been carried out on the 'the upper apartment of the mistress', originally planned and decorated for Mme de La Tournelle, later duchesse de Châteauroux, and Louis's second titled mistress.[25] On becoming, in her turn, Louis's 'very official' consort Pompadour moved into a social and architectural space prepared in advance.[26] No doubt because this first apartment does not have her personal signature upon it, because, indeed, in the case of both her Versailles apartments she had had to make do with re-used spaces and inherited elements of decoration, comparatively little attention has, until recently, been paid by art historians to Pompadour's cultural life at court.[27] If not commissioned by or for her, what can such interiors tell us about her? According to Cröy and, indirectly, Luynes, it was her manner of inhabiting and using space, rather than her minor acts of embellishment, that were significant, even original.

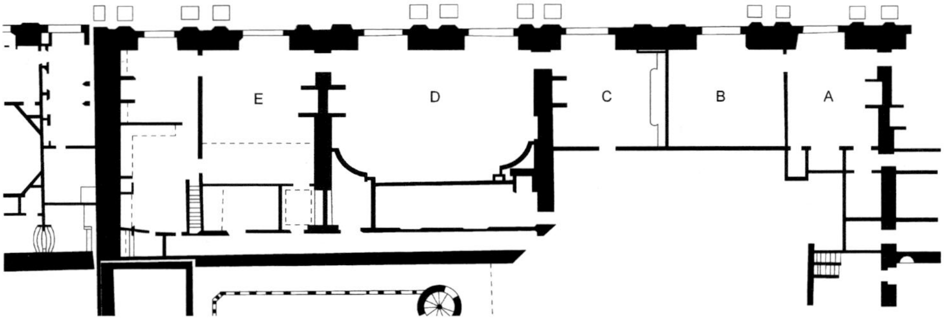

6.8 Plan of the attic apartment of Mme de Pompadour: A first antechamber; B second antechamber; C cabinet; D bedchamber; E cabinet.

When using the testimonies of Cröy and Luynes it is important to remember the different circumstances under which they wrote. Luynes, as the husband of one of the queen's ladies-in-waiting, was a permanent resident at court, a native of the 'country'.[28] Inevitably, his attention was concentrated on a legitimate female authority to which Pompadour related only secondarily. He was concerned to preserve the status quo and his journal recorded and, on occasion, actually served to protect, the interests of established privilege and traditional ritual.[29] Cröy, like Luynes, a member of the high, sword nobility, had, by contrast, no such ceremonial or ministerial appointment to secure him a place and an apartment.[30] Consequently, for him, Versailles was not so much Louis Le Vau's and Hardouin Mansart's classical monument as a field of operation within which to manoeuvre for the rank of fieldmarshal, for the governorship of Condé, for the honour of a *Cordon bleu*, and for the advantageous marriages of his children. As an outsider (*externe*), he was obsessed with the interior, with that elusive place, that was the seat of power.[31] The word 'interior' recurs significantly in his journal.

Architectural theory of the period (by Cordemoy, Daviler, Blondel, Brisseux) represented the distribution of internal domestic space in terms of the apartment, or group of units of accommodation arranged in sequence – *en enfilade*.[32] Likewise, Luynes related the conduct or manners of courtly life in terms of the number and identity of rooms that should, for example, be hung in black to mourn the death of a *dauphine*;[33] the number and identity of rooms that, to take another example, should be traversed for the proper reception of ambassadors and their wives;[34] or the number and identity of rooms that must separate the queen from her musicians in order that she might dispense with court dress as she listened to their playing.[35] In articulating his experience of the court by reference to the 'interior', Cröy set aside this rigidly differentiated, additive space, regulated by custom (*bienséance*),[36] and seemingly discovered a place that was, by contrast, amorphous and intimate. One of his earliest close encounters with the king took place in December 1748, at Pompadour's neighbouring château of La Celle, and is joyfully described as an occasion 'in the greatest intimacy' ('le plus grand intérieur');[37] several years later, at Versailles, he was moved to endorse Louis in his intimacy ('the king was very well in this interior');[38] and in February 1754 he noted with not a little satisfaction that he was himself 'more intimately in the interior of the court'.[39] 'Interior' referred not just to an architectural space but a social one. In the case of the former, Cröy mostly had the king's *petits appartements* in mind,[40] rather than Pompadour's, with which they were contiguous, but in terms of the latter Cröy recognized her as the condition of Louis's intimacy. Thus, on 30 September 1747 Croy described entry to the king's *souper* in the *petits cabinets* as having taken place via the 'small staircase of Mme de Pompadour', an evening at which the king appeared only in time to sit down at table with the ladies, Pompadour foremost among them, with whom he later played *comète*.[41] A party of eighteen, these were the 'real intimates' of the 'petit intérieur'.

The repeated characterization of the 'interior' as small – whether architectural or social – is impossible to ignore.[42] Indeed, Cröy draws attention to it; he uses it to dramatize his account of the evening by picturesque shifts of scale between the diminutive context and the grandeur and magnificence of the royal content. At one level he no more than reiterated a commonplace of classical theory, which, from Vitruvius, located the character and proportions of the first orders, the Doric and the Ionic, in the bodies of man and woman.[43] That is, Louis and Pompadour. However, where Vitruvius and his followers were concerned with typology, with the definition and separating out of difference, Cröy is interested in composition, in the bringing together of opposites, or, as he put it, in '*contraste*'. Contrast was, in the sphere of ornament, the adjective used by architects and critics in the 1730s and 1740s to describe the effects of asymmetry in the rococo.[44] And as with the rococo, Cröy later acknowledges that, notwithstanding his continued pleasure in the effects of 'liberty' and 'gaiety' created by contrast, displacement and confusion arise in the 'petit intérieur'.[45] At a supper in February 1753 he accused Pompadour of so 'lengthening the list' of invitees that invitation was 'singularly extended to include all ages, all degrees, all kinds'.[46] He qualified the statement after a dash with '– of nobility, of course'. The delay of the dash was intended to exaggerate momentary feelings of rancour, if not outrage, at Pompadour's irrational regime, its license contrasted unfavourably with the proper choice of Louis XIV and a younger Louis XV.[47] The 'interior', it seems, undermined the 'apartment', displacing privilege and confusing the distinctions that the *enfilade* articulated along its finely calibrated length.

WALKING THROUGH DOORS

Pompadour, without changing the architectural form of Versailles significantly, introduced a new, a 'singular', exercise of social space, one that was flowing, or, better, slurred rather than staccato, and which progressed to a diminuendo of inner, and inner-inner spaces, of interiors *within* interiors.[48] In this she not only effected a rococo movement behind the classical façade, she also established new pathways or routes inside the palace – a new rhetoric of walking, to borrow from Michel de Certeau. In developing a theory of the way space is appropriated by its users, made over to another's intentions, de Certeau draws on the model provided by language.[49] He argues that tropes (figures of speech entailing the use of words or phrases in a manner other than that which is proper to them)[50] can stand for the manipulation of elements of the constructed order, for derivations from literal or original function. De Certeau is concerned with the practices of today's everyday and with the city, but his framework of analysis seems apposite, too, to yesterday's baroque palace, not least because the theory of the sister arts encouraged analogies between language and architecture.[51] Parallels were, for the most part, confined to metaphors of structure, but according to the eighteenth-century vocabulary of architectural terms, management of movement about a building was an art of 'communication'.[52] The kinds of trope that de Certeau selects as especially important are synecdoche (the use of the part in place of the whole) and asyndeton (the omission of conjunctions in or between sentences),[53] tropes, here, of the door and the stairs.

As the only public person of the realm, the king was, theoretically, always accessible, his domain without enclosure.[54] Court ceremony ushered subjects into his presence through a sequence of casements – or triumphal arches – the leaves of the double doors opened or half-opened, the *portières*, or door curtains, fully or partially drawn aside, according to status.[55] In practice, however, there was a politics of the door. In 1753 Cröy's ambition was boundless; he knocked at 'all doors'.[56] However, favours falling notoriously to Pompadour, the door soon became specific. To deliver thanks for the realization of one particular ambition the following year, Cröy 'forced the door of the Marquise.'[57] At the most delicate moment of negotiation for the *survivance* of the governorship of Condé, his optimism rose by degrees as the doors, first on her *toilette secrète* and then to her 'rear, red lacquered cabinet', closed discretely behind him.[58] That the door was moreover an attribute of gender and not simply of personal identity is suggested by an entry in Cröy's journal on 18 January 1754. In further pursuit of his cause the duc had sought out the comte d'Argenson, minister of war, but on arrival at his apartment had found Mme d'Estrades (allegedly d'Argenson's mistress) blocking the threshold. 'Door shut, I realized the necessity of passing via her.'[59] Mme d'Estrades assumed the function, even the form, of a door. Women/doors were the power of communication between men – an informal, illegitimate means to a public authority. By amplifying the detail, violence was done to the whole. The door as synecdoche simultaneously maximized a place of movement, of the forced, fêted or frustrated comings-in or goings-out of the interns of the court,[60] and minimized the static built forms of ceremonial space. The part stood for the whole but in doing so transformed it, feminized it, dynamically.

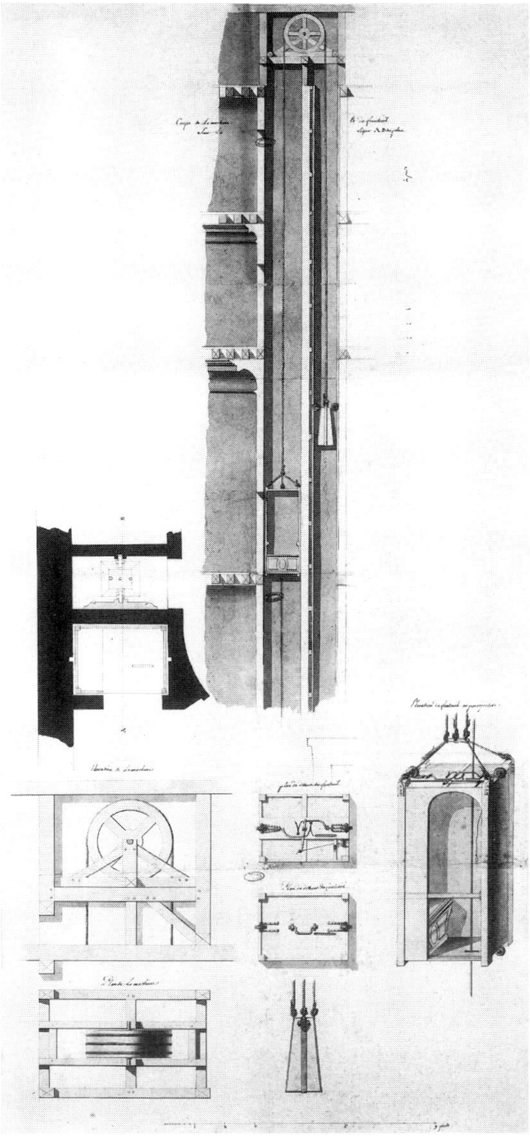

6.9 *Chaise volante*, 1743. Pen and wash, 12.3 × 5.5 cm. Paris: Archives nationales. Copyright: Archives nationales de France.

The staircase was also a figure of movement, of a particular quality or style of gait. Not the ceremonial stairs, the *Escalier des Ambassadeurs* (1672–78) that, grandly decorated and broadly lit, rose in stately measure between landings, but the backstairs, steeply vertical, unadorned and sometimes dangerously obscure.[61] According to Luynes, the dauphin's apartments were removed to the ground floor in 1747 partly because the entourage and fuss prescribed by etiquette to accompany him down the formal stairs when he went out had made the crown prince sedentary.[62] Backstairs were, by contrast, a means of passage – *dégagement*, to use the technical term. Rather than extending the space of ceremonial, they freed up circulation by establishing vertical short cuts through the building.[63] '*Dégager*' involved clearing spaces, creating gaps, where '*engagement*', its opposite, had built binding conjunctions. Movement by stairway, by skipping over the spaces of ceremony, quickened pace in the palace, admitted change. Architectural manuals of the period identified such stairs with the traffic of servants.[64] Luynes recollects, however, their constant use by members of the court and the royal family.[65] Pompadour's identification with stairs was particularly close during the period of her residence in the attics because the 'small' staircase, *her* small staircase, was the primary means of access, a means to which attention was additionally drawn by the novelty installation in 1743 of the *chaise volante*, or lift (plate 6.9).[66] Moreover, in contemporary fiction stairs fulfilled a ludic function, staged the breathless, hasty rise of the lover, leaping over the legitimate rights of father or husband. In Pinot Duclos's *Confessions du comte de* *** (1741), the hero secretly reaches the beloved but married Antonia by mounting 'a little staircase inside a tower'.[67] At Versailles, the 'tower' similarly housed the beloved; its inner spring, the stairs, reconfigured the settled order of the castle by elliptical movements of favour.

What do these tropes add to the understanding of Pompadour's interior politics? In one sense they appear to articulate afresh and with some originality the tired misogyny of men of letters who, from Montaigne to Montesquieu, had confidently attributed the ills of the state to the inside, informal and illegitimate authority of women.[68] But to the figure of Venus, the cause of this 'other' authority, may now be added that of Fortuna, the particular idiom – irrational (contrast), unstable (hinged) and elliptical (spiral) – of Pompadour's power. Some, notably those outside the court, interpreted that idiom literally. By the playwright Charles Collé, for instance, Pompadour stood accused of having transformed the court into a money economy in which specie was not only the universal equivalent of things (from posts in finance to coats of arms on the portal) but also the determining feature of all relationships.[69] While fortune, in the context of absolutism, did not produce power as such, by continually and capriciously redistributing parts of it in exchange, Fortune/Pompadour, according to Collé, 'did violence to the king's authority.'[70] Arguably, the violence was more symbolic than actual: by exposing the pathways of royal power Pompadour demystified, de-sacralized, its substance. Meanwhile, for Pompadour herself to embody movement, chance, was to lack a proper place: initially Luynes could not find her; thereafter, friends and enemies anticipated her disappearance.[71] *Her* power was the mystery.[72] Movement 'is the indefinite process of being absent and in search of a proper', according to de Certeau.[73] The rest of this essay is devoted to Pompadour's search for presence: to her acts of construction not locomotion.

CHÂTEAU DE BELLEVUE

Between 1746 and her death Pompadour bought, built or leased a total of fifteen properties: some, hermitages in the neighbourhood of the royal châteaux at Versailles, Fontainebleau and Compiègne; some, larger country houses in the Ile de France; and others, town houses, though conspicuously fewer of these. Bellevue (plate 6.10) and the hôtel d'Evreux were, by their location in or near Paris, and by the investment Pompadour made in them, among the most important. All – but these two most especially – spoke of a desire not simply to spend but to spend in order to establish an independently powerful identity.

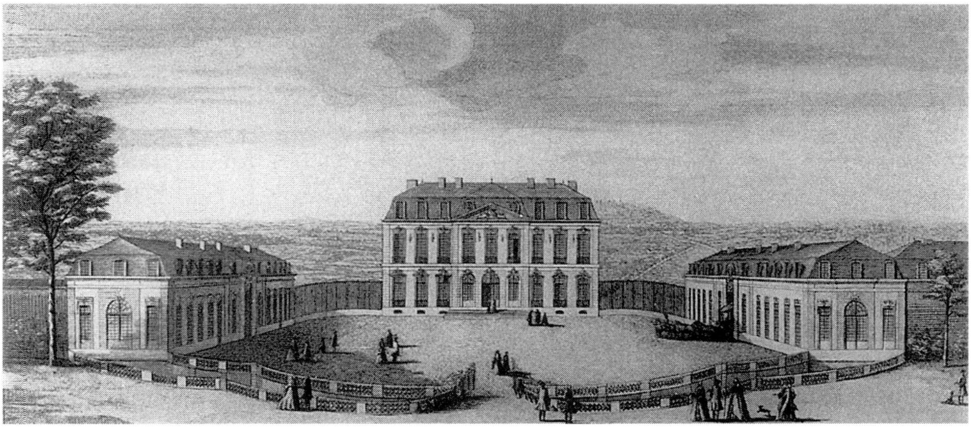

6.10 Courtyard elevation of the château of Bellevue, *c.* 1750. Engraving.

Luynes made two quite unrelated remarks about Pompadour's taste in buildings, neither of them about Bellevue, but both of them suggestive of the distinctive nature of her architectural enterprise. In May 1747 he noted that she had visited the château de Maisons, situated on a terrace overlooking the Seine, with a view to purchasing it in exchange for her more distant château at Crécy, near Dreux.[74] In November 1748 he remarked at the sight of her newly finished miniature hermitage on the northern periphery of the great park at Versailles that it inevitably prompted recollection of an incident at Clagny, the property opposite: Louis XIV had there built an analogous 'petite maison' for his mistress Mme de Montespan, but she had rejected hers as 'fit only for an opera girl', and a proper château had had to be built in its stead.[75] In both instances Pompadour's constructions were compared with monuments of the French classical tradition. Luynes's joke about Clagny turned first upon the double meaning of small, a literal description of scale and a euphemistic allusion to function, and secondly, on a contrast between the grand and noble (architectural and sexual) passions of Louis XIV and the petty ones of Louis XV: Pompadour was no better than an opera girl and, in fact, in view of her frequent appearances from 1747 in amateur productions by the *théâtre des cabinets*, was one – regularly.[76] The larger significance of the visit to the château de Maisons is not immediately obvious from Luynes. However, the architect Jacques-François Blondel later remembered that Mansart's 'masterpiece' had been passed over, notwithstanding its acknowledged beauty, because it lacked *commoditiés*, or the conveniences of everyday.[77] Setting aside Pompadour's paraded dependence, what Luynes's remarks tend to suggest is the unconventionality of her taste in living. It broke with the past, embracing the miniature when status and propriety were seemingly on the side of the gigantic. Moreover, it put comfort and function before beauty and order: comfort in the sense of interior distribution and the spatial support of bodily wellbeing, and function in the eighteenth-century sense of *caractère*, or the expression of a building's type and a proprietor's person.[78]

The Versailles hermitage had been designed and built by Pompadour's official architect, Jean Lassurance, in the summer of 1748, at exactly the time when, according to the registers of the Conseil d'État, the king was negotiating the complex purchase of some sixty-two *arpents* of land on the plane of Meudon overlooking the Seine, upon which to build a 'pavilion'.[79] When, in the following year, Louis ceded the property to his lover and Lassurance was charged with the realization of the pavilion, there emerged within a year and upon an expansive terrace a dwelling that substantially repeated, except on a larger scale, the design of the earlier hermitage. Thus a building of nine bays, set between a terrace and a garden, replaced one of five, and the simple tripartite division of the earlier façade was enlarged proportionately, the central pavilion breaking forward under a pediment, its exposed lines (like the corners of the buildings) elegantly reinforced with quoins. The shapes and distribution of the windows were similarly related; only the amount and distribution of ornament created a note of variation. The resemblance is significant, not so much with respect to authorship[80] but because it suggests that Bellevue was at heart a hermitage, a place where, in Pompadour's words, 'I am alone . . . or with the king and few others, and am therefore happy.'[81]

This is not to deny that Bellevue was a château; indeed it conformed remarkably closely to the fourth of Blondel's models for country houses in *De la distribution des maisons de plaisance* (1737–8). Rather, it is to recognize that Bellevue was shaped additionally by poetry. The château, as idyllic refuge, as Cythera, or pastoral redoubt, was a well-established poetic genre by the mid-eighteenth century.[82] Where Blondel offered country houses in a descending order of size and complexity in step with a corresponding scale of patronage determined by rank and means,[83] poetry's châteaux were, as figures of happy isolation, security and intimacy, always already small, no matter what their actual dimensions. In poetry, pleasure and comfort prescribed an intimacy of scale; in Blondel simplicity and comfort served rather to compensate those unable to secure a larger beauty.[84] Poetry, thus, assigned a positive value to the small and the simple, where architecture merely recognized constraints imposed by 'economy'.[85] In '*Le Hameau*', for instance, Gentil-Bernard, poet and protégé of Pompadour, matched

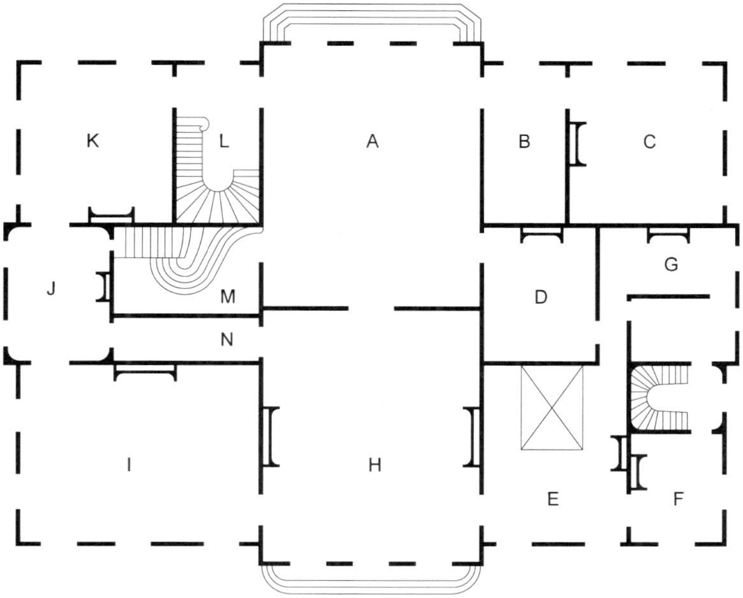

6.11 Plan of the château of Bellevue: A vestibule; B guards' room; C room of the Swiss guards; D antechamber; E Pompadour's bedchamber; F cabinet; G library; H dining room; I salon; J small gallery; K music room; L back stairs; M grand staircase; N closet.

the subject of the simple pastoral idyll to its poetic form: a short, four-syllable line and a naïve hop, hop, skip, skip, hop end-rhyme:[86]

> Rien n'est si beau
> Que mon hameau,
> Oh! Quelle image!
> Quel paysage
> Fait pour Watteau!

Simplicity is not lack but the power to isolate and concentrate: a tree for a landscape, a wave for a stream and, by extension, a hermitage for a house. Bellevue's smallness and simplicity[87] stood in determined contrast to the 'grands châteaux' and 'grands voyages' that constituted the permanent existence of the court.[88]

Inside Bellevue the conflicting demands of hermitage and palace were manifest in the distribution of ceremonial, social and private spaces. On the ground floor (plate 6.11), entering from the courtyard, the two guards rooms to the left of the vestibule, instead of initiating a ceremonial tour of a grand apartment, were cut off from their life's work and reduced to a cul-de-sac. Priority was removed to the society rooms, to the dining room, salon, 'gallery' and music room, arranged along the terrace and the east front. Likewise, in the distribution of the Pompadour's apartment the antechamber can scarcely have served as pompous introduction: landlocked and benighted, it was related to no other room in the apartment *en enfilade*. Greater value, in terms of location and decoration, was assigned to the *cabinets* arranged one above the other in a mezzanine (*en entresol*) at the northwest corner. These *cabinets* were not like those that preceded the bedchamber in Pompadour's Versailles apartments, and which served as important spaces of reception; they were smaller, beyond the bedchamber, and dedicated rather to the promotion of the mistress's physical wellbeing. According to Paul Biver, the lower *cabinet de toilette* was furnished with a closed stool, bidet and night table, in addition to the usual seat furniture.[89] The room was light, from the windows giving in two directions, bright, from the reflection produced by the mirror set above the fireplace, and warm.[90] Its decoration further enhanced the impression of comfort: above a varnished and gilded dado the walls were upholstered with elaborately embroidered silk hangings, and the gilt bronze of the andirons and the porcelain flowers (plate 6.12) of the wall-brackets – a striking novelty – drew attention to light and fire.[91]

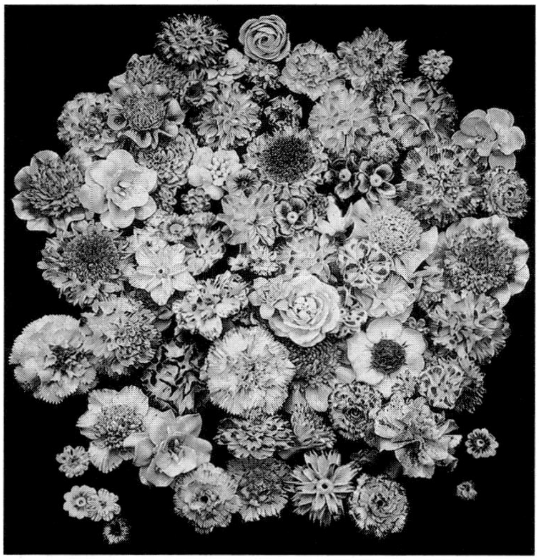

6.12 Porcelain flowers, *c.* 1747–50. Vincennes. Copyright: Christie's, New York.

Architectural theory early identified a conflict between comfort and beauty. Germain Boffrand argued in his *Livre d'architecture* (1745) that the master (or mistress) of a house could not count himself [herself] 'properly housed if everything which surrounds him [her] is not conveniently arranged for his [her] use, and easily to hand'.[92] So saying, Boffrand indicated that making comfortable and convenient was not only an art on a human scale (the unit of measurement an arm's length) but one that, in its responsiveness to the body, shaped buildings from the inside. He regretted the credit that it enjoyed in France and the consequent neglect of the decoration of the exterior.[93] Werner Szambien has pointed out that the opposition between comfort and beauty, interior and exterior, was also understood as a conflict between patron and architect, between the satisfactions demanded by the former and the aesthetic aspirations cherished by the latter.[94] Such a patron was, according to most, bourgeois; a person whose horizon was governed by the narrow demands of domesticity.[95] One argument that might be made with respect to Bellevue is that Pompadour 'brought her (bourgeois) lair with her', just as, according to Luynes, she arrived with her tongue twisted by vulgar expressions.[96] It is not one that will be made here because Bellevue was conspicuously not a *family* house in either the noble and genealogical or the bourgeois sense.[97] Rather, by reference to the poetic image of the château, this essay proposes that comfort constituted a politics of the interior.

Such a hypothesis gains support from the fact that Bellevue was not unusually well fitted with amenities, but rather made an extraordinary feature of those it did possess. Nowhere was this more apparent, perhaps, than in the *appartement des bains*, housed in one of the two pavilions that flanked the courtyard and, like its companion, introduced to the château to which it was linked by C-shaped scrolls of gilded iron railings. Entered through French windows from the terrace, the apartment consisted of a main room with a fireplace at the far end to either side of which doors opened – left onto the bathroom and right onto a closet with a closed stool. The principal room, though north-facing for freshness,[98] must have appeared the epitome of comfort. Like Pompadour's *cabinet*, the walls were upholstered above low panelling with a 'tapestry' made of fine cotton, striped and edged with *cordonnet* and chenille, upon which silk Chinese figures had been appliquéd – the roughness of the *cordonnet*, the soft, fluffiness of the chenille and the thickness of the appliqué creating a highly textured, supple surface in contradiction to the rigidity of the wall.[99] To describe the effect differently, instead of drawing *out* space in the straight lines of a geometrical shape, such a surface, by its address to touch, advanced to meet the bather, crowded *in* to comfort the body. Further folds of cotton stuff printed with flowers and butterflies hung in curtains about the windows, draped the day bed and upholstered the chairs and armchairs whose sculpted wooden frames were painted in contrasting tones of green. Above the doors hung paintings in elaborately carved frames: François Boucher's *Bath of Venus* (1751; National Gallery, Washington DC) and *Toilette of Venus* (1751, plate 6.13).

The *Toilette of Venus* depicts the interior it decorates. Fabric again dominates the scene: sky-blue drapery encloses the goddess in a reversible skin, interior by convention, exterior by colour. She sits propped in the 'arms' of a rose-tinted day bed and beneath her foams white and gold brocade, the flambé pattern turning to ripples of water. The folds of this elemental, 'smooth' space accommodate, moreover, the nesting instincts of doves.[100] To this natural image of habitation amidst so much artifice, Boucher added another: the shell – the place of Venus's birth, her original abode, in fact – appropriately depicted near her feet, and repeated both in plan and in section on the upper and lower rails and in the corners of the carved and gilded frame (plate 6.14).[101] Cröy's description of the *petits appartements* at La Muette as '*nids de rats*' (rats' nests) and the abbé Pluche's account of shells as houses drawn to a universal plan to which each species adds 'its own perfections, its own charms and *conveniences*' suggests that primal images of the interior as tangible outcroppings of the body were readily understood at the

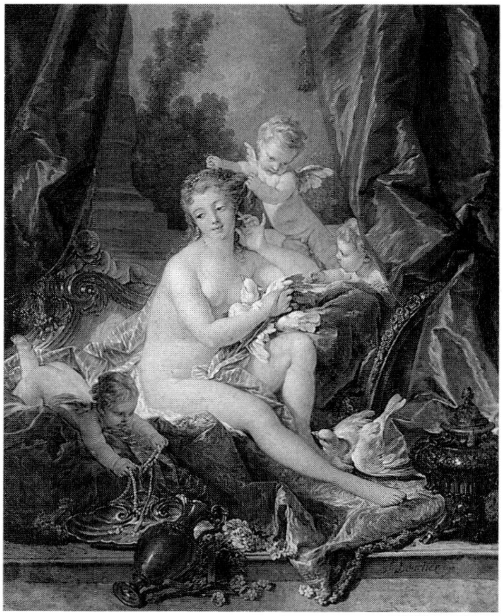

6.13 François Boucher, *The Toilet of Venus*, 1751. Oil on canvas, 108.3 × 85.1 cm. New York: The Metropolitan Museum of Art. Copyright: The Metropolitan Museum of Art.
6.14 Louis XV picture frame, *c.* 1750. Carved and gilded wood, 125 × 55 cm. Paris: Musée des arts décoratifs. Copyright: Musée des arts décoratifs.

time.[102] This, however, was not the dynamic, questing body (of doors and stairs), but a body profoundly rooted and at rest, literally implanted upon the bed. Comfort, in its particular manifestation and articulation in the *appartement des bains*, thus begged to contradict the image of Pompadour as '*conduit*' (to use an eighteenth-century diarist's metaphor) between places – between, that is, the king and his subjects – and cast her as a place of destination, one of such primal force that it naturalized the king's periodic visits as returns to origin.[103]

Dominique Massoumie has questioned the necessity of the connection between the emergence of the bathroom in the eighteenth century and the advent of modern notions of comfort, pointing out that many bathrooms at that time were located at too great a distance from living quarters for convenient daily use.[104] Bellevue's decoration has suggested, however, that its bath was discursively, if not actually, *commode*, or, to make the same point differently, that the furnishings and paintings in the room performed the comforts and conveniences that planning apparently denied. Comfort was an aspect of the château's character quite as much as a dimension of its function. To say so is to pursue, with respect to architecture, an argument made persuasively by Ewa Lajer-Burcharth about the tangible as a modality of vision in painting, and as a means of self-differentiation, but to see it raised on this occasion to the status of an attribute, a device.[105] The susceptibility of contemporaries to this impression can only have been heightened by the symmetrical disposition of the theatre opposite the bathhouse in the courtyard.[106] Pompadour's reputation as an actress was well established; moreover, in 1750 she had played the part of Venus in a *ballet héroique* by Pierre Laujon – recently related by Alastair Laing to Boucher's pictures in the bathroom.[107] In chinoiserie the two spaces partook, moreover, of the same language of decoration.[108] The stage was Pompadour's domain, performativity an attribute of her character and, by a unity of impulse that linked stage and bath, comfort and pleasure emerged further to define her.

Character as a principle of architecture was of relatively new conceptualization.[109] In 1734 Boffrand, who is credited with having introduced character to architectural discourse, presented his first lecture on the subject at the Academy of Architecture, a lecture twice repeated and later published in the *Livre d'Architecture*.[110] Adapting Horace's famous analogy between poetry and painting, Boffrand proposed two senses of architecture as theatre. First,

> Through its composition a building expresses, *as if in a theatre*, that the scene is pastoral or tragic; that this is a temple or a palace, a public building destined for a particular purpose or a private house. By their planning, their structure and their decoration, all such buildings must proclaim their purpose to the beholder.[111]

The building assumed, in this sense, the role of an actor, announcing in the case of Bellevue that the 'scene' was pastoral. Towards the end of the essay Boffrand attributes to it another role, that of stage set:

> If you are setting out to build a music room, or a salon in which to receive company, it must be cheerful in its planning, in its lighting, and in the manner of its decoration.[112]

The interior as stage set construes rooms as discrete spaces, spaces disengaged from any larger sequence or narrative; it is significant in this respect that Boffrand illustrates his argument with examples of 'society' rooms which did not belong, properly speaking, to the apartment, or ceremonial space of the house. Moreover, from a contrast in the following sentence of music room and mausoleum, Boffrand's spaces emerge as not only discontinuous but mutually exclusive. To return briefly to Gentil-Bernard's château poem, there, too, scenes of country pleasure replace, 'efface', one another:[113]

> Là chaque place
> Donne à choisir
> Quelque plaisir
> Qu'un autre éface.

At Bellevue, the bathroom and theatre, by their advanced position, served perhaps as a prologue to the production of the house, but the reception rooms

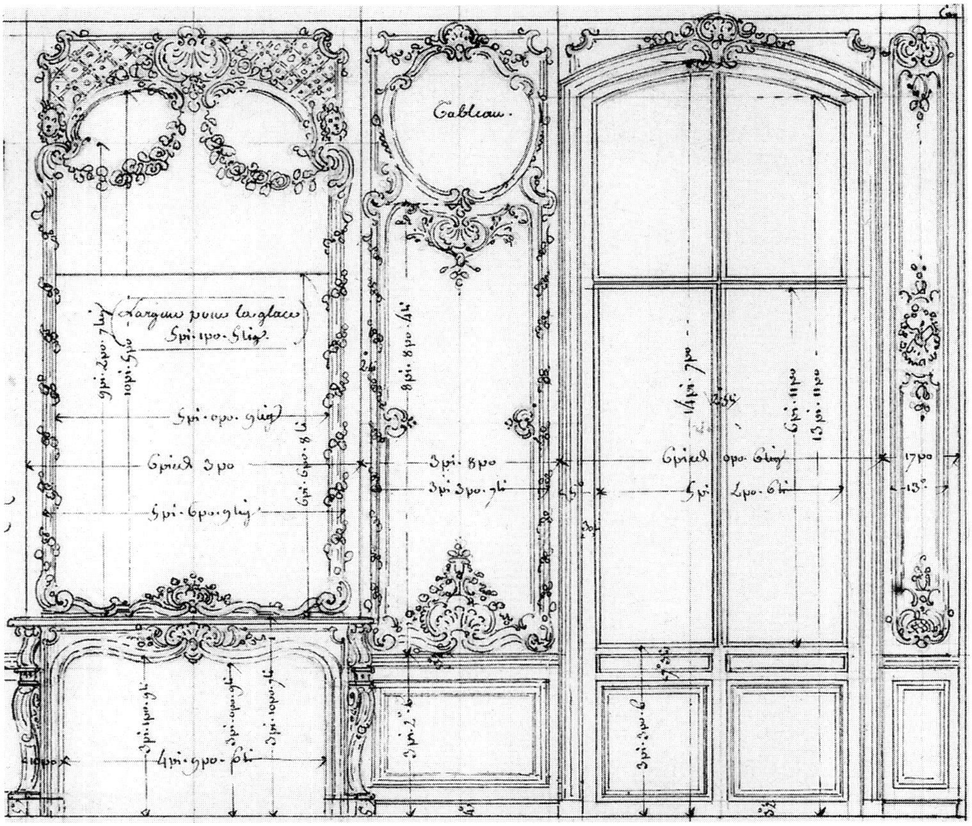

6.15 Jacques Verberckt, *Design for the panelling for the salon of Bellevue*, c. 1749. Pen and ink. Paris: Archives nationales. Copyright: Archives nationales de France, Paris.

within the *corps de logis*, distributed according to no obvious logic, seem rather to have shared in this new, disintegrative aesthetic.

Bellevue had both a music room and a salon at adjacent corners of the château; however, sufficient evidence for a reconstruction survives only for the second and more important room. Entered from the dining room (plate 6.15), the walls of the salon were decorated with carved and painted panelling by Jacques Verberckt, into which were set mirrors and paintings.[114] Mirrors filled the spaces between the windows, surmounted the chimney mantle and occupied the centre of the west wall. Carle Van Loo's paintings of the Arts – *Painting*, *Sculpture*, *Architecture* and *Music* – and of *Comedy* and *Tragedy* were distributed in pairs on three walls: two of the Arts were positioned high to either side of the chimney piece, the other two took up positions opposite, above pier-glasses. The last, larger couple covered doors, real and false, on the west wall. To judge by the preparatory drawings, Verberckt anticipated deploying a floral iconography of palms and garlands appropriate to a château rather than a scheme exclusive to this room;[115] it was left to the paintings to set the salon apart. *Comedy* (plate 6.16) and *Tragedy* invoked the theatre. Moreover, by their appropriation of the type of allegorical actress portrait devised by Jean-Marc Nattier, they alluded perhaps to Pompadour's own comic and tragic roles.[116] The salon was not, of course, a theatre but a place for the performance of unscripted though not unregulated sociability, in this instance, the playing of games: the inventory of furniture included six '*voyeuses*' (chairs designed especially for a comfortable, over-the-shoulder observation of the card table), and a backgammon table supplied by Lazare Duvaux.[117] It is not impossible that playing a part served wittily to evoke playing a hand, and that the genres of comedy and tragedy indirectly described the swings of fortune at the table. Playing also accounts for the activity of the children performing arts evidently beyond their years. These, too, were performances to which the marquise could, with imagination, be related: as model in *Painting*, as patron in *Sculpture* and *Architecture*, and as artist in *Music* (plate 6.17). They, too, were appropriate to the character of the room by the summary of taste and refinement they elaborated.

The pictures not only distinguished the salon by their number and subject matter; more significantly, they also contributed to the theatricalization of its space. The tendency of the pictures to break down formally and thematically into pairs – *Painting* and *Sculpture*, *Architecture* and *Music* – worked to flatten space in so far as it encouraged the beholder 'to read' each wall separately. The sense of the wall as *tableau*, or surface, can only have been heightened by the treatment of the doors. Two of them were covered with mirror glass to enhance the brightness or 'cheerfulness' of the room, but reflection also held them to the surface by the scenes in the room that they enclosed and reproduced.[118] Blondel explained that interior doors could be decorated differently on their two sides to coordinate with the rooms into which they faced; as such, the door was imagined no longer as part of the mobile fittings (*menuiserie mobile*) but as annexed by the wall (*menuiserie dormante*).[119] The Bellevue salon included false as well as real doors; no multiplication, then, of the idea of openings, of flowing space, but evidence that doors offered a means, among others, of articulating the sedentary wall symmetrically, even dramatically. The shadows cast across closed doors in the engraved illustrations of *De la distribution des maisons de plaisance*, and Blondel's later discussion of the aesthetic possibilities of the surface depth created by the casement and its moulding, suggest that doors in the hands of the eighteenth-century architect could produce sublime effects as

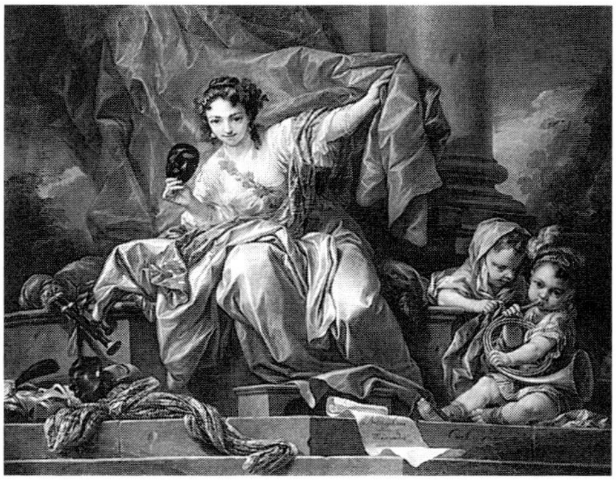

6.16 Carle Van Loo, *Comedy*, 1752. Oil on canvas, 122 × 151 cm. Moscow: The Pushkin Museum. Copyright: The Pushkin Museum.

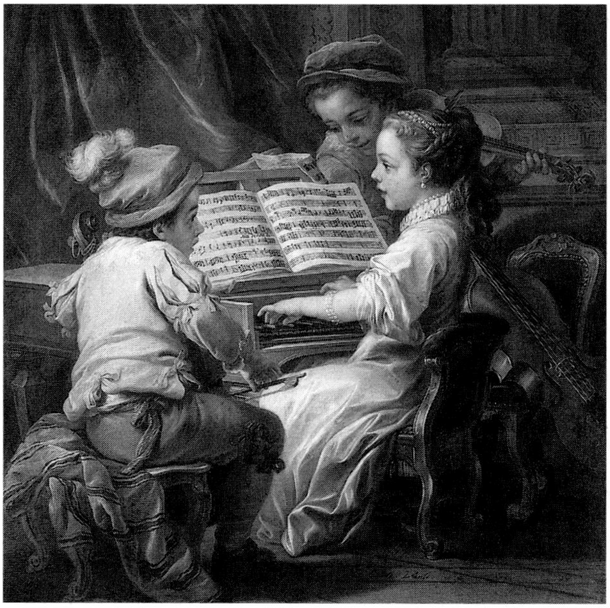

6.17 Carle Van Loo, *Music*, 1752–3. Oil on canvas, 87.5 × 84 cm. San Francisco: Fine Arts Museum. Copyright: The Fine Arts Museum, San Francisco.

well as classical order for the treatment of interior elevations.[120] Meanwhile, above the doors on the west wall, Van Loo's paintings offered further inducements to stillness; by Bernard Lépicié's account, they were painted to such a high finish as to warrant the focused attention of cabinet pictures.[121] Comfort had stilled by touch; the stilling of arrested vision was achieved by analogous appeal to the materiality of the sign.[122] But not only by that. *Comedy*'s action of raising the curtain and removing her mask redoubled the effort to engage the beholder's attention. It integrated the viewer's response into the work and held the gaze captive.

Such analysis might be repeated, evidence allowing, in other rooms in the château: the music room, the gallery, or the bedchamber. With considerable originality, this last was decorated 'à la Turque', a treatment seemingly fitting to the character of both room and resident. The exotic, upholstered realm of oneiric retirement that constituted the harem, according to the West, was recreated imaginatively at Bellevue with 'tapestries' of layered Chinese silk and gauze, lacquer furniture and paintings by Van Loo, in one of which Pompadour appeared dressed *en Sultane*.[123] The polysemy of Van Loo's image has been analysed at length by Perrin Stein, according to whom the picture simultaneously articulated novelty in decoration, alluded to Pompadour's theatrical roles – the Saracen Hermione in a production of *Tancrède* in 1748, for instance – and made witty reference to her new-found status – in 1752 no longer the mistress but the favourite of the king's expanding harem.[124] In the bedchamber she was reframed as alluring, in the music room, perhaps, as a siren. Bellevue unfolded an identity for

Pompadour that was not one, but multiple, social. There were many rooms, many Pompadours.

Such proliferation of forms and functions by 'character' had, according to Dalibor Veseley, the paradoxical effect of introducing into architecture significant simplifications of space and time.[125] Concerned as it was with representation, character, as Veseley notes, drew attention to the surface of buildings at the expense of depth and the complexities of distributing the world according to a moral order.[126] Boffrand may have urged that character were conventional, dependent, that is, on the status and role of the patron, but representation had not the same power of ritual to distinguish nobles and non-nobles, the field marshal, the judge and the prelate, men and women, master and servants, according to their several domains. Character in this sense was anti-apartment, anti-*enfilade*. Influenced by theories of physiognomy and expression character was, moreover, a matter of appearance and therefore largely independent also of tradition, precedent and socially sanctioned norms.[127] At Bellevue *turquerie* could frame sleep and masquerade a mistress, though it had done neither before. Pompadour's taste may not have been innovative but her house was fundamentally modern. Character offered her legitimate identities denied her by her bourgeois origins and disorderly occupation.

In black on the balconies, in gold and encircled by garlands on the console tables in the dining room, interlaced with palms and embroidered on the silk furnishings in the salon, Pompadour's tower multiplied and playfully recombined with other motifs throughout the château.[128] An heraldic device, symbol of the status conferred on her by the king, Pompadour had taken full and independent possession of her ornament and remade it in her own image on the inside.

HÔTEL D'EVREUX

On Christmas Eve 1753 Pompadour bought the hôtel d'Evreux located between the rue Saint Honoré and the Champs Elysées.[129] Rumours of the sale had been circulating for some months.[130] She had at her disposal an apartment at the hôtel des Ambassadeurs, rue Neuve des Petits Champs, but, according to the marquis d'Argenson, the changed nature of her relationship with the king (platonic from 1751) made a property of her own essential.[131] So keen, apparently, was Louis to retire his former mistress to Paris that he offered to buy Bellevue from her to finance the purchase of the house.[132] The rumour was almost certainly groundless but the pairing of Bellevue and Paris and the anticipation of an exchange of properties found an echo elsewhere. Marc-Antoine Laugier, in the second edition of his *Essai sur l'architecture* (1755) so far commended Bellevue for its situation that he anticipated its status as a royal château.[133] He imagined a magnificent extension of the terrace in either direction as far as Meudon and Saint Cloud, the Seine made straight and monumental with trees in rows of four planted on either bank, a vista of the dome of the Invalides in one direction and access to the king, via a gently ramped causeway, in the other. Capital and court would face one another; form a spectacle for one another, and in so doing foster good relations between them, so necessary to both. Of course, the two fantasies differ in genre: d'Argenson's critical exposé bristles with buildings brought into play by political event; Laugier's utopia assigns to architecture the power to shape a better world. Both, however, construe the house as primarily visual and symbolic, not spatial. Indeed, the act of looking – to discern a motive or command a height – is consciously staged. Instead of the doors, staircases and rooms that have featured so far as emblematic of the processes of moving through, or being contained by, social and built space, this last part of the essay focuses on windows: first metaphorically, in the sense of the pointed 'looking-in', or in-spection, performed by critics; and thereafter, in relation to patterns of actual fenestration and the views they sought to frame for those 'looking out'. How did the dialectic between inner and outer, the patron and her critics, redefine her interior?

René-Louis de Voyer de Paulmy, marquis d'Argenson (1694–1757) was one of Pompadour's bitterest critics. A member of the *robe* and a staunch supporter of the Paris *parlement*, he had served briefly as secretary of state for foreign affairs until dismissed from office in 1747 for mishandling the War of the Austrian Succession. He divided his time in retirement between Paris and Segrez, his country estate, both of which offered him, so to speak, a window on the world of politics and the court that was, he alleged, detached and disinterested.[134] It was an upstairs window, in the sense that the view was panoptic, all encompassing. The journal reviewed at the day's end not the court (Cröy, Luynes) but the court-in-the-nation. Exile had turned d'Argenson into a voyeur and the bewitching world of Versailles that had formerly possessed him into a text for his jaundiced eye. Moreover, it was the 'sight' of Pompadour that often precipitated his most sustained and intense political fantasies.[135]

The portrait of her to emerge from the copious pages of the journal was shaped by the reactionary ideology of the *robe* nobility, deeply hostile to the money economy and to the interests of finance that Pompadour represented, and it is consequently framed by the luxury debate, familiar negative tropes of which are mobilized to discredit her cultural ambitions. Thus, Bellevue is denounced by eloquent contrast of the allegedly extravagant cost of its realization and the manifestly miniature size of its production.[136] Royal revenue was poured into the ground, into foundations which, he claimed, exploiting parable, were built on sand and naturally subsiding.[137] Enormous forces of labour were set to trivial tasks: whitewashing, varnishing, gilding.[138] Finally, tokens of the chatelaine's comforts became, under d'Argenson's pen, infamous symbols of *luxe*: for example, the closed stool that allegedly secured the furniture-maker Migeon a pension of 3,000 *livres*;[139] or the porcelain flowers that decorated lights and filled vases at Bellevue and were the talk of Paris for their scandalous and unprecedented *superflu*.[140]

D'Argenson's critique of Bellevue and *luxe* Pompadour was, however, more than a petty assault on the moneyed vulgarity of any woman and any house. In ways not always coherent, Pompadour figures in the journal as a cause *and* an effect of decadence, as a symptom of the mounting tyranny *and* of the imminent collapse of absolutism. The appointment by her influence of Machault d'Arnouville as *contrôleur général des finances* and successively of her relations Le Normand de Tournehem and the marquis de Marigny at the Bâtiments du roi had seemingly liberated her galvanic powers to spend by putting the public purse at her disposal.[141] Her *luxe* was thus conspicuously unjust, arising from an abuse of power and resulting in the increasingly unequal distribution of wealth. In d'Argenson's texturology of the kingdom her prodigality and ambition is regularly juxtaposed with the destitution and misery of town and country, of peasant and weaver, in the immediate aftermath of the Peace of Aix-la-Chapelle (1748).[142] To Pompadour's privatization of parts of the state apparatus, d'Argenson adds, in 1756, her domestication of monarchy, which he describes strikingly as a 'chiffonage de femme', a ragging, creasing, or crimping of the fabric of the state by her feminine touch.[143] He paints an allegorical portrait of her and Louis as Omphale and Hercules, the latter utterly alienated from his regal self: 'he is a lover enslaved and subjugated, who fears displeasing his mistress.'[144] The dominatrix kept her king spinning, in constant movement, from one place to another, from one distraction to another, so that he was prevented ever from thinking about, never mind concerning himself with, serious matters of state.[145] Instead, her trivial tastes became state affairs: she interested the crown in Sèvres and 'a building the size of the Invalides' was built not to succour the casualties of the recent war but to manufacture soft paste porcelain flowers.[146]

For every striking example of luxury's softening, dissipating and corrupting effects, d'Argenson fashioned another that illustrated its tendency to monopolize and desensitize power.[147] Drawing heavily on Montesquieu, he repeatedly describes the court as a seraglio. In an entry for 11 February 1748 the interior of Versailles is described in terms of imprisonment, a harem/prison within which Pompadour assumes the role not of Sultana (which she later played at Bellevue) but of head eunuch, implicitly enforcing the will of the master, explicitly policing access to his presence by stopping up independent entrance to the palace.[148] By 1750 the seraglio stood more generally for Louis's pursuit of his pleasure in contempt of a suffering nation.[149] There was widespread anger that the end of war had brought no immediate lifting of taxes; that indeed, in 1749, Machault had introduced a new tax, the *vingtième*, a 5 per cent tax on all incomes without exception, for the sole purpose, seemingly, of financing the excesses of the court. The parlements and the provincial estates had had to be compelled to register the edict; D'Argenson warned of the dangers of public anger, of possible acts of 'defenestration'.[150]

D'Argenson's journal was, of course, not an open book, though Pompadour was certainly aware of the enmity in which she was held, if not the detail of that of which she stood accused by d'Argenson. His angle of vision, his perspective, was, however, shared by others: the parlements and some Salon critics, notably

La Font de Saint Yenne, and the *peuple* whose reported actions and opinions feature prominently in the journal.[151] In 1753 ten works commissioned for Bellevue were shown at the Salon, and though the response of the critics was generally favourable, La Font spoke out forcefully in the name of the public against the technical facility and intellectual bankruptcy he perceived in Boucher's *Rising* and *Setting of the Sun*, en route for the king's bedchamber at the château, and the humiliating triviality he discerned in Van Loo's allegories of the Arts.[152] He was especially critical of the compressed space and stacked figures in the art of *Music* (see plate 6.17) and identified the cause of such perversities in the disorderly demands of the rococo interior and the necessarily private-minded patronage of women.[153] More or less concurrently, he had expressed dismay at the corresponding neglect of public architecture, notably the Louvre. A dialogue between the Louvre and the City of Paris published in 1756 saw the complacent self-satisfaction of the latter in the everyday beauties of its private houses pricked by the former's bleak sketch of a capital without squares, fountains, theatres or bridges worthy of the name.[154] Since the glory days of Colbert, Paris had turned inwards, into an interior, so to speak, a place not of public virtues but of private tastes and appetites.

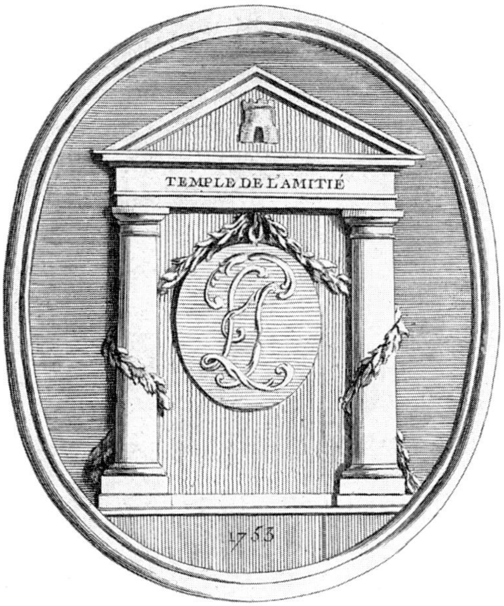

6.18 Mme de Pompadour, *The Temple of Friendship*, c. 1752–3. Etching, 15.3 × 13.1 cm. London: Victoria and Albert Museum. Copyright: Victoria and Albert Museum.

Pompadour's contemporaries liked often to represent her as either oblivious to criticism or vengefully over-reacting to those with the temerity to attack her.[155] Her actions indicate otherwise and suggest that she essayed a number of strategies to meet the criticism to which her patronage had become vulnerable with the increasing currency of notions of character and expression in architecture. Self-parody was one. A ballet performed at Bellevue in 1751 and entitled *L'Amour architecte* adapted La Fontaine's fable in which, after enormous fuss and stupendous effort, a mountain gives birth, not to a city 'the size of Paris', but to a mouse or, in this case, a house: Bellevue.[156] As 'author' of the house, the ballet implied that Pompadour and her patronage were not to be taken seriously.[157] In the same year Pompadour moved to her new apartment on the ground floor at Versailles, a move, as d'Argenson had foreseen, calculated to raise her dignity so far that it eliminated the need for interior politics.[158] That presumption of her influence was not forestalled thereby and required further allaying is suggested by a gesture she made five years later: with a touch of melodrama she had the staircase between the king's apartment and her own walled up and thus apparently ended all secret congress between them.[159] The purchase and elaboration of the hôtel d'Evreux constituted another such symbolic gesture, a further formalization of relations between them that coincided, moreover, with a new architectural device (plate 6.18): a classical temple.

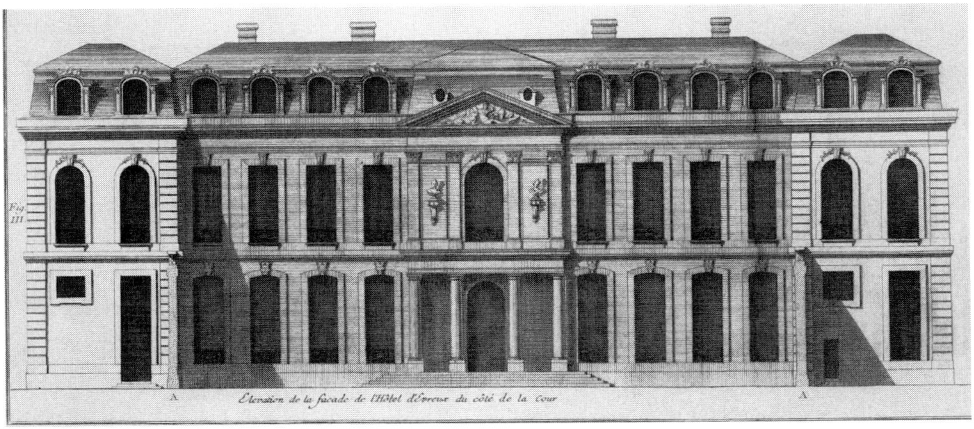

6.19 Courtyard elevation of the hôtel d'Evreux, 1752–6. Engraving. From Jacques-François Blondel, *Architecture françoise*, 1752–6. London: The British Library. Copyright: The British Library.

Much has been written about the iconography devised by and for Pompadour around 1753 to represent anew her relationship with the king.[160] In addition to the paintings and sculpture that elaborated the theme of friendship at Bellevue, Pompadour engaged Jean Guay to engrave a new seal for her. Upon one of its three facets the 'gallant' tower made way for a 'Temple of Friendship', as did azure for the tincture topaz.[161] A medallion combining the monograms of Louis and Pompadour hangs by a garland of oak leaves from the classical entablature; the text that accompanied Pompadour's etching of the gem explained that the Doric order and the associated species of ornament symbolized respectively the properties of solidity and endurance that characterizes true friendship, one that never changes.[162] The Temple of Friendship was thus also a Temple of Taste: not the circular *tempietto* familiar from Boucher's pretty pastorals and landscapes, but a plainly classical one, one almost primitive in the manner of Laugier's 'first' house, first published in the spring of 1753.[163] In complete reversal of the turret, the temple has no walls, no interior.

Coincidentally, the entrance to the vestibule of the hôtel d'Evreux (plate 6.19) was also not enclosed but open to the elements, and though the *hôtel* as a whole was scarcely primitive in its vast expansiveness, it nevertheless presented a magnificently classical face to the courtyard with a central pavilion of Doric columns, Tuscan in their simplicity, according to Blondel.[164] Built by

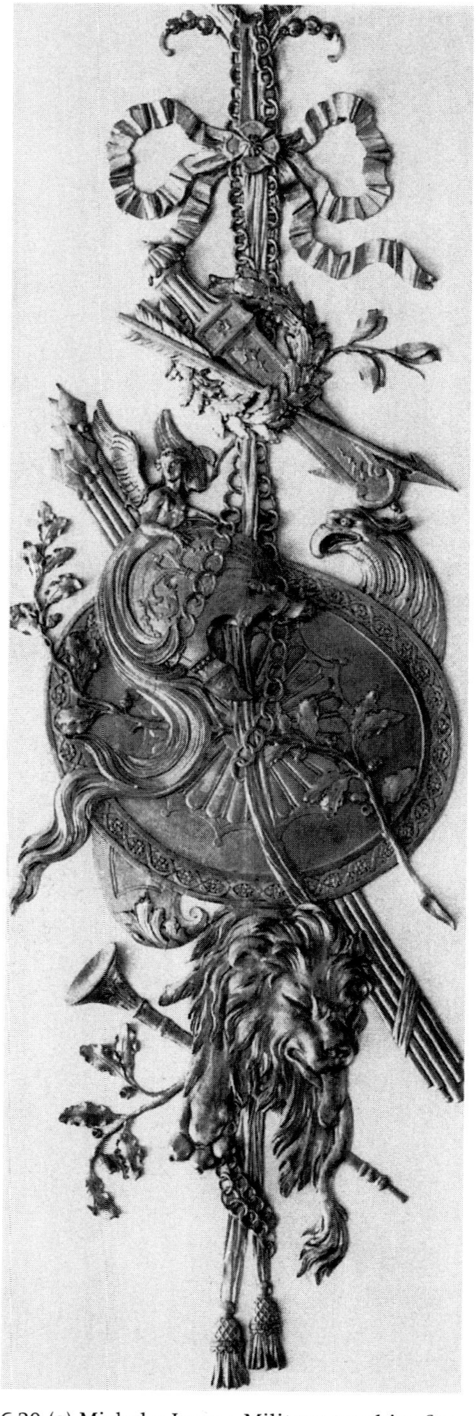

6.20 (a) Michel II Lange, Military trophies for the panelling of the Salon, 1722.

Armand-Claude Mollet between 1718 and 1720, the *hôtel* was chiefly commended by architects and critics mid-century for the splendours within and for the pleasing aspect of the garden. The adjectives 'grand', 'magnificent', 'beautiful', and 'rich' flowed from the pens of guidebook writers such as Germain Brice and Dezallier d'Argenville;[165] it was left to Piganiol de La Force to strike a rather more critical note. According to him, the architecture, though properly vast, lacked proportion.[166] He was especially critical of the disproportion of the windows, as Blondel later noted, in height three times their width;[167] openings that by their number and size seemed to engross the façade. However, Paris in the 1750s apparently experienced a veritable '*fureur*' for such tall, arched windows,[168] their large panes and high-grade transparency dissolving the boundary of the interior.[169]

The principal room with a view was the salon. Located on the main axis between the court and the garden, it occupied the three bays of the central pavilion, its French windows giving onto the garden which stretched away towards the Champs Elysées. This, the most richly decorated room in the house, combined mirrors and panelling to a design by Jules-Michel Hardouin. Sculpted by Michel II Lange, the *lambris* incorporated military trophies (plate 6.20): elaborate, antique armories of helmets, shields, swords, quivers and arrows, suspended in a magnificent jumble by beribboned chains from tautly depressed mouldings below shell-like clasps.[170] The masculine hyperbole of military triumph had suited Henri-Louis de La Tour d'Auvergne, *colonel-général de la cavalerie*, for whom the interior had originally been realized in 1722. Pompadour might have been expected to have had this space particularly in mind when she hatched plans to decorate and redecorate parts of the house but initially she did little to temper its aggressive, gilded grandeur.[171] Arguably, indeed, she reinforced its character by having fitted into the panelling a Gobelins tapestry bearing at its centre the interlaced 'Ls' of her former lover.[172] Framed in the panelling, the tapestry, large with armorial significance, is unlikely to have disguised or softened the solidity of the wall, that is, rendered comfortable the interior (as at Bellevue); rather the tapestry assumed the wall's structuring rigidity.

How to understand Pompadour's retention and minor improvisation of the Evreux scheme? As evidence of disinterest? – she used the house but occasionally.[173] As an instance of particularly adventurous masquerading? – her previous excursions into cross-dressing having been limited to pastoral shepherds.[174] Or as the attachment of caution to the sanctioned taste of another, to the sober and sculptural *style Régence* once favoured by the sword nobility and potentially fashionable anew in the wake of war and in the context of early neoclassicism? In favour of the last hypothesis, which would find Pompadour first experimenting with an overtly classical and heroic language of decoration in Paris, is the complicity of the medium. Panelling (*menuiserie*) belonged to architecture, shared its preoccupation with geometry and proportion. Moreover, Laugier's powerful evocation of architecture's origin in the primitive hut, in post and lintel structures made of trees, encouraged

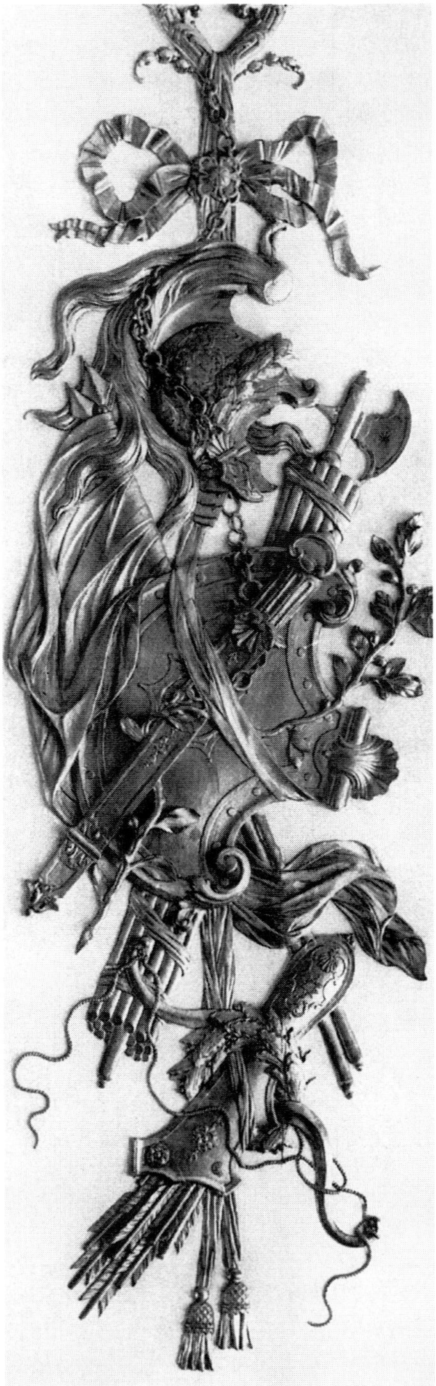

6.20 (b) Painted oak. Paris: Palais de L'Elysées. Copyright: The Courtauld Institute of Art, London.

architects and patrons to think of woodwork as the first, and thus, the authentic medium of the interior.[175] In contrast to Bellevue, where the spell of the interior lay in its having, seemingly, been moulded inside out, the authority of the hôtel d'Evreux sprang from its having apparently brought the outside in: the martial trophies from the entablature of the garden façade for the panelling, the semi-circular crowns of the windows for the tops of the mirrors, and more allusively for the whole, the spirit of a primitive classicism and the principle of reform that it implied. The windows, their apertures sidelined in red by expensive crimson curtains, were an essential component of this switchback.[176] What did they admit and make tangible to sight?

Later in the century the guidebook writer Louis-Victor Thiéry elaborated the verdict of excellence generally passed on the view from the salon by noting that the transparent, railed boundary of the property encouraged the appropriation of the Champs Élysées as park to the Évreux house and garden.[177] The garden was not prized for its privacy and seclusion but on the contrary for the public realm it admitted: Thiéry described the view as 'happy' and 'animated' by the quantity of public strolling by. The relation between the spaces was the stronger at the time of Pompadour's residency because she purchased land from the king that projected her garden into the public way.[178] D'Argenson implied, not surprisingly, that the public aspect of Pompadour's private garden had been created only under public pressure,[179] but it seems more likely, in fact, that Pompadour was actively seeking public recognition of a relation between her *hôtel* and royal places in the vicinity. She signed the contract of purchase for the *hôtel* in December 1753, paid over the odds for it, but only after a final decision had been made in August to locate the Place Louis XV, a royal square in the planning since 1748, at the entrance of the Champs Élysées.[180] The square was, probably, the single most important urban project in the capital during Louis XV's reign. The equestrian statue of the king had been commissioned by the City of Paris in 1748 to commemorate the Peace of Aix-la-Chapelle and to the king fell the task and the expense of clearing space for its display. Pompadour had taken an active interest in the project from its inception and it was her architect, Lassurance, who, in 1748, first drew attention publicly to the potential of the site between the Pont du Tournon and the Champs Élysées.[181] Five years later when initiating proposals for the remodelling of the hôtel d'Evreux and its garden, he was still working on those plans; the two projects proceeded simultaneously. Although the square and Edme Bouchardon's bronze statue were never visible from the salon, plans sent to Pompadour by an obscure architect, one Louis-Jean Laurent, proposing to drive an avenue through her garden to give her a 'beautiful view of the square and the beloved object that is its spirit', indicate that the view was a picture in more than one mind if not actually before the eye.[182] And, when Marigny came to redistribute the Champs Élysées in 1758, trees were felled to create a view from the salon to the Seine and beyond to another icon of Bourbon monarchy, the Invalides.[183] By the expansion and arrangement of the garden and the planning and realization of the square, the salon d'Evreux made a spectator rather than a spectacle of Pompadour.

Studies of the relation between sight and site in early modern French architecture have focused classically on Versailles. According to Louis Marin's reading of Louis XIV's château, the axis (or sightline) palace–park–beyond marked the projection of the king's body into space according to 'the law of the gaze'.[184] An absolute gaze, the aim of its radial view was all encompassing, infinite. A dominant gaze, the effect of its power was 'to develop' or structure space according to the symmetries, the classic order, of a Bourbon place. Although gender is no part of Marin's argument, his use of the gaze conforms in essentials to the active form of scopophilia – the drive to look and thereby to master or control others by objectification. This 'point of view' or manner of deploying vision, notionally monopolized under Absolutism by the king, was one to which royal subjects reacted either by subjection or by legitimate or illegitimate identification. D'Argenson, would-be first minister, is a particularly explicit example of the latter, of appropriation in fantasy of the governance of the gaze. Pompadour, self-styled object of desire, might be expected to have exemplified the former: the passive, exhibitionist role of being looked at and displayed. Indeed, Luynes maintained in the case of her hermitage at Fontainebleau that she had had it built under the king's windows that he might gaze out upon her.[185] However, at the hôtel d'Evreux Pompadour's look conformed to neither model. Hers was not imperial or promiscuous like the king's but set precisely at an object. According to Luynes, again, her dissatisfaction with Crécy, which she eventually sold to the duc de Penthièvre, arose from its lack of a view: it had a terrace and sightlines enough but nothing significant to look at.[186] Projection afforded no pleasure as such. Rather, Pompadour's look reversed the direction of sight through windows which, by design, assigned priority neither to the outside nor the inside,[187] and introjected or enveloped the king, represented indirectly by the Invalides (seen, but not of Louis XV's creation) and the place Louis XV (unseen but contiguous, palpated).

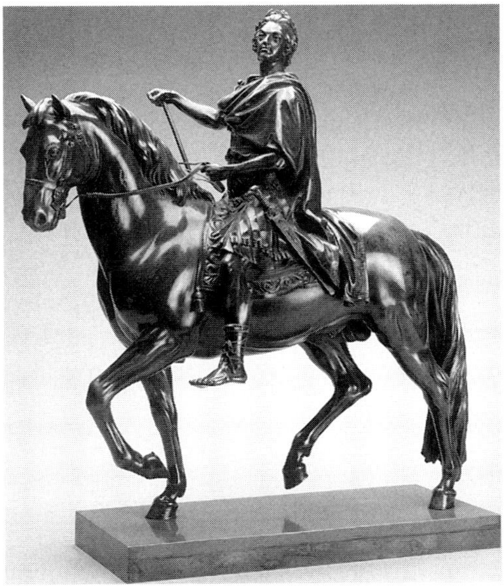

6.21 Louis-Claude Vassé, after Edme Bouchardon, *Equestrian Statue of Louis XV*, 1764. Bronze. London: Buckingham Palace. Copyright: Her Majesty the Queen.

Pompadour's look was qualitatively different from the gaze. It made of sight a broader faculty of vision that resisted absolute distinctions of inside/outside, subject/object, between, that is, what is seen 'objectively' and what is imagined emotionally. However, of itself, this does not explain why Pompadour chose to construct herself as a spectator at the hôtel d'Evreux, a spectator fully satisfied at last in 1763 when, thanks to a gift from the City of Paris and in the wake of the inauguration of the square, she was able to erect in the salon a miniature replica of Bouchardon's statue (plate 6.21) and thus complete the effect of the 'square' in the room.[188] The realization of the actual square had seen rivalries played out between different sources of authority in the state, between the Crown, represented by Pompadour and her clan at the Bâtiments and the Treasury, and the City of Paris, and between different ideals of the square, civic and royal. In 1753 La Font de Saint Yenne had argued energetically against a peripheral location in the 'fields' and in favour of Boffrand's plan, which had located the king at the heart of the city, in Les Halles, and thus in the hearts of his people.[189] It is not impossible that Pompadour's staging of the square at the heart of her house was an attempt not only to thwart criticism of her taste by a display of borrowed classical rectitude but also to articulate, via a tender perception of the capital from the windows, the faithfulness of one particular person to the king. It was to her 'heart', after all, that Bouchardon addressed an urgent plea in 1758 to delay a precipitate inauguration of the statue and square that would have compromised 'the king's glory and the satisfaction of the public'.[190] The salon d'Evreux, a temple of friendship, staged the final performance of a loyal beholder in contrast both to the 'voyeurism' of a d'Argenson and the critical spectatorship of a La Font. It suggested an ambition tamed, framed.

At the outset, this essay invited a judgement of Pompadour in answer to the question of whether her patronage of architecture was significant, a question no less contested now than it was then. Bellevue, by the distribution, decoration and typology of its rooms, has suggested that she played a part, indeed a vital part, in the early transformation of the house from a ceremonial or partly ceremonial space, into an intimate and personalized one. Moreover, Pompadour's graduation from the modern pastoralism of her château to the antique tenor of the hôtel d'Evreux has indicated a swing in the mid-1750s towards classicism, though in her case towards the classicism of the late baroque rather than the new *goût grec*. More significant, however, than these crude benchmarks of art-historical 'progress', has been the realization that the interior was drawn about a body, or to put it more strongly, that it is always materialized by a subject. At Versailles Pompadour's space, and the use of it she imposed upon others, remade the apartment as 'interior'. Source of her authority, this social space was, however, in conflict with architectural space, with representation, upon which devolved Pompadour's ambition for legitimacy. Frames, doors, stairs, rooms and windows, as architectural features and sociopolitical metaphors, have been the means of charting Pompadour's struggle for control of her interior self. Critical to this account has been the interplay between the tangible and the visual, specifically, between

Pompadour as movement and enclosure and Pompadour as spectacle and spectator – that, for her, 'looked-at-ness' was a quest for legitimacy indicates, if indication is needed, that the conditions of early modern subjectivity were the conditions imposed by patriarchy. Its absolute terms cast her as Fortuna or Omphale, agents of chaos and disorder; she pretended to the status of Venus, shell of the king's happiness, and later, if the allusion is not too fanciful, to that of Echo, she who to the last looked in love at the glory of another and was ultimately consumed.

Notes

This essay owes a great deal to the encouragement, advice and generosity of students. I thank first and especially my research assistant Mia Jackson. My warmest thanks next to those present at the research seminar at which the gist of the essay was presented and who, by their critical comments, helpful suggestions and invaluable references, have improved the text considerably: Michael Hall, Florian Knothe, Edouard Kopp, Joanna Gwilt, Ofer Mansour, Janice Mercurio, Anissia Morel, Jamie Mulheron, Abigail Price and Alicia Weisberg-Robert. The result is offered in memory of Haruko Matsubara (1947–2004).

1 M. Dennis, *Court and Garden. From the French Hôtel to the City of Modern Architecture*, Cambridge, Mass., 1988, 152.

2 A.T. Friedman, 'Architecture, Authority and the Female Gaze: Planning and Representation in the Early Modern Country House', *Assemblage*, 18, 1992, 40–61; T. Hinchcliffe, 'Gender and the Architect: Women Clients of French Architects during the Enlightenment', in *Gender and Architecture*, eds L. During and R. Wrigley, Chichester, 2000, 114–34; T. Hinchcliffe, 'Women and the Practice of Architecture in Eighteenth-century France', in *Architecture and the Politics of Gender in Early Modern Europe*, ed. H. Hills, London, 2003, 83–92.

3 On portraits, see, especially: E. Goodman, *The Portraits of Madame de Pompadour*, Berkeley and Los Angeles, 2000; M. Hyde, 'The "Makeup" of the Marquise: Boucher's Portrait of Pompadour at her Toilette', *Art Bulletin*, 82: 3, 2000, 453–75; E. Lajer-Burcharth, 'Pompadour's Touch: Difference in Representation', *Representations*, 73, 2001, 54–88. On patronage, see *Madame de Pompadour et la floraison des arts*, exhib. cat., David M. Stewart Museum, Montreal, 1988; D. Posner, 'Mme de Pompadour as a Patron of the Visual Arts', *Art Bulletin*, 72: 1, 1990, 74–105; *Madame de Pompadour et les arts*, exhib. cat., Musée national des châteaux de Versailles et de Trianon, 2002.

4 In addition to the full treatment of them in the recent *Madame de Pompadour et les Arts*, see also P. Biver, *Histoire du château de Bellevue*, Paris, 1933; J. Vittet, 'Le décor du château de Crécy au temps de la marquise de Pompadour et du duc de Penthièvre. Essai d'identifications nouvelles', *Bulletin de la société de l'histoire de l'art français*, 2000, 133–55.

5 A. Laing, *François Boucher 1703–1770*, The Metropolitan Museum of Art, 1986, no 64; Hyde, 'The "Makeup"', 463; Lajer-Burckharth, 'Pompadour's Touch', 68–9.

6 Though the point being made here is slightly different, I build on, and readily acknowledge a debt to, Ewa Lajer-Burkharth's analysis of the Munich portrait and most particularly on the ambiguities of space that it makes manifest. I warmly thank her for her comments on a draft of this essay.

7 G. Bachelard, *The Poetics of Space*, trans. M. Jolas, Boston, 1994, 67–8. Although there is no contemporary record of Pompadour's 'housework', the duc de Luynes had occasion to record the queen's concern for the dusting of her apartment, because it gave rise to a dispute over etiquette. See C.P. d'Albert, duc de Luynes, *Mémoires du duc de Luynes sur la cour de Louis XV (1735–1758)*, eds L. Dussieux and E. Soulié, 17 vols, Paris, 1860–63, 7: 264–5.

8 See *Livre-Journal de Lazare Duvaux, marchand-bijoutier ordinaire du Roy, 1748–58*, ed. L. Courajod, 2 vols, Paris, 1873, 2: 294.

9 On social space, see H. Lefebvre, *The Production of Space*, trans. D. Nicholson-Smith, Oxford, 1991, chap. 2.

10 Luynes, *Mémoires*, 7: 5.

11 See, in a different context, D. Posner, 'The Time Path of Fragonard's Progress of Love', *Burlington Magazine*, 114, 1972, 526–34.

12 Luynes, *Mémoires*, 8: 76–7.

13 Michel de Montaigne, 'On three kinds of Social Intercourse', in *The Complete Essays*, trans. M.A. Screech, Harmondsworth, 2003, 933–4; significantly, in the present context, the description of his library follows his discussion of the ideal forms of intercourse between men and women. Others have read Pompadour's towers as having a discursive as well as an heraldic value. Jean Vittet finds her blazon given a *chinoiserie* twist in a pair of pagodas ordered for Crécy, and in another instance converted into chess pieces in the ornamentation of her chandeliers, now at the Bibliothèque Mazarine. See Vittet, 'Le décor ... de Crécy', 144–45, 150–51.

14 J. Mosley argues, in '"O Tower Worthy of Praise!": The Paradox of Freedom, Captivity and Gender in Literary Architecture of Sixteenth-century France', in *Gender and Architecture*, eds Durning and Wrigley, 29–43, that Montaigne's perspective was culturally determined as masculine.

15 See *Pompadour et les arts*, no. 153.

16 All eighteenth-century architectural treatises singled out chimneys, doors and windows as the principal decorative components of the interior. See, for example, J.-F. Blondel, *De la distribution des maisons de plaisance*, 2 vols, Paris, 1737–38, 2: 65–80; C.E. Briseux, *L'Art de bâtir des maisons de campagne*, 2 vols, Paris, 1741–42, 2: 129–35.

17 This essay attempts to retrieve the behavioural element of architecture so effectively and persuasively accomplished with respect to furniture by Mimi Hellman. See, M. Hellman, 'Furniture, Sociability and the Work of Leisure in Eighteenth-century France', *Eighteenth-Century Studies*, 32: 4, 1999, 415–45.

18 See D. Gallet, 'Madame de Pompadour et l'appartement d'en bas au château de Versailles', *Gazette des Beaux-Arts*, 118, 1991, 129–38; *Pompadour et les arts*, 78–84.

19 See E. duc de Cröy, *Journal inédit du duc de Croy (1718–1784)*, ed. Vicomte de Grouchy and P. Cottin, 4 vols, Paris, 1906, 1: 168–9; Luynes, *Mémoires*, 10: 117.

20 Cröy, *Journal*, 1: 56.

21 Luynes, *Mémoires*, 6: 352.

22 Luynes, *Mémoires*, 6: 421.

23 Luynes, *Mémoires*, 7: 60.

24 Cröy, *Journal*, 1: 61.

25 For Châteauroux's apartment, see W.R. Newton, *L'espace du roi. La cour de France au château de Versailles*, Paris, 2000, 61–5, 177–8.

26 Pompadour also inherited Châteauroux's apartment at Fontainbleau. See Luynes, *Mémoires*, 7: 80.

27 Pierre-Xavier Hans made an especially valuable contribution to the *Pompadour et les arts* exhibition with his essays and entries on these apartments.

28 In 1732 Luynes married Marie Brulart de la Borde. On Luynes, see, in addition to the introduction to the *Mémoires*, J.-L.-A. Huillard-Bréholes, *Notice sur le duc de Luynes*, Paris, 1868.

29 Luynes's diary was not infrequently used for establishing precedent in matters of etiquette, see *Mémoires*, 8: 366, n.1.

30 On Cröy, see the introduction to the *Journal*, 1: vii–lxiv. In January 1747 he had loan of the apartment of the comte d'Estrées. On the advantages of being so lodged, see Cröy, 1: 65. See also Newton, *L'espace du roi*, 394.

31 On the vocabulary referring to those not properly of the court, see Cröy, *Journal*, 1: 148–9.

32 On the apartment, see, for example, J.-F. Blondel, *L'Architecture françoise*, 4 vols, Paris, 1752–6, 1: 26–31. Hugh Murray-Baillie has argued in 'Etiquette and Planning of the State Apartments in Baroque Palaces' (*Archeologia*, 101, 1967, 169–99) that French court ritual was temporal rather than spatial, a view with which I beg to differ. See K. Scott, *The Rococo Interior*, London and New Haven, 1995, 103–17.

33 Luynes, *Mémoires*, 8: 152, 158.

34 Luynes, *Mémoires*, 8: 198–9.

35 Luynes, *Mémoires*, 7: 439.

36 *Bienséance*, also known as *convenance*, was, according to eighteenth-century architects, an essencial principle of good architecture. See, for example, Brisseux, *L'Art de bâtir*, 1: 18. For a general discussion, see W. Szambien, *Symétrie, goût, caractère. Théorie et terminologie de l'architecture à l'âge classique*, Paris, 1986, 92–8.

37 Cröy, *Journal*, 1: 115–16.

38 Cröy, *Journal*, 1: 196.

39 Cröy, *Journal*, 1: 231–2.

40 On the *petits appartements*, see, most recently, A. and J. Marie, *Versailles au temps de Louis* XV, *1715–1745*, Paris, 1984; J.-C. Le Guillou, 'La creation des cabinets et des petits appartements de Louis XV au châtau de Versailles, 1722–1738', *Gazette des Beaux-Arts*, 1985, 137–47; J.M.J. Rogister, 'From Louis XV to Louis XVI: Some Thoughts on the *Petits Appartements*', *Eighteenth-century Life*, special issue *The Art and Architecture of Versailles*, eds P. Maccubin and D.F. Mor, 17, 1993, 146–66.

41 Cröy, *Journal*, 1: 73.

42 'Petit' recurs so often to describe her houses (*hermitages*), her rooms (*cabinets*), her staircases, her taste, her detail, that it achieves the status of a cliché. See, Cröy, *Journal*, 1: 135, 148, 149, 190 etc.

43 C. Perrault, *Les dix livres d'architecture de Vitruve corrigez et traduits nouvellement en français*, 1684, facsimile edn, Brussels and Liège, 1979, book iv, 106; for a modern and slightly different translation of the Latin, see *Vitruvius. The Ten Books of Architecture*, trans., M.H. Morgan, New York, 1960, 104.

44 See, for instance, the puff for prints after Juste-Aurèle Meissonnier in the *Mercure de France*, March 1735, 558–9 and later critical comments by, for example, the abbé Leblanc, *Lettre d'un françois*, The Hague, 1745, 2: 46

45 Hostile critics linked contrast with displacement (things not in their proper places) and confusion. For an eighteenth-century instance, see Blondel, *De la distribution des maisons de plaisance*, 2: 67. For a broader discussion, see Scott, *The Rococo Interior*, 252–65.

46 Cröy, *Journal*, 1: 196.

47 For a reassertion of this view, see Cröy, *Journal*, 233.

48 Cröy noted, with a touch of despair, that the 'real' interior was always elsewhere, in an inner cabinet, or inner-inner cabinet, receding in a '*mise en abyme*'. See *Journal*, 1: 71. A contrast is implied here with the *enfilade* that progressed towards a crescendo, towards the most important, often the largest rooms in the sequence.

49 M. de Certeau, *The Practice of Everyday Life*, Berkeley and Los Angeles, 1984, 97–105.

50 *Shorter Oxford Dictionnary*, 5th edn, 2002.

51 See H. Coulet, 'La métaphore de l'architecture dans la critique littéraire au xviie siècle', *Critique et création littéraires en France*, Paris, 1977, 291–306; W.A. McClung, 'The Matter of metaphor: Literary Myths of Construction', *Journal of the Society of Architectural Historians*, 40: 4, 1981, 279–88; A. Guilheux and D. Rouillard, 'Échanges entre les mots et l'architecture dans la seconde moitié du xviie siècle à travers les traits de l'art de parler', *Cahiers de recherches architecturales*, 18, 1985, 18–27; G. Boffrand, *Book of Architecture containing the general principles of the Art*, ed. C. Van Eyck, London, 2002, xxii–xxiii.

52 Though the abbé Cordemoy's innovative glossary of architectural terms at the end of the *Nouveau traité de toute l'architecture ou l'art de bastir*, Paris, 1714 does not include 'communication' it was in those terms that he discussed, for example, the location of the staircase (105).

53 De Certeau, *The Practices*, 101–102.

54 H. Murray Baillie, 'Etiquette and Planning', 184; Roggister, 'From Louis xv to Louis xvi', 147.

55 See, for example, Luynes, *Mémoires*, 7: 230; 8: 198–9.

56 Cröy, *Journal*, 1: 191.

57 Cröy, *Journal*, 1: 271.

58 Cröy, *Journal*, 1: 207.

59 Cröy, *Journal*, 1: 214–5.

60 The duc de Lyunes's diary also makes frequent reference to doors and to the tactics of looking through key-holes, and boring holes through door panels in order to see and listen in spaces into which access was denied. See Luynes, *Mémoires*, 7: 89, 90–1. In contradiction to the argument made here the door did, on occasion, constitute a place or 'locale' rather than an interval. See Cröy, *Journal*, 1: 211, for an account of a conversation between the prince de Soubise and Cröy that took place in a doorway.

61 On the Escalier des Ambassadeurs, see most recently *Charles Le Brun 1619–1690. Le décor de l'escalier des Ambassadeurs à Versailles*, exhib. cat., Musée national du château de Versailles, 1990–91. For a discussion of the planning and decoration of grand staircases in the first half of the eighteenth century, see Blondel, *De la distribution des maisons de plaisance*, 1: 38–41; 2: 145–6; Brisseux, *L' Art de bâtir*, 1: 18–21, 2: 112–14; C.A. Daviler, *Cours d'architecture*, 1760 edn, Paris, 1760, 222–67. According to Luynes, one guard's fortune was made by the fact that he saved the dauphin from falling down some back stairs at Versailles. See Luynes, *Mémoires*, 8: 458–9, 468.

62 Luynes, *Mémoires*, 8: 14–15.

63 On *dégagement*, see Blondel, *De la distribution des maisons de plaisance*, 1: 38–9 and Brisseux, *L'Art de bâtir*, 1: 20. On the alternative and more progressive use of corridors for this purpose, see V. Droguet, 'Le couloir central dans la distribution: son apparition et son développement au xviiie siècle', *Bulletin monumental*, 160: 4, 2002, 379–89. I thank Alexandre Gady for this last reference.

64 On servants and architecture in the eighteenth century, see R. Benhamou, 'Parallel Walls, Parallel Worlds: The Places of Masters and Servants in the Maisons de plaisance of Jacques-François Blondel', *Journal of Design History*, 7: 1, 1994, 1–11.

65 See, for instance, Luynes's account of the 'escalier de communication' installed to link the dauphin's and the dauphine's apartments to one another at Fontainbleau (*Mémoires*, 6: 80), or the one between Pompadour's apartments and the king's *petits cabinets* in the same palace (6: 111–12), or the staircase that linked the king's and queen's apartments at Versailles to the dauphin's (8: 258–9).

66 See *Pompadour et la floraison des arts*, David M. Stewart Museum, no. 40.

67 Confessions du comte de *** (1741) in *Romans libertins du XVIIIe siècle*, ed. R. Trousson, Paris, 1995, 190. For a suggestive discussion of the literary motif of the staircase in the sixteenth century, see M.M. Fontaine, 'Images littéraires de l'escalier', in *L'escalier dans l'architecture de la Renaissance*, Paris, 1985, 111–16. My warmest thanks to Mia Jackson for this reference. In an anecdote recounted by Denis Diderot, Mme d'Aine, d'Holbach's mother-in-law, on being pursued up the backstairs at the château de Grandval by M. Le Roy, called out between smothering embraces, 'À moi mes gendres. S'il me fait un enfant, tant pis pour vous.' D. Diderot, *Lettres à Sophie Volland*, ed. A. Babelon, Paris 1978, 1: 256–7. Cited in Droguet, 'Le couloir', 379.

68 See Montaigne, 'On restraining your will', *The Complete Essays*, 1134–1159; Montesquieu, *Lettres persannes*, Paris, 1906, 236. For an examination of these texts in the context of politics, see J.H. Brumfitt, 'Cleopatra's nose and Enlightenment Historiography', *Woman and Society in Eighteenth-century France. Essays in Honour of J.S. Spink*, eds E. Jacobs et al, London, 1979, 183–94; S.P. Conner, 'Women and Politics', *French Women and the Enlightenment*, ed. S.I. Spencer, Bloomington, 1984, 49–60.

69 *Journal et mémoires de Charles Collé (1748–1772)*, ed. H. Bonhomme, 3 vols, Paris, 1868, 3: 349.

70 Collé, *Journal*, 3: 349–50.

71 The marquis d'Argenson was always anticipating her demise (see *Journal et Mémoires du marquis d'Argenson*, ed. E.J.B. Rathery, 9 vols, Paris 1859–65, 5: 73, 80, 112, 252, 282, etc) but the duc de Cröy saw her position as exceptionally vulnerable only in the aftermath of Damiens's attempted regicide. See Cröy, *Journal*, 1: 366, 368.

72 D'Argenson was amazed at Pompadour's capacity to preserve her looks and her power and claimed that in the past it would have been explained as the consequence of a spell, or a talisman. See *Journal*, 6: 77.

73 De Certeau, *The Practices*, 103.

74 Luynes, *Mémoires*, 8: 208. On Crécy, see Vittet, 'Le décor ... de Crécy'.

75 Luynes, *Mémoires*, 9: 255–6.

76 Luynes's is in fact the most extensive and detailed source on Pompadour's performances. See especially vol. 7 of the *Mémoires*. See also W. H. Kaehler, 'The Operatic Repertoire of Madame de Pompadour's Théâtre des Petits Cabinets (1747–1753)', PhD diss., University of Michigan, 1971; D. Gallet, 'Madame de Pompadour et le théatre', *Pompadour et la floraison des arts*, David M. Stewart Museum, 73–9. For the political consequences of her theatricality, see T.E. Kaiser, 'Madame de Pompadour and the Theaters of Power', *French Historical Studies*, 19: 4, 1996, 1025–44.

77 J.-F. Blondel, *Cours d'architecture* (1771), ed. J.-M. Pérouse de Montclos, 9 vols, Paris, n.d. 3: 88.

78 On *comodité* and *caractère* as notions in French eighteenth-century architecture, see Szambien, *Symétrie, goût, caractère*, 85–91, 174–99.

79 See the account given in P. Biver, *Histoire du château de Bellevue*, Paris, 1933, 13.

80 Biver was the first to doubt the attribution to Lassurance though Bellevue was formally that architect's responsibility (see *Histoire de Bellevue*, 18). He suggested that Ange-Jacques Gabriel drew up the plans and designed the elevations and that Lassurance merely delivered the building. Biver's view has largely been accepted. See, most recently, *Pompadour et les arts*, 99. The planning of the first floor, the king's apartment, does seem to anticipate in significant ways – for instance, the placing of the council chamber rather than the bedchamber at the centre of the garden façade – Gabriel's grand scheme for remodelling Versailles, but the elevations are absolutely consistent with Lassurance's known work.

81 Pompadour to the comtesse de Lutzelbourg, 27/1/1749, quoted from Biver, *Histoire de Bellevue*, 18.

82 S. Menant, 'Lieux de bonheur: les châteaux poétiques au XVIIIe siècle', *La Quête du bonheur et l'expression de la douleur dans la littérature et la pensée françaises. Mélanges offerts à Corrado Rosso*, Geneva, 1995, 141–8.

83 Blondel's *De la distribution des maisons de plaisance* offers, in volume 1, five different plans for châteaux from the largest at 50 *toises* to the smallest at 15 *toises*.

84 Blondel, *De la distribution des maisons de plaisance*: see the discussion (1: 146–62) of 'un edifice de vingt trios toises de face' or 'une Maison d'oeconomie'.

85 Architectural opinions on size were related to social appropriateness of bienséance, see n. 36.

86 'Nothing is as beautiful/As my cottage,/Oh! What a picture!/What a landscape/Made for Watteau!', quoted from *Anthologie de la poésie française du XVIIIe siècle*, ed. M. Delon, Paris, 1997, 100.

87 It was described as such by contemporaries. See Dézallier d'Argenville, *Voyage pittoresque des environs de Paris*, Paris, 1755, 27; E.J.F. Barbier, *Journal historique et anecdotique du règne de Louis XV*, ed. A. de la Villegille, 4 vols, Paris, 1847, 3: 100, 196.

88 On 6 September 1752 Cröy noted that 'les petits voyages des châteaux comme Choisy, la Muette,

Bellevue, Crécy, Trianon etc. remplissaient tout l'intervalle des grands voyages de Compiègne, Fontainbleau, et Marly. *Journal*, 1: 185–6.

89 Biver, *Histoire de Bellevue*, 44–5. In *Pompadour et les arts*, no 140, the furniture in question is attributed, without explanation, to the king's *cabinet* on the first floor.

90 Elaborate firedogs and fire-backs were ordered for the fireplaces throughout the house (see Biver, *Histoire de Bellevue*, 46, for the 'feu' in the Cabinet en entresol and 39–43 for the andirons in the chamber) though those for this room are not recorded. Bellevue was not the only residence for which Pompadour actively sought these comforts.

91 This careful preparation notwithstanding d'Argenson was delighted to note that on the king's first visit the chimneys smoked. See d'Argenson, *Journal*, 6: 298, 302. For the porcelain flowers, see T. Préaud and A. d'Albis, 'Bouquets de Sèvres', *Connaissance des arts*, 1992, 68–76; T. Préaud, 'The Origins and History of Porcelain Flowers', *The French Porcelain Society Journal*, special issue, *A Symposium in Memory to Genevèive Le Duc (1930–1999)*, 1 (2003) pp. 47–55.

92 G. Boffrand, *Livre d'architecture (1745) La figure equestre de Louis XIV (1743)*, Farnborough, 1969, 11. Mine is an explicit interpretation of 'convenablement à son service' which merely implies physical proximity.

93 Boffrand, *Livre d'architecture*, 41.

94 Szambien, *Symétrie, goût, caractère*, 85–91.

95 See, for example, A.F. Frezier, *Dissertation historique et critique sur les ordres d'architecture*, Paris 1738, 6.

96 See Luynes, *Mémoires*, 7:119. On her early habitations, *Pompadour et la floraison des arts*, David M. Stewart Museum, 51.

97 It is significant that her coat of arms did not decorate the main pediment but lateral façades.

98 On the orientation and decoration of the bathroom, see Blondel, *De la distribution des maisons de plaisance*, 1: 71–5; 2: 129–33.

99 The fabric was described in detail in an inventory of Bellevue taken in 1763. See Biver, *Histoire de Bellevue*, 66–7. Warmest thanks to Lesley Miller for her help in interpreting the description.

100 The notion of 'smooth' space as a metaphor is adapted from G. Deleuze and F. Guattari, *A Thousand Plateaus. Capitalism and Schizophrenia*, trans. B. Massumi, London, 1999, 474–7.

101 For differing opinions on the authencity of the frame first connected with Boucher's painting in *Cadres et bordures de tableaux de la fin du XVIe siècle au Premier Empire*, Paris, 1910, see Laing, *Boucher*, 258 and *Pompadour et les arts*, no 47, n. 4. The frame appears to be contemporary with the picture but the dimensions of the frame have almost certainly since been altered.

102 Croy, *Journal*, 1: 250, 264, and also d'Argenson, *Journal*, 5: 464; N.A. Pluche, *Le Spectacle de la nature*, 8 vols, Paris, 1732–51, 3: 226–37. Pluche uses a range of architectural vocabulary to describe shells, dividing them into those with a 'corps de logis' of one or two 'pieces'. On natural metaphors of habitation, including shells, see Bachelard, *Poetics*, chapters 4 and 5.

103 Barbier was among those who described Pompadour as a 'canal', a simile chosen for the comparison it afforded between the operations of her favour and the circulation of money on which it was supposedly based. See Barbier, *Journal historique*, 3: 175.

104 D. Massoumie, 'L'usage, l'espace et le décor du bain', in *Paris, capitale des arts sous Louis xv*, ed. D. Rabreau, Paris and Bordeaux, 1997, 197–210.

105 Lajer-Burcharth, 'Pompadour's Touch'.

106 D'Argenson, *Journal*, 7: 185; Biver, *Histoire de Bellevue*, 70–1.

107 Laing, *Boucher*, 1986, 257.

108 See d'Argenson, *Journal*, 7: 185. See also, E.G. Landau, '"A Fairy-tale Circumstance" The influence of stage design on the work of François Boucher', *Cleveland Museum of Art Bulletin*, 70, 1983, 360–78.

109 See Szambien, *Symétrie, goût, caractère*, 174–99.

110 For the evolution of Boffrand's ideas see Boffrand, *Book of Architecture*, xiv–xvii.

111 Boffrand, *Livre*, 16.

112 Boffrand, *Livre*, 27.

113 Gentil-Bernard in *Anthologie*, 101. 'There, each place / Offers to choice / Some pleasure / That another replaces.'

114 For a full description of the room see Biver, *Histoire de Bellevue*, 28–34.

115 The design derived ultimately from the redecoration of the Chambre de la Reine at Versailles. On Verberckt, see B. Pons, 'Jacques Verberckt (1704–1771) sculpteur des Bâtiments du roi', *Gazette des Beaux-Arts*, 119, 1992, 173–88.

116 See, for example, Nattier's *Thalia, (presumed portrait of Silvia Balleti)* and *Terpsichore*, Palace of Legion of Honor, San Francisco.

117 See Biver, *Histoire de Bellevue*, 34; Duvaux, *Livre-journal*, no 1960 (10/12/1754). On *voyeuses*, see M. Jarry, *Le siège français*, Fribourg, 1973; B.G.B. Pallot, *L'Art du siège au XVIIIe siècle en France*, Paris, 1987.

118 For a discussion of these effects in relation prints after Oppenord's designs for interiors published at the mid-century, see Scott, *The Rococo Interior*, 158–9.

119 Blondel, *De la distribution des maisons de plaisance*, 2: 74. On the different kinds of *menuiserie*, see Blondel, *Cours*, 5: 11–12.

120 Blondel, *De la distribution des maisons de plaisance*, 2: pl 70–1, 73; Blondel, *Cours*, 5: 48.

121 See an unpublished letter by Bernard Lépicié to the marquis de Marigny, 13 December 1752, written in support of the invoice submitted by Van Loo for the work. Lépicié claimed to have a followed the work on a daily basis and therefore to have a perfect knowledge of its merits and assures Marigny that 'bien loin de tenir des dessus de portes ordinaires, on doit les regarder comme des tableaux de chevalet des plus finis. L'esperance de meriter les suffrages de Madame de Pompadour a engagé M. Vanloo a ne se permettre aucune negligence; je l'ai vû sacrifier des semaines entieres pour en epurer les compositions, et les repeindre jusqu'a trois fois pour les donner cette durée que n'ont jamais les ouvrages peints au premier coup.' Archives nationales, 392.AP.1. Pompadour seems to have had a marked preference for highly worked and finished paintings.

122 On the issue of the materiality of the sign, see Lajer-Burcharth, 'Pompadour's Touch'.

123 See *Pompadour et les arts*, no 49.

124 P. Stein, 'Madame de Pompadour and the Harem Imagery at Bellevue', *Gazette des Beaux-Arts*, 123, 1994, 29–44.

125 D. Veseley, 'Architecture and the Politics of Representation', *Daidalos*, 25, 1987, 25–36.

126 On distribution and distinction, see Scott, *The Rococo Interior*, 81–117.

127 This point is illustrated by Veseley with a passage from Blondel's *Cours*, 2: 318.

128 For the balconies, see Barbier, *Journal historique*, 3: 175; for the console table, see *Pompadour et les arts, musée national des châteaux*, no. 12; for the upholstery fabric in the salon, see Biver, *Histoire de Bellevue*, 33.

129 Archives nationales, Minutier central CVII/475, 24/11/1753. The house had been valued for the heirs and creditors of Henri-Louis de La Tour d'Auvergne, comte d'Evreux, at 450, 000 *livres* and sold to Pompadour because she offered a sum above the estimate and 'personne n'en ayant offert d'avantage'.

130 See d'Argenson 9/4/1753, *Journal*, 7: 449.

131 D'Argenson, *Journal*, 5: 229, 373; *Pompadour et la floraison des arts*, 104.

132 D'Argenson, *Journal*, 7: 462–3.

133 Laugier, *Essai*, 141–2.

134 As an example of d'Argenson's statements of disinterestedness, see his *Journal*, 5: 83–4. For the particular 'perspective' afforded by Segrez a place away from the world, see *Journal*, 6: 181, 197. The same trope of engagement (court) and retreat (Paris) occurs in Cröy's *Journal*, 1: 126–7, 297, 331–3, etc, though in his case detachment is the prize not just of distance but religious conscience.

135 In 1752, in a remarkable imagined speech, D'Argenson, as prime minister, starts his reforms by upbraiding the king for his taste, a taste described in exactly the terms he used to characterize Pompadour's. See *Journal*, 7: 299–300.

136 D'Argenson, *Journal*, 6: 24.

137 D'Argenson, *Journal*, 6: 24, 137.

138 D'Argenson, *Journal*, 7: 173.

139 D'Argenson, *Journal*, 5: 466.

140 D'Argenson, *Journal*, 6: 222.

141 D'Argenson, *Journal*, 5: 229.

142 See, for instance, d'Argenson's criticism of the king's expensive country jaunt in 1749 to Le Havre so that Pompadour could see the sea, and his account of depression in agriculture and manufacture in the Tourraine (*Journal*, 6:35, 49–52).

143 D'Argenson, *Journal*, 9: 202.

144 D'Argenson, *Journal*, 9: 202.

145 D'Argenson, *Journal*, 6: 20.

146 The comparison with the Invalides is made in D'Argenson, *Journal*, 8: 408. For complaints about the '*curieuses bagatelles*' made by the manufactory, see *Journal*, 7: 384.

147 In 1751 d'Argenson seconded the characterization of the régime as '*une anarchie dépensière*' and warned of the growing attractions of another constitutional form of monarchy provided by Britain. See *Journal*, 6: 463–4.

148 D'Argenson, *Journal*, 5: 185. For her control of the valets ('eunuchs'), see 183.

149 D'Argenson, *Journal*, 6: 274.

150 In June 1750 Pompadour nearly came to grief in Paris when a mob assembled on the perimeter of the hôtel of a friend whom she was visiting. Violence to her or to it was only just averted. See d'Argenson, *Journal*: 6, 212–13, 220.

151 See T.E. Crow, *Painters and Public Life in Eighteenth-century Paris*, New Haven and London, 1985, chap. 4.

152 For an overall discussion of Pompadour's paintings at the Salon see H. Wine, 'Afficher une image: Madame de Pompadour au Salon', in *Pompadour et les arts*, 17–25. That the *Rising of the Sun* and *Setting of the Sun* were destined for the king's bedchamber is the recent discovery of Jo Hedley in *François Boucher, Seductive Visions*, The Wallace Collection, London 2004, 105–108. Pompadour owned a copy of La Font's *Sentiments* and was thus presumably aware of the criticism levelled against her. In the case of the

Rising of the Sun and *Setting of the Sun* La Font reported the self-imposed exile of clerics from the Salon and anticipated the anxiety of mothers ('Sentiments sur quelques ouvrages de peintures, sculptures et gravures, écrits à un particulier de province' (1754) in *La Font de Saint Yenne, Oeuvre critique*, ed. E. Jollet, Paris 2001, 288); in the case of the *Arts* he reported speech overheard concerning their descent into puerility (285).

153 For a more extended discussion of this issue, see Scott, *The Rococo Interior*, 255–7.

154 La Font de Saint Yenne, 'Le Génie du Louvre aux Champs Élysées' (1756), in *Oeuvre critique*, 340.

155 According to d'Argenson, Pompadour would not allow discussion of the country's miseries in her presence (see *Journal*, 7: 83) and she allegedly had imprisoned those who disclosed the sums of money spent on her residences (*Journal*, 6: 251). Charles Collé affirmed, on the contrary, however, that she showed mercy to her critics. Collé, *Journal et mémoires*, 2: 349.

156 Account given in d'Argenson, *Journal*, 6: 348–9; J. de La Fontaine, *Fables*, Paris, 1966, book 5, fable 10: 'La Montagne qui accouche', 148.

157 La Fontaine states the moral of the fable as follows: 'Quand je songe à cette Fable/Dont le récit est menteur/Et le sens est veritable,/Je me figure un Auteur/Qui dit: Je chanterai la guerre/Que firent les Titans au Maître du tonnerre. /C'est promettre beaucoup: mais qu'en sort-il souvent? Du vent.'

158 D'Argenson, *Journal*, 5: 400.

159 Cröy, *Journal*, 1: 356.

160 See especially K. Gordon, 'Mme de Pompadour, Pigalle and the Iconography of Friendship', *Art Bulletin*, 50, 1968, 249–62; Stein, 'Pompadour and Harem Imagery'.

161 Azure was the heraldic colour of the field of her towers; the Temple of Friendship was engraved on a three-faceted topaz and topaz was also a 'tincture' of heraldry. On the gem, see *Pompadour et les arts*, no. 117.

162 See J.-A. Poisson, marquise de Pompadour, *Suite d'estampes gravées par Madame la marquise de Pompadour, d'après les pierres gravées de Guay, graveur du roi*, Paris, 1782, 10, and pl. 44. The two other facets are shown on pls 41 and 43.

163 It seems to me entirely possible that Pompadour and/or Guay were aware of the *Essai*, which received the censor's approbation in November 1752 and was being reviewed by the spring of the following year. Moreover, the abbé Leblanc mentioned it favourably in his Salon review of that year. Wolfgang Herrmann thinks it likely that Leblanc brought Laugier to Pompadour's attention. See W. Herrmann, *Laugier and eighteenth century French Theory* (1962), London, 1985, 5.

164 Blondel, *Architecture française*, 4: 3: 156–8; Blondel, *Cours*, 3: 119.

165 G. Brice, *Description de la ville de Paris*, 3 vols, Paris, 1752, 1: 315–6; A. Dezallier d'Argenville, *Voyage pittoresque de Paris*, Paris, 1757, 167. See also Antonini, *Mémorial de Paris et de ses environs*, Paris, 1732, 76–8.

166 Piganiol de La Force, *Description de la ville de Paris et de ses environs*, 10 vols, 1765, 3:26–8.

167 Blondel, *Cours*, 3: 119.

168 Laugier, *Essai*, 50.

169 On the advancing technology of window production in the eighteenth century, see J.-F. Belhoste and G.-M. Leproux, 'La fenêtre parisienne aux xviie et xviiie siècles: menuiserie, ferrure et vitrage', in *Fenêtres de Paris, xviie et xviiie siècles, Cahiers de la Rotonde*, 18, Paris, 1997, 15–43, esp.27–35.

170 Only the window wall and the one facing it remain as originally designed; the other two walls were remodelled in the late 1770s by Étienne-Louis Boullé. On Lange's panelling, see M. Gallet, 'Trois décroateurs parisiens du xviiie siècle: Michel II Lange, J.B. Boistou, Joseph Métivier', *Bulletin de la société de l'histoire de l'art français*, 1976–77, 76–87, especially 78–9, 84–5; B. Pons, *De Paris à Versailles 1699–1736. Les sculpteurs ornemanistes parieiens et L'art décoratifs des Bâtiments du roi*, Strasbourg, 1986, 120.

171 Blondel, *Architecture française*, 3: 156.

172 Luynes, 3: 442, cited in *Pompadour et les arts*, 124.

173 See C. Leroux-Cesbron, 'Le palais de l'Elysé, I Ancien hôtel d'Evreux, II Mme de Pompadour à l'hôtel d'Evreux', *Bulletin de la société historique et archéologique du xviie et xviiie arrondissements*, 4, 1924, 265–92, esp. 279–80.

174 Pompadour played the role of Colin in a production of Jean-Jacques Rousseau's *Le Devin de Village* at Bellevue on 4 and 6 March 1752.

175 Blondel, *Cours*, 5: 6–10. The full title of the publication is *Cours d'architecture ou traité de la décoration, distribution et construction des bâtiments contenant les leçons donnés en 1750 et les années suivates par J.F. Blondel*. Thus, while only published in 1771–1777 it expresses ideas that were current twenty years earlier.

176 Luynes, *Mémoires*, 13: 442.

177 L.-V. Thiéry, *Guide des amateurs et des étrangers voyageurs à Paris*, 3 vols, Paris, 1787, 1: 82–3.

178 See the plans of the house and garden attached to the sale of the property to Nicolas Beaujon in 1773 at which point the garden was retrenched to its former lines. Archives nationales, Minutier central LIII/500, 2/10/1773.

179 D'Argenson, *Journal*, 7: 366.

180 See Jean Ducros, 'La place Louis XV', in M. Gallet and Y. Bottineau, *Les Gabriel*, Paris, 1982, 254–77.

181 Ducros, 'La place', 258.

182 See Bibliothèque nationale, département des manuscripts, n.a.f. 23621 (*Receuil de lettres, requêtes, placets et poesies addresses à marquise de Pompadour*), fol. 101. See also from Laurent, fols 100, 102–107.

183 See C. Leroux-Cersbron, 'Le palais de l'Elysée: I, ancient hôtel d'Evreux; II, Mme de Pompadour à l'hôtel d'Evreux', *Bulletin de la société historique et archélogique du VIIIe et XVIIe arrondissements*, 1924, 289.

184 L. Marin, 'Classical, Baroque: Versailles, or the Architecture of the Prince', *Yale French Studies*, 80, 1991, 167–82.

185 Luynes, *Mémoires*,14: 200.

186 Luynes, *Mémoires*, 8: 208.

187 See Blondel on the design of window aperture, *Cours*, 5: 53.

188 J. Cordey, *Inventaire des biens de mme de Pompadour, rédigé après son décès*, Paris, 1939, 36, no 342: 'une statue équestre de Louis Quinze sur sa gaine'.

189 La Font de Saint Yenne, 'Examen d'un *Essai sur l'architecture*, avec quelques remarques sur cette science dans l'esprit des beaux-arts, 1753', in *Oeuvre critique*, 242–3.

190 Edme Bouchardon, *Réflexions présentées à Madame de Pompadour au sujet de la statue équestre que l'on doit placer dans un mois, le 6 juillet, 1758*, Fondation Jacques Doucet, Carton 36, Sculpteurs.

7

INSIDE/INTERIORS: CHARDIN'S IMAGES OF THE FAMILY

RENÉ DÉMORIS

'Low subjects without being lowly': it was by this formulation that in 1747 Jean-Bernard Le Blanc saluted the outstanding success achieved by Jean-Siméon Chardin (1699–1779) in his scenes of everyday life.[1] In 1753 the *Mercure de France* echoed the salutation:

> The painter's compositions, although simple, and subject to the manners of the day, do not pretend to grandeur. But the choice selection and the charm of the images present a lively critique of Flemish painters in general. Smoke-filled rooms, fist-fights, the exercise of bodily functions, in short nature caught at her most abject, are in fact the subjects most usually treated by a Brauwer, an Ostade, a Teniers, etc. Mr Chardin has always avoided these images humiliating for humanity.[2]

The allusion to Flemish art indicates the risk run by Chardin in representing 'domestic life', that is, subjects dealing with private life and family relations.

The unprecedented interest in the family that marked the eighteenth century may be related to an evolution in the sum of ideas, or *mentalités*, of feudal society under Absolutism – an evolution in which the economy became a significant force for change to the traditional order – and to an interrogation of the social at a moment when belief in its divine origin was no longer universally accepted. Correspondingly, artists and writers of the first half of the century turned their attention towards interior, domestic space.

Was family a remedy for society's ills? Marivaux gave almost too illustrative an answer in a story published in the *Spectateur français* in 1724: briefly, the scene is set by an honest but ruined family, the mother and father despairing for the children, until the moment when the children catch them mid-conversation (a pre-eminently Freudian moment) and remind them of the present joy of their conjugal love.[3] The context is the family's poverty, the *mise en scène* provided by the children and the importance accorded to the often unspoken bond between mother and son, the story being, moreover, inconceivable without the coming together of all the characters in the space of the home – the setting of some of

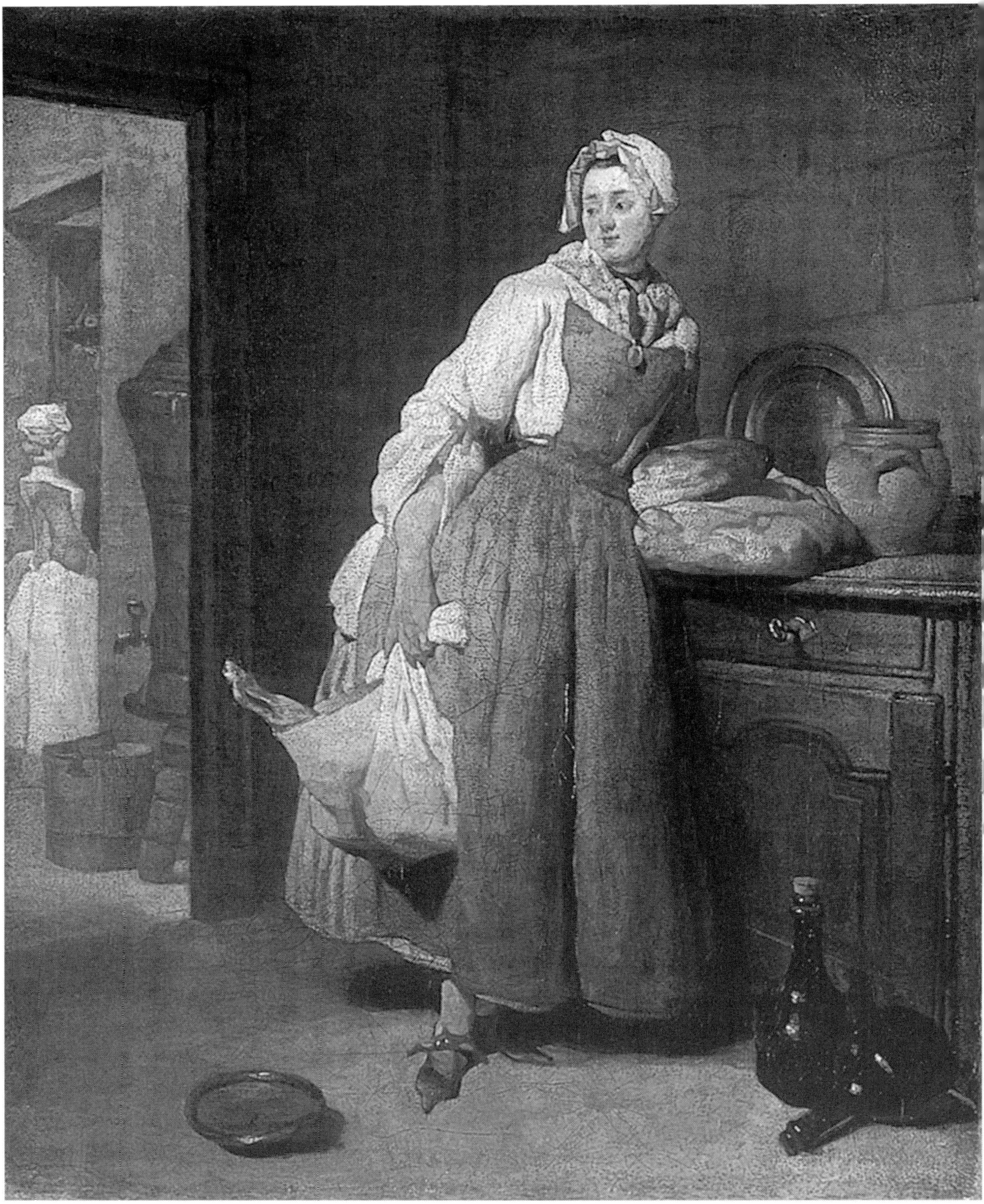

7.1 Jean-Siméon Chardin, *The Kitchen Maid*, 1739. Oil on canvas, 47 × 38 cm. Paris: Musée du Louvre. Photo: Réunion des musées nationaux.

Marivaux's plays that portray the complex web of relationships forged in this space between parents and children, servants and masters. That family love could even take priority over affairs of the heart is evident from his novel *La vie de Marianne* (1731–42) in which the love of a foundling for a rich young man gives way before the discovery of an adoptive mother in the person of the young man's parent. Meanwhile, *Le Paysan parvenu* (1735–6) is the archetypal example of the 'lowly' subject: a rich and pious woman in her fifties marries a young peasant who had been her valet. Despite the novel's title, however, the story is not about the conquest of social space (the incursions into the exterior are, in fact, not always happy ones), but consists rather of a series of interior scenes before which the couple is constituted as such, according to a sort of neo-family model, and not without Marivaux also painting a picture of bourgeois life through the eyes of the valet. There is even the glimpse of a still life to be caught, when Jacob first penetrates the *dévote*'s interior: 'The remnants of lunch were there on a small table; it had consisted of a half bottle of Burgundy, almost all drunk, two fresh eggs and a small brioche. I think this detail not wearisome; it plays a part in the portrait of the person of whom I speak.'[4] He was referring, in fact, to the lady's delicate sensuality that self-indulgence had preserved for love's tomorrows. With this 'detail', the author was conscious of skirting the realm of the trivial. Danger notwithstanding, he suggested that between food and love there existed a bond, and did so even though it meant possibly provoking the reader's further indignation at the conflation of bodily and spiritual appetites. The perspective adopted by Marivaux implies at one and the same time a possible devaluation of love and an eroticization of supposedly elementary needs (on first meeting his *dévote*, Jacob finds her 'appetizing').

Defined by Antoine Furetière at the end of the seventeenth century as a 'household consisting of a head and his *domestiques*, either wives, children or servants', the interest in 'the family' remained during the first half of the next century largely unconnected to notions of filiation, or to a genetically rooted understanding of family feeling, with which the eighteenth century later became obsessed.[5] It was unconnected also to the idealization of the family. For Marivaux (and Chardin) attention is given to a primary and fundamental relationship between beings and objects in a space occupied not only by children and parents but also by servants. Such a configuration of the family, manifest, for example, in *Le Paysan parvenu*, was alive to the transgression of social barriers.

Marivaux, the recognized enemy of the higher literary genres, aimed to release this rudimentary relationship from the traditional codes of its narration according to which it was cast as comic, that is to say, was treated to derision. He was closely allied in this to the collective desire of a public grown weary of the pomp of the higher genres – tragedy, epic, history painting – but one that feared descent into the 'low'. Marivaux who, around 1715, had proclaimed that the depiction of a 'peasant' could well be worthy of that of a 'great princess' and who had plumbed the resources of 'travesty' and 'parody' (that is to say, of a conflation of high and low), found a solution to this dilemma largely in the portrayal of domestic space which at least partially avoided constraints of genre.[6] In so doing, he elaborated a fiction of the private person in direct contrast to libertine fiction, in which characters fail to escape their social roles and exhaust themselves playing out their private lives on a social stage, in order to become the heroes of a pseudo-history.

The resources of the writer and those of the painter are different, even if one eighteenth-century critic brought Marivaux and Chardin closer together in the inimitable character of their eminently elusive methods.[7] But the painter and the novelist (to a greater extent than the playwright) dealt with analogous expectations and taboos. Marivaux's endeavour may thus serve to illuminate the use that Chardin made of the everyday in the domestic space.

STILL LIVES

One quality is remarkable from the very first still lifes. Chardin eschews the example provided by his predecessors who were anxious to elevate and enhance the status of still life – situated on the lowest rung of the hierarchy of genres. For example, Chardin passed over the use of luxury items or things possessed of an intrinsic beauty that pleased the eye even before being committed to canvas. Another of the strategies of ennoblement practised by Jean-François Desportes and Jean-Baptiste Oudry was opening up the genre to exterior space, notably in depictions of animals (living or dead). The hunting scene that glories in the noble connotations of the sport readily arrays itself in a landscape or around architectural ruins, even attaining the monumentality of a work like Oudry's *The Dead Wolf* (1721, London: Wallace Collection). The depiction of exotic animals pricked curiosity and alluded also to royal taste at the Ménagerie. Chardin rarely had recourse to the exterior space of the hunt, and then only with extreme moderation: in *Dog and Game* (1730, Pasadena: the Norton Simon Museum of Art), *The Spaniel* (1724, private collection) and also in *The Dead Hare* (1750, Paris: Musée de la Chasse). If the lighting most often suggests an interior space, sometimes no more than a wall, there are none of the pictorial clues present in seventeenth-century Dutch paintings: the glimpse on the silver, reflective body of a ewer, of a window, of the person who has eaten the herrings whose remains remain visible on the table. In Chardin's still lifes it is from the objects that a place can be inferred, often most imprecisely: simple objects, useful wares that belong, with few exceptions, to the world of the kitchen. They are, in all senses of the word, *common* objects, which is to say that they connote no social group in particular (the opposite, in fact, to vessels used in the consumption of food, to which Chardin later gave limited play). They are ubiquitous and so utterly banal that they are overlooked, in fact, by the leisured class. Chardin detaches this useful ware from prior usefulness, which had seemingly often linked it to the peasantry, or at any rate, to poverty, with its marks of use and breakage. Unspoilt by use, Chardin's objects are not the things of the poor. They are strangers to property, de-socialized, and in

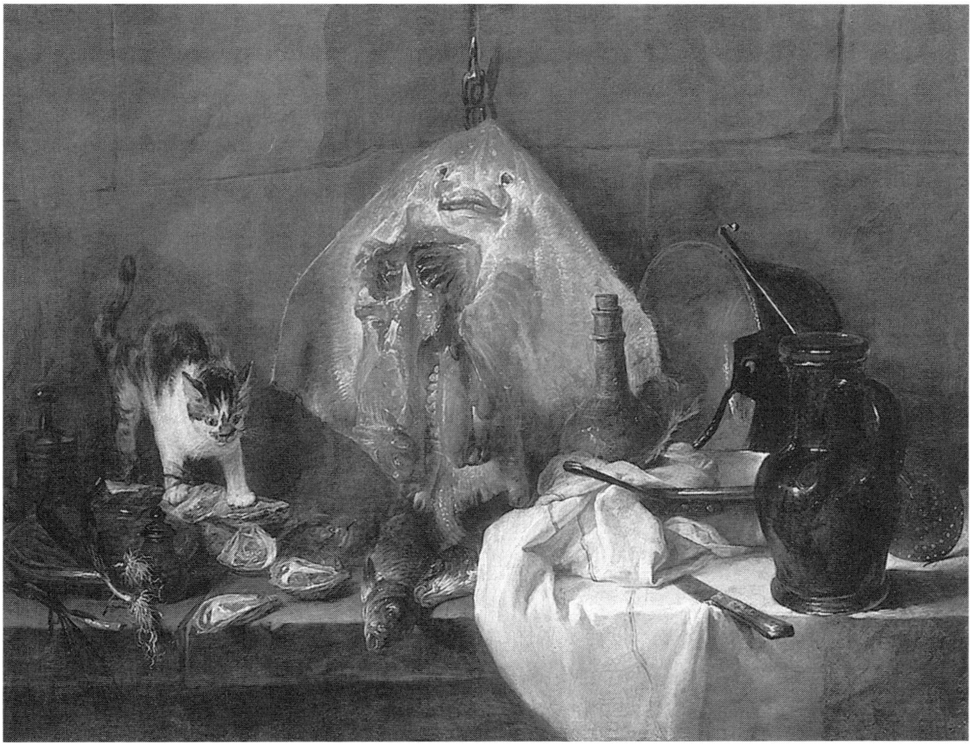

7.2 Jean-Siméon Chardin, *The Ray Fish*, 1728. Oil on canvas, 114.5 × 146 cm. Paris: Musée du Louvre. Photo: Réunion des musées nationaux.

this sense outside language's scope. The will not to distract the viewer from the object is manifest in Chardin's avoidance, 'probably systematic', of objects that figure as symbols of *Vanitas* – neither candle nor butterfly, watch nor insect (with the exception of a smoking pipe in *The Smoker's Case*, 1737, Paris: Musée du Louvre).

While Chardin's choice of subjects should be recognized as 'invention' (a noble artistic category that Roger de Piles did not attribute to the painter of still lifes), his choice could nevertheless provoke displeasure. When Denis Diderot thought of improving genre painting (still life), he seemed to address Chardin specifically:

> Why put our tiresome cleaning utensils on this buffet? Are these flowers any more brilliant in a Nevers vase than in one of more attractive shape? And why don't I see, around this vase, a group of dancing children, the joys of harvest, a bacchanal? If this vase has handles, why not cast them in the form of two intertwining snakes? Why not have the tails of these snakes descend onto its lower portion, making a few serpentine curves there?[8]

This is an excellent example of how not to understand the painter's project. Diderot, like others, is of the opinion that the painter expends energy on objects that do not merit it. In this he fails to recognize that the gap between the quality of the painting and that of the object leads to awareness of its interest, hitherto ignored, disavowed, one could even say repressed, by the edicts of the prevailing aesthetic. It is an effect that Diderot came to recognize elsewhere; he noted when standing before a Chardin that there are 'hardly any unworthy objects in nature'[9] (another sidestepping of the issue).

Did Chardin anticipate the *affetti* (or affect) of his presentation of objects in the domestic sphere? It would be difficult to deny it before *The Ray Fish* (plate 7.2) where the angle of vision makes of the fish's head a carnival mask that suggests, in turn, a human face, compelling the viewer to identify with the wounded hanging body of the dead fish. What makes this painting remarkable in Chardin's œuvre is not so much the magical harmony of colour, noted by C.N. Cochin, but this juxtaposition of burlesque and horror and the sexual connotations it engenders. Elsewhere the author has attempted to draw analogies between the human body and those of the hanging hares, evoking the idea of martyrdom or crucifixion that the frame's isolation of the animal from precise surroundings makes possible.[10] After 1750, during Chardin's second period of still-life painting, a tonality of pity rather than horror animates the scene. With *The Ray Fish* (plate 7.2) Chardin confronted the risk of the 'disgusting', to use Diderot's term, one also used by Charles Joseph Mathon de la Cour, an extreme term for the ugliness ascribed by the critic to the objects depicted in the still lifes.

Blood and deadly violence belong normally to the history painter's register. Seemingly, Chardin reminds us that they are already present in the primitive experience of the individual, regressing to a child's view of the connection the kitchen has with death – and opening to view the dark and disturbing side of the domestic domain.

LITTLE WOMEN AT THEIR HOUSEWORK

For his debut in depicting scenes of animation, figure pictures – and supposing that *Woman at the Urn* (plate 7.3) and *The Laundress* (plate 7.4) were his first attempts – Chardin again chose to confront the disgusting. At that time the term was virtually a natural attribute of the servant. Moreover, in these works the figures devote themselves to the elimination of dirt: one draws water, another sweeps, one washes, the other hangs out the laundry. This is the beginning of the cycle of women's activities that ensure the smooth running of the domestic sphere: looking after children, educating them, feeding them, peeling vegetables, going to market, caring for the sick. They were described as 'utterly uninteresting' subjects by La Font de Saint-Yenne.[11] 'Little women busy with their housework', wrote the *Mercure de France* of the two pictures – exhibited in 1734.[12] Did avoidance of the term 'servant' register doubt about identity (servant girls or middle-class women?) or did it allow censorship of a degrading descriptor? Within the space of a household, tasks are shared, but without the figures talking to or looking at one another. In *The Laundress* (plate 7.4) the child borrows soapy water from his mother's tub, but remains in his own bubble. As for her, she looks

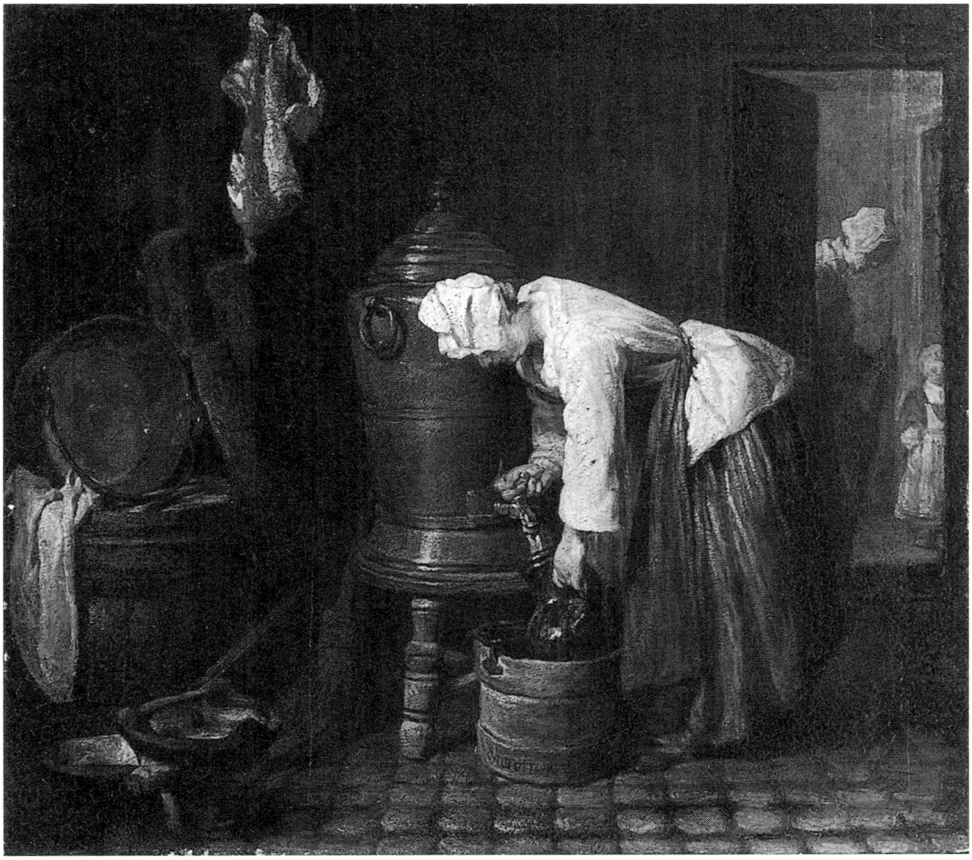

7.3 Jean-Siméon Chardin, *Woman at the Urn*, 1733. Oil on panel, 38 × 43 cm. Stockholm: Nationalmuseum. Copyright: Nationalmuseum, Stockholm.

elsewhere. Not a word is uttered – viewers might think themselves transported back to that age of 'action language' that Étienne Bonnot de Condillac attributed to primitive humanity, before the advent of verbal language.[13]

Criticizing Bachelier, Diderot wrote about *The Scullery Maid* (1738, Glasgow: The Hunterian Museum and Art Gallery) exhibited in 1738 and again in 1757, that,

> . . . without doubt it's permissible for Chardin to show a kitchen with a servant bent over a tub washing dishes, but note how truthful are this servant's movements, how her jerkin shows off her upper body, and how the folds of her skirt reveal everything that's beneath them; note the astonishing truth of all the household utensils, the colour and harmony of the whole small composition.[14]

Chardin's 'astonishing technique' allows the omission of a 'powerful, ingenious or striking' idea. Is it necessary to point out Diderot's enigmatic formulation of

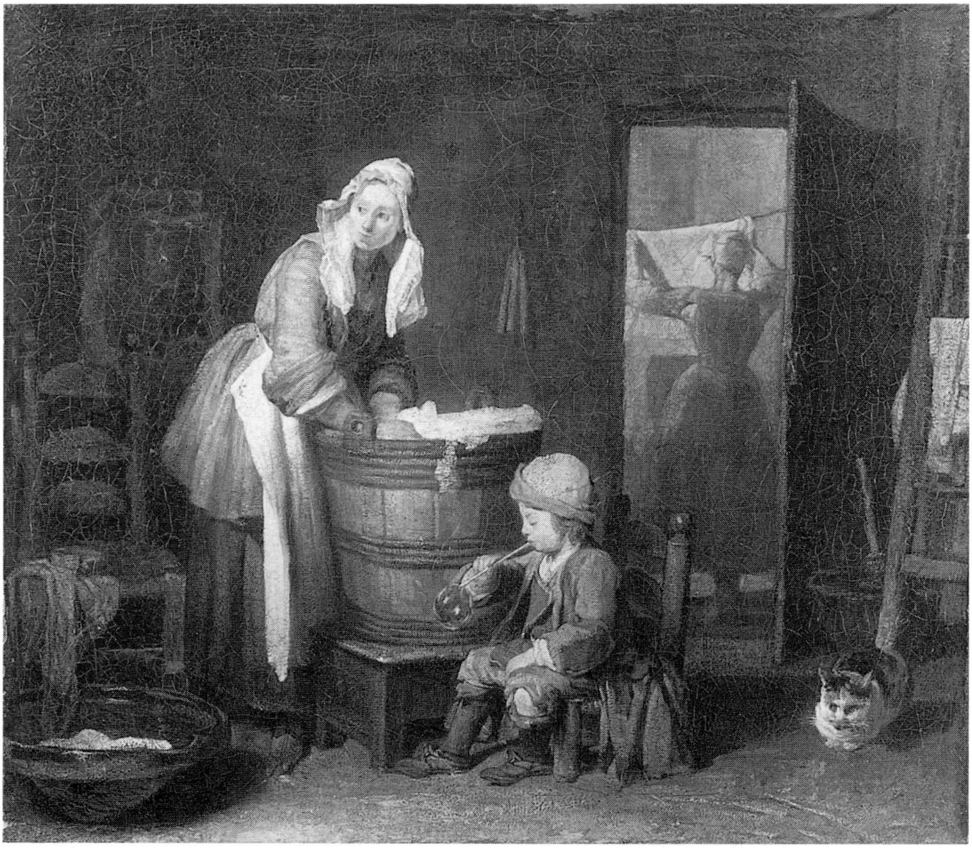

7.4 Jean-Baptiste-Siméon Chardin, *The Laundress*, 1733. Oil on canvas, 37.5 × 42.5 cm. Stockholm: Nationalmusum. Copyright: Nationalmuseum, Stockholm.

'sublime technique', deployed in order to avoid having to examine an erotic response to the servant? Diderot recognizes in Chardin the talent of the history painter, the talent, that is, to suggest the nude through drapery, in his case by everyday clothes remarkable for their volume and simplicity. These heavily dressed bodies are surprised at a moment when they are grappling with a task, yet momentarily interrupted: the laundress gazes to the left (plate 7.4); the scullery maid lifts her eyes from her barrel; the kitchen maid (plate 7.1) glances towards the couple conversing on the threshold. This looking-elsewhere, also seen in *The Turnip Scraper* (see plate 7.7), indicates a person who is detached from the task in hand. The female body is the subject of these canvases, the composition leaves no room for doubt; the curved or broken line of the body stands out against a skilful grid of verticals and horizontals within which objects from the still lifes are located. Whether Diderot likes it or not, a woman who has her hands plunged in dirty water is made desirable. Is it because of this potentially erotic effect (but not signified as such) that Diderot refrains from commenting on Chardin's genre scenes, unlike his contemporaries, who recognized his achievement in inventing a 'new genre'? It is perhaps this misplaced seduction that is indirectly suggested by the caption to Bernard Lépicié's engraving, which claims that only fraud can account for the kitchen maid being so well-dressed. It could be the effect of the pendant that both she and her companion wear, suspended on blue ribbon around their necks? Such discreet signs of femininity indicate that desire operated in the domestic world, though usually concealed from view. But there is no story in *The Laundress*, and no expression of the passions. Between the mother and the son there is not the least trace of affect. If La Font de Saint-Yenne speaks of 'utterly uninteresting' moments, it is because of the absence of that narrative part of painting, essential according to the abbé du Bos, because it conditions the identification of the viewer with the subject in the picture and allows him or her to be 'touched'. Chardin makes no use of that movement of the soul. He retains only that distracted attention that indicates life.

RED AND WHITE

Chardin seemingly portrays the domestic sphere completely differently in *Lady Sealing a Letter* (plate 7.5), a large canvas that cannot be securely dated either before or after the two paintings of 1733 (plates 7.3 and 7.4). A 'common' action borrowed from the Dutch tradition, the painting is possibly about the writing of a love letter. In a rather opulent setting a valet holds a lighted candle, with which he lights a taper to melt the stick of red wax that his mistress ('a very charming person', according to the *Mercure de France*) extends to him, so that she may seal the letter that she is holding in her other hand.[15] The gazes of the two figures converge on the flame, the point where the projection of the lines, the candle and the stick of wax also meet. It is difficult to deny that this *mise en scène* – the red of the wax and the white of the letter – puts into circulation an incendiary lexicon of desire. Everything works to bestow a strong erotic intensity to the poses of those two bodies awaiting the intermediary contact of a flame. One might think that Chardin, who borrows a baroque red curtain from the repertoire of *scènes galantes* and the restless greyhound from a *Declaration of Love* (1725, New York: Metropolitan Museum of Art) by Jean-François de Troy, was not entirely ignorant of these effects, all the more so as he selects a rather attractive male figure whose brown attire hardly bears the mark of his condition. Moreover, one might ask if it is rouge, a flush or a blush that charmingly colours the lady's cheeks. The reproductive engraver's tendency to eroticize appears to have been checked and he has contented himself with imagining, as did the editor of the *Mercure de France* (who found the print 'very piquant'), 'impatience', in order to animate the scene (a typical response in this situation), and to urge the valet: 'make haste ... Frontain / Ah Frontain, for you to move so slowly / Cupid must never have touched your heart.'[16] This expresses fairly well the troubling effect provoked by a ceremony in which the two participants must, in this silent scene of gestures, have some awareness of the eloquence of the objects they handle. The subject bears

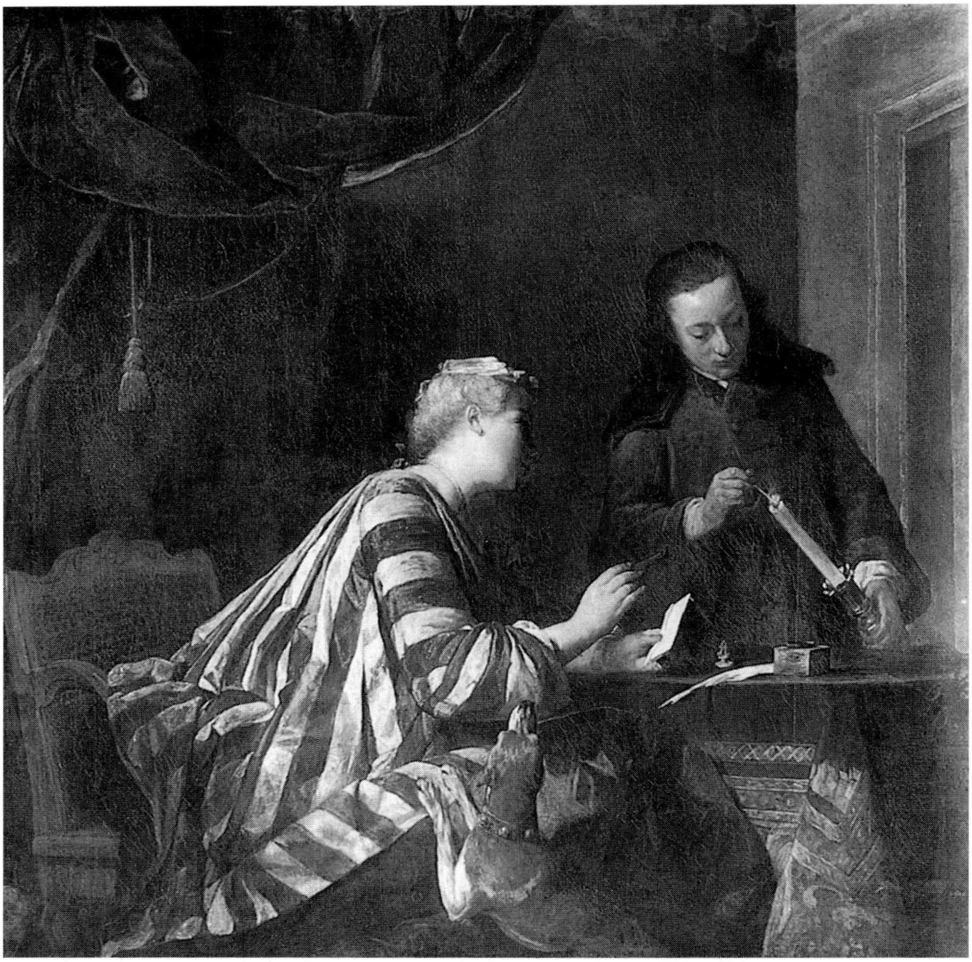

7.5 Jean-Siméon Chardin, *Lady Sealing her Letter*, *c*. 1733. Oil on canvas, 146 × 147 cm. Berlin: Staatliche Museen zu Berlin Preussischer Kulturbesitz. Copyright: Staatliche Museen, Berlin.

comparison to Marivaux's *Le Paysan parvenu*: a valet seduces his mistress. With this painting – overall perfectly innocent – Chardin reveals the libidinous tensions born of the fleshly proximities of the domestic domain. A separation between the figures – their poses, dress and physical beauty – does not set aside the possibility of an amorous relationship. In Marivaux, the two partners have the length of the story to explore this artificial social division and to develop a relationship that does not rest on physical need alone. As for Chardin, he has one dream of touching hands and looks through the objects in hand, the red of the wax, the white of the letter. Meanwhile, something is certainly happening, but something which the very situation withdraws from legibility, from the kind of legibility occasioned by the expression of the passions.[17]

CHILDREN'S GAMES

In 1737 a commentator praised the 'naive, noble and fine' taste with which Chardin had painted 'the innocent games of childhood', describing him as the 'painter of the sprightly laugh / and friend to the graces'.[18] But, in fact, Chardin's children neither laugh nor really jest. The relationship between the *Lady Taking Tea* (1735, Glasgow: The Hunterian Museum and Art Gallery) and *The House of Cards* (1737, London: National Gallery) sheds light on the seriousness that marks nearly all Chardin's domestic scenes, but those with children most especially, to the point where laughter – often in painting their natural attribute – is denied them.

Chardin's first child is at the feet of the laundress in the painting of the same title (plate 7.4); he makes soap bubbles and is interested in nothing else. With his torn clothing, he hardly conforms to the nobility and refinement that the author quoted above bestows on the painter. He exhibits no more than attention, which betrays nothing of what he feels. Chardin must have been aware that he was putting into play a motif with a completely different past to that of washing and hanging out laundry, a motif that belongs to the symbolic register of *Vanitas*. The full lexicon is elaborated in paintings containing knucklebones (used as jacks), card castles, a *jeu de l'oie*, or a top. Things and actions give rise to the thorny question of interpretation. The symbolism is certainly hackneyed but it nevertheless conjures up ideas of death, in order to quicken the believer's concern for salvation, or to remind the Epicurean to live for the moment. Conventionally, the figures in *Vanitas* imagery are no more than bearers of emblems. They may even laugh at objects whose meaning they do not grasp. Chardin tends, by contrast, to focus the viewer's interest on the attention that the handling of the object necessitates: the coordination of the eyes, hands, breath that this apprenticeship requires. The deathly and antiquated significance of things can thus be legitimately set aside; and yet at the same time the child does *indeed* experience the fragility of his object from which an awareness of mortality may *in fact* arise. That fragility does not trouble him, however, because it is *given*: before long the top must keel over; the house of cards must collapse; the bubble must burst. This is part and parcel of the game that consists only of delaying the inevitable. It is without consequence: unlike adult activity, play (or at least this type of play) is not aimed at a goal in the future, does not suppose a project, does not become alienated by deferred gratification. It would perhaps be worth remembering Rousseau's diagnoses, according to which a principal alienation of modern and civilized man arose from the imperative ceaselessly to make the present moment depend on its possible future consequences, thus imposing a delay to fulfilment. By this account, child's play belongs to the same order as the distracted look of the servants who turn away from mechanical tasks (washing, hanging out laundry etc.) which entail a plan, even if its accomplishment brings no anguish. The relationship between the two can be found in the servant playing jacks in Chardin's *Game of Knucklebones* (*c.* 1733, Baltimore: The Baltimore Museum of Art).

The captions to the prints do not necessarily convey Chardin's thought or intention and his print-makers never intended that they should. However, they do reveal the associations to which the images lent themselves, albeit under the cover of comedy. None of them assumes a radical form of the biblical indictment; instead they offer variations on the moral theme: the bubble mirrors the inconstancy of Iris; the game of the goose represents life's obstacles; the house of cards symbolizes the instability of man's endeavours; and the top denotes man in thrall to Fortune. The 'lesson' sometimes suggests the potential superiority of play over adult activity; Lépicié versifies, 'Charming child, beguiled by pleasure, / We smile smugly at your frail *travaux* / But, between us, which is the more solid / Our endeavours or your *châteaux*?'[19] The viewer is thus inspired with a certain nostalgia for the *immediate* pleasures harboured by the domestic space. The address to the child, it should be noted, assumes him to be capable of reflection.

Perhaps because he is already old enough to do so. In relation to *The Game of Knucklebones*, the engraver Fillœul comments, 'Already grown and full of charms, / It does not suit you, Lisette, / To play knucklebones alone, / And henceforth you are made, / To make a young man happy, / By condescending to give him a part in your games.' A wink at the painter perhaps, to say that the viewer is not duped by the ludic context. This servant with her apron adrift is in fact already a woman. The observation could be repeated of other scenes of play which feature adolescents, no longer children – unlike the absolute child in *The Laundress*, the little brother in *The Young Schoolmistress* (1735–6, London: National Gallery) and the accomplice in the background of *Soap Bubbles* (1735–6, Washington: National Gallery of Art), who wears a bonnet, apparently the distinctive mark of the child. The unfocused handling of these figures seems to emphasize the relatively 'unformed' character of the child's body. In *The Young Schoolmistress* and *Soap Bubbles* Chardin has underlined the distance that separates these secondary figures from the main protagonists, who are undoubtedly possessed of sexuality, the real children having been assigned the passive roles of spectator or pupil. It is this that justifies the sexual reference, more or less veiled, of the legends appended to the prints – the 'charming child, beguiled by pleasure', or Iris in *Soap Bubbles*, the 'dissemblance and deception'[20] attributed to *The Young Schoolmistress*. It operated also by negation. Of the *Young Girl with a Shuttlecock* (1737, private collection), the print relates, 'Without cares, without sorrows, tranquil in my desires, / A Racquet and a Shuttlecock provide all my pleasures.'[21] The shape of her body, which announces other pleasures, leads to the surmise that this tranquillity cannot last long.

Chardin dresses potentially seductive adolescent bodies with extreme attention to detail – more pronounced in the pictures of card castles and in *Boy with a Top* (1738, Paris: Musée du Louvre) than in *Soap Bubbles* – which links them more closely to *Lady Sealing her Letter* (1733, plate 7.5) and *Lady Taking Tea* (1735, Glasgow: The Hunterian Museum and Art Gallery) than to the pictures of servants. Their clothing is that of well-to-do, middle-class children. It eschews the ostentation of luxury associated with *mondain* society and calls attention rather to upright

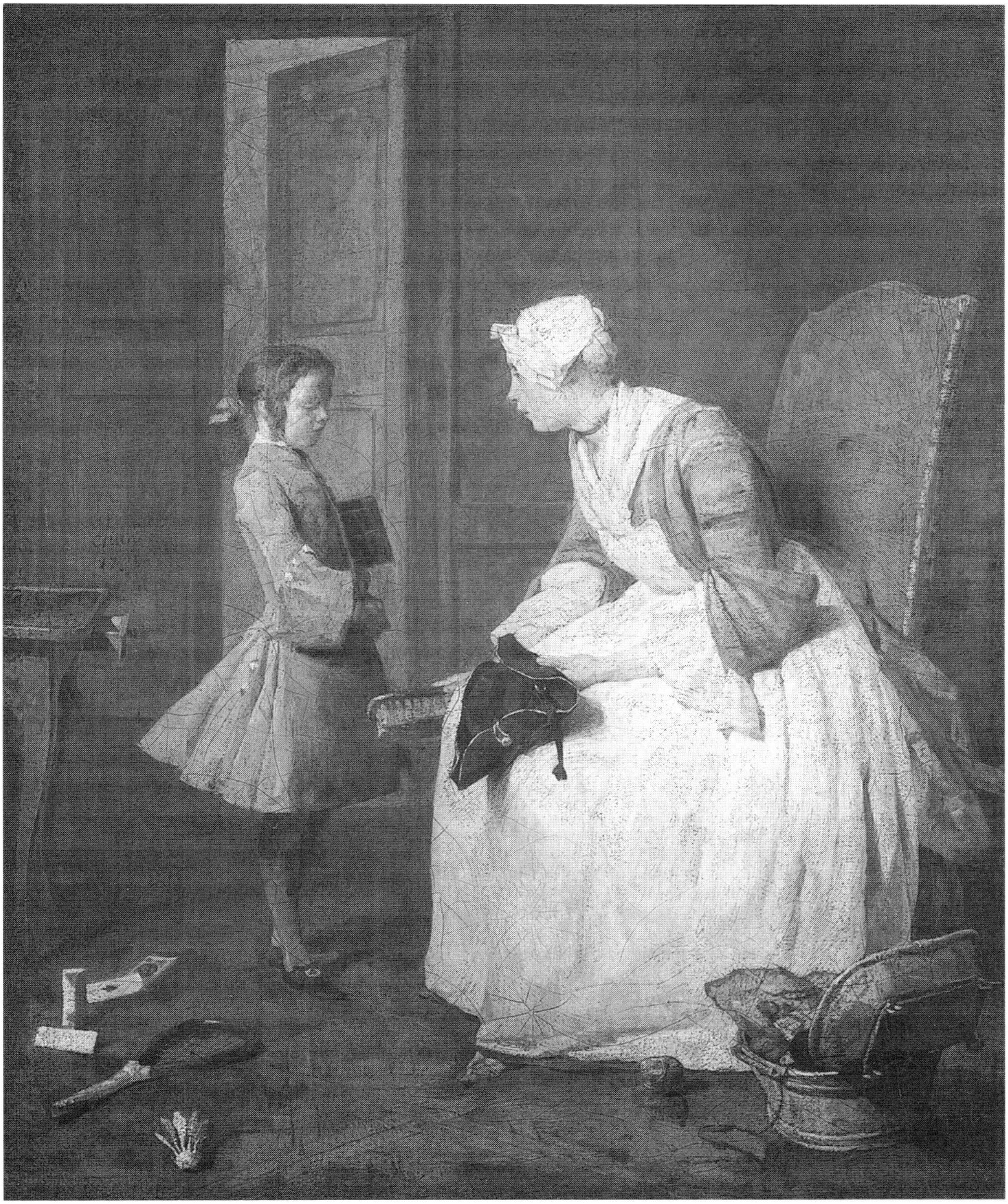

7.6 Jean-Siméon Chardin, *The Governess*, 1738. Oil on canvas, 46.5 × 37.5 cm. Ottawa: National Gallery of Canada. Copyright: National Gallery of Canada, Ottawa.

posture and to the exercise of control over the body. These are bodies that could appear with dignity in the social realm beyond the home; the tricorn attests to it. *The Governess* (plate 7.6) captures a moment of departure, abandoned toys strewn upon the floor. In *Boy with a Top* this relationship to the exterior is emphasized by pens, ink and compass, that point to schoolwork from which the child turns in order to become absorbed in a game which is not, perhaps, entirely suitable for his age or soon will not be.

Domestic space is where the adolescent still has a right to unproductive play, to the fascination with nothing or next to nothing. This is a libidinous place where bodies that will seduce put themselves on display, which licenses dreaming. It is even possible to imagine that across the paintings the young girl with the shuttlecock looks at a boy building a castle of cards. The same may be said of *The Scullery Maid* and *The Cellar Boy* (1738, Glasgow: The Hunterian Museum and Art Gallery). Scenes of play also reveal the space of the home as a place of shelter for libidinous relationships with the self, a happy narcissism, evidence of which is to be found in the look that the little girl casts at her reflection in *The Morning Toilet* (1741, Stockholm: Nationalmuseum).

This is a happy world, though serious, but one that is marked nevertheless by signs of death.

FOOD

Not surprisingly something funereal also touches food, another function of the family, conjured up by the ingredients and utensils of the still lifes. While cruelty and horror are implied, portrayals of food also risked being castigated as vulgar and lowly. Was it for this reason that the only painting by Chardin to depict the consumption of food (the painting portrays the instant immediately preceding it, but the table is set) is placed under the sign of the word of God? *Saying Grace* (1740, Paris: Musée du Louvre) is the first picture in which Chardin hazards the representation of an exchange of looks between mother (or maybe governess) and child, a complex exchange, moreover, because additionally an older sister looks at the child seated in the foreground, his hands joined together, his dress an indication of his extreme youth. The expression of affect remains discreet in the mother / governess; her slender silhouette, hands resting on the table, inclines towards the child. Critics responded to the smiling atmosphere of this picture, imagined that the 'sister is surreptitiously laughing at her little brother', who rushes his prayer, casting 'an impatient look' at his soup.[22] This scene that the nineteenth century saw as emblematic of 'holy respect for the family' and 'bourgeois virtues' is without religious gravity, and if the child is being schooled, it is done so lightly. Domestic space is one of happiness shared, bathed in smiles; 'the connoisseur', writes a poet for the *Mercure de France*, 'Smiles at these children and allows himself be charmed / Feels even more than he can express.'[23]

The contrast is evident in the tonality of other contemporary scenes of education, but also in works where Chardin is concerned with food, the first being *The*

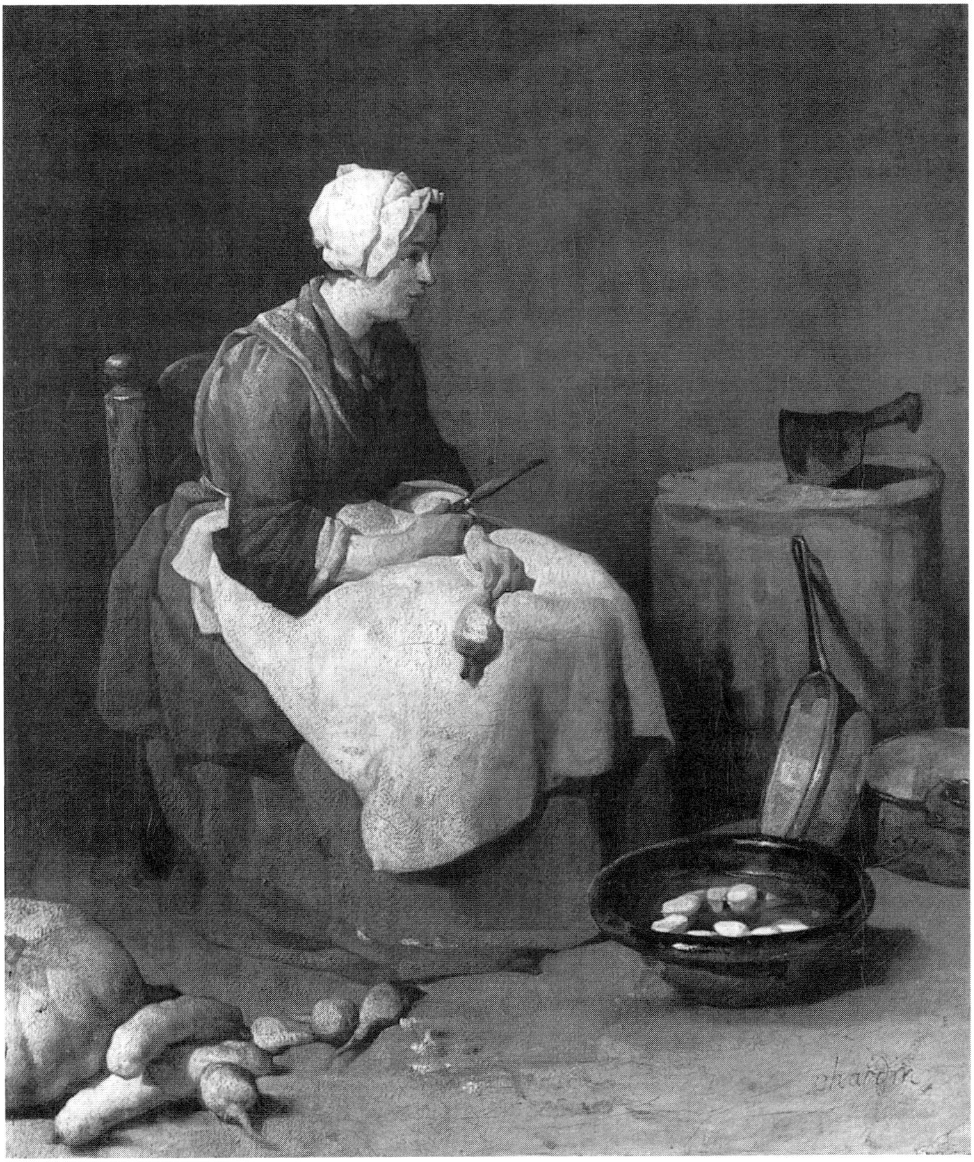

7.7 Jean-Siméon Chardin, *The Turnip Scraper*, 1738. Oil on canvas, 46.2 × 37.5 cm. Washington, DC: National Gallery of Art. Copyright: National Gallery of Art, Washington.

Turnip Scraper of 1738 (plate 7.7), a scene of its preparation. A woman, seated and surrounded, more than is usual in Chardin, by brightly coloured still-life objects (gourds, cucumbers, a pot, an earthenware dish), peels turnips, or more precisely scrapes them, that is to say removes the skin with the blade of a knife that, in a moment of rest, she holds vertically in her lap. She stares vacantly at the space above and beyond a blood-stained block into which a cleaver is stuck. It is tempting to follow the path of that scarlet stain from the *Ray Fish* (plate 7.2) and the trickles of blood that escape from the mouths of hares, to the joint of meat hung above the laundress (plate 7.4), to this point, which invokes the slaughter of animals. *The Turnip Scraper* (plate 7.7) succeeds the 'cleaning-women' exhibited in 1734. This conjunction of blood, knife and a look that loses itself rather than focusing on some object unseen is unsettling. It is as if her daydream is coloured by the violence suggested here, and implied by the civilizing process that transforms the raw into the cooked (violence conveyed perhaps by the use of colour). The quatrain that Lépicié appends to his print expresses this uneasiness: 'When our ancestors took from Nature's hands / These vegetables, proof of their simple way, / The art of making food into poison / Had not yet seen the light of day.'[24] This malediction cast on cooking renders the servant either a poisoner or a representative of nature (the vegetables are, after all, held in her hands). It seems that the art of cooking is associated with death suggested by the spot of blood (necessarily invisible on the print).

It is not impossible that *The Attentive Nurse* – also known as *The Convalescent's Meal* (probably *c.* 1747, Washington DC: National Gallery of Art) – was intended as a late pendant to *The Turnip Scraper*. If so, Chardin has played on contrasts, because all is softness and harmony in the objects and in the figure, tall, finely dressed (too finely, in fact, for a servant), and occupied in peeling a hard-boiled egg upon which her somewhat dreamy gaze is fixed. But there is softness and harmony of colour also; it is an artful play of pastel tones. Convalescence excludes meat and blood. Yet the setting suggests the presence of sickness and death, which confer on the otherwise seductive figure of the nurse a quasi-maternal role, echoed in the egg, a familiar symbol of birth (a reminder too of the 'fresh eggs' and 'brioche' which preserve Mlle Habert's freshness in *Le Paysan parvenu*). The cooked here responds to the world of the raw over which *The Turnip Scraper* reigned. In these two works the ambivalence of an orality at once happy and destructive may be rediscovered, both images in their different ways being marked by death.

OPEN DOORS

The Kitchen Maid (plate 7.1) also belongs to this cycle of food; she who presides over the bringing of food into the interior. Diderot found this kitchen maid, who, leaning on the sideboard, deposits the load she has brought back from the market, 'somewhat colossal in proportion and mannered in attitude', whereas Brunaubois-Montador wrote of her: 'she is the most correct figure I know.'[25] The judgements 'colossal' and 'mannered' may be partly explained: the mass of the kitchen maid is emphasized by comparison with the silhouette of the young girl seen on the threshold to the left, and the contrapposto of her body (she leans to the right but faces left) finds its explanation in the attention she pays to the conversation between the girl and a man, of whom no more than a hat and half a face is seen. He towers over the young girl, accentuating her smallness. She is perhaps very young, but her body's sexuality is evident in the size of her breasts and her choice of clothing. Could she be a younger servant or the daughter of the house? A triangle of blue sky confirms that the exchange is taking place on the threshold. This kitchen maid is also an 'eavesdropper', though she is more discreet than the surreptitious listeners portrayed by Nicolas Maes in the 1650s. Diderot, always in search of a story, no more so perhaps than other critics, did not notice this anecdotal detail, which is nevertheless brought to the viewer's attention by the light of the hall, against which the outline of the majestic copper urn is silhouetted.

Even without assigning the role of temple guardian to this water urn, one has the feeling that the world of food leaves the idyllic at the threshold because one cannot but attribute an undercurrent of gallantry to the dialogue at the door, all the more remarkable for its uniqueness in Chardin's œuvre. The kitchen maid's expression, excepting the attention revealed by the direction of her gaze, remains indecipherable, though we can say for certain that she is not smiling, nor passionate (yet again Chardin exploits an affect of weak intensity and the ambiguities that it allows). This elegantly dressed woman keeps under covert surveillance what is taking place on the threshold. Moreover, her stature (and the physical strength that it implies) is a little daunting. A subtle thread of conflict seems to slip into the weave of the domestic sphere.

Such conflict is more obvious in *The Governess* (plate 7.6), where the space opens once more to the left – as in *The Kitchen Maid*, but without the latter's effect of perspective – and the boy's silhouette stands out against an open door. That the scene depicts an act of reprimand is evident from the lowered eyes of the child, but the expression of the seated governess (she too is elegant and massive, but fine featured) lacks the anger anticipated. The *Mercure de France* commended 'the affability, gentleness and moderation that the governess retains whilst reprimanding the young man for dirtiness, messiness and carelessness'.[26] In order to characterize the woman's expression further it is tempting to say that it betrays a certain surprise, as if the child were some kind of foreign object (it is the very look levelled three years earlier by the young schoolmistress at her still younger pupil in *The Young Schoolmistress*). In his reproductive print Lépicié suggests that the boy 'is planning / to return to his shuttlecock.' This seems highly unlikely. The tricorn being brushed (or that has just been or is about to be brushed) and whose blackness stands out against the whiteness of the apron, is an emblem of masculinity retained by the governess. It heralds an imminent departure, which would put an end to chastisement, and thus to displeasure.

The half-open door (albeit almost totally obscured by a large screen) and conflict reappear in the *The Diligent Mother* (1740, Paris: Musée du Louvre), and serve Lépicié as an alibi for putting sharp and moralizing talk into the mouth of the parent. The child's face certainly does not glow with happiness as she gazes at the length of embroidery held at the other end by her mother (similarly, in *The Governess* and in a sketch for *Saying Grace* two characters are yoked by an object they share). On close inspection, the mother, notwithstanding the 'imposing air and austere mien' attributed to her by one critic,[27] and reinforced by her disproportionate size, does not look at her daughter, nor at the sewing, but rather at a point in space, which suggests a moment of suspended action, of reverie or introspection. The settings of these scenes of chastisement are distinguished by richer furnishings, emphasizing the enclosed nature of the space, and they offer displays of tools for feminine, domestic labour: a work basket in *The Governess*, a large yarn-winder in the foreground in *The Diligent Mother*. Similar motifs recur much later in *The Good Education* (1749, location unknown, a later version at Houston: Museum of Fine Arts), a scene of recitation in which the door ajar in the depth of the room is replaced by a window to one side from whence comes light. The wider angle upon the scene and the frieze-like composition confine the bodies of the mother and daughter to a narrower place upon the canvas. Moreover, they are set further apart; the mediating object (brush or piece of material) is gone, the link of one to the other no more than the spoken recital of a written text. It is rather difficult to follow the abbé Leblanc who, seeking to praise Chardin's handling of the passions, refers to 'a fire and an action which astonish' and reads in the little girl's expression 'the internal distress that she feels because she does not know her lesson properly'.[28] However, the bowed head of this rather stiff figure, strikingly captured in profile, is enough to indicate the child's displeasure. This is certainly a far cry from the gentle humour aroused by saying grace in *Saying Grace*.

This series of open doors, suggesting an exterior where the child would rather be, lends a slightly oppressive character to a domestic space now linked to an educational activity, which substitutes a register of mother–governesses for that of servants. This educational theme was apparently first treated by Chardin in 1735 in his first *Young Schoolmistress* (London: National Gallery), in which a young girl takes it upon herself to instruct a much younger child, to whom she teaches his letters. Lépicié had noted the gracefulness of the female figure, recognizing in the role she plays a foreshadowing of other seductions: 'May one not think that such dissemblance and deception / Are granted to the fair sex at birth.'[29] The young girl's expression does not suggest that she has any passion for her task; it is more a kind of astonished withdrawal before the child and what she is making him do. As in *The Lady Sealing a Letter* (plate 7.5), the relationship between the two figures is articulated by the activity of the hands around a common object, the large knitting needle held by the young girl corresponding to the child's index finger as he points to a letter.

The Morning Toilet (1741, Stockholm: National Museum) expresses clearly the delight of escaping from the domestic sphere. The missal and muff on the stool to the left and the clock to the right indicate imminent departure for Mass, a place of encounters, often amorous ones; Marivaux's Marianne meets her future lover in church, after having long hesitated over the choice of her *cornet*.[30] Contemporary critics responded sensitively to Chardin's compositional invention: 'This *little* girl, whose *Mother* arranges her hair, turns away to look in the *Mirror*. In the gesture of the Head turned aside one reads the stirrings of vanity. Her little heart is in the eyes which interrogate the Glass, and which are on the look-out for those little Graces she believes will escape her.'[31] The contact, if not the complicity of the two figures, is essential here. The mother dressing her daughter's hair takes possession of her, and in so doing adds to the pleasure the child takes in looking at herself in the mirror. Chardin has concentrated his efforts on the clothes, the relative luxury of which indicates the triumph of an *honnête coquetterie*, situated outside the fashionable world. It was in relation to this painting that the author of the *Lettre à M. de Poiresson-Chamarande* wrote: 'It is always the members of the *Bourgeoisie* that he treats [. . .] There is no woman of the Third Estate who does not see in his work an image of her figure, her domestic household, her comfortable manners, her day-to-day occupations, her moral code, the moods of her children, her furnishings, her wardrobe.'[32] Charles-Etienne Pesselier noted the sexual nature of the subject in a commentary curiously close to Lépicié's on *The Young Schoolmistress*: 'In the desire and art of pleasing / Beauties, I see, are never children.'[33] In his treatment of the *toilette*, Chardin was doubtless aware of having appropriated in his own way a notoriously libertine subject: Boucher's *Lady Fastening her Garter, with her Maid* (1742, Madrid: Thyssen-Bornemisza Museum of Art) and such parodies as Coypel's *Children Playing at Make-up* (1728, private collection) come to mind.[34] In spite of the smoking candle, it is hard to see in this little girl a Magdalen at her mirror. Chardin has scarcely revealed with more clarity the libidinous dimension of the domestic world. Yet he does so only to move away from it.

SINGLE WOMEN

In the absence of children, can the woman in her home, the mistress of the house, know a self-sufficiency analogous to that of the children playing? *Household Economy* and *Domestic Pleasures* (*c*. 1764–7, Stockholm: Nationalmuseum) suggest an answer. Both describe the relationship a woman can entertain with the written word: with the account book kept by the first, a woman surrounded by household objects, and employed to control the relationship with the exterior space via the reduction of objects to signs. The second painting, notwithstanding the spinning wheel on the table, an emblem of female work, depicts a moment of leisure given over to reading – a novel, according to contemporaries. The reading has been interrupted, however; the book lies in her lap as she sits and she raises her eyes to the spot where the spectator stands: 'an amiable idler in the guise of a lady, carelessly yet fashionably dressed, with a rather attractive physiognomy', opines La Font de Saint-Yenne,[35] while the author of *Observations sur les arts* (1748) observes that Chardin,

> portrays an idle woman carelessly seated in an armchair and holding in her hands which rest in her lap, a brochure. From the sort of languor that fills her eyes, trained on a corner of the picture, one may guess that she is reading a novel, and that the tender impressions that she has drawn from it have led her to dream of someone she would very much like to see arrive![36]

Idleness, nonchalance, carelessness, languor: the tone brings La Font to the brink of censure. With this figure, who fixes the gaze of the spectator, half-smiling, one is at the opposite extreme to the social whirl. Has someone just arrived or, as the critic suggests, is she dreaming of someone who might arrive? This ambiguity makes her into a figure of welcome, open to an exterior object, imaginary or real. Was this another way of escaping the enclosed space of the house?

This feminine self-sufficiency is also apparent in *The Bird Organ* (plate 7.8). But the object of attention, a canary, is real enough and doubly enclosed – in a cage in the interior – whilst the seated woman, leaning on her embroidery frame, occupies the background of the composition. It is impossible to ignore the visual iconography of the bird, symbol of an amorous liberty which the bird's-nesting swain offers to his shepherdess as an invitation to 'that felicity which is the portion of birds'.[37] In both painting and poetry, the bird symbolizes as much the male as the female sex; it is Boucher's 'poorly defended bird', or Diderot's question to Jean-Baptiste Greuze's *Weeping Girl with a Dead Canary* (1765, Edinburgh: National Gallery of Scotland), 'is she thinking of her bird?'. The canary had the potential to become an object of passion: Mouhy's *La Mouche* (1736) tells the tale of a lady who offers herself in marriage to whoever returns her lost canary and the reunion forms the occasion for a love scene comparable to that depicted in *La Femme à la Cage*, a print by Blondel d'Azincourt (after a drawing by Boucher) over which Jean-Jacques Rousseau raved and in which a bird freed from its cage pecks the lips of his mistress. But the canary also provokes innocent amusement. In his *Nouveau Traité des Serins de Canarie* (1709) Hervieux de Chanteloup praises the 'sweet and innocent pleasure of canaries' and gives methods for educating them; the bird is treated like a child who thinks of nothing but play if left to itself. And in 1745 he advocated the use of the 'mechanized flageolet', otherwise known as the bird-song organ, described in detail in the *Encyclopédie* as a superior alternative to the flageolet, which tires the lungs, and above all, 'because it is rather unseemly, above all for the [fairer] Sex, to play it . . . .'[38] It is in this context that the abbé Raynal interprets Chardin's *The Bird Organ* (plate 7.8): 'Indeed, one can say without fear of hyperbole, that the model Mr. Chardin has chosen on this occasion indicates a woman devoted to her duty, *honnête*, full of gentleness, a woman all in all who knows how to amuse herself.'[39] And he approves of this manner of making one 'love' and 'envy' the 'common life'. 'Varying her amusements' (an alternative title for the work), the lady avoids the boredom which would lead her to seek adventure, to risk herself in the exterior world.

Chardin could not, of course, have been ignorant of these different uses of the bird motif, and still less of its relationship to his own scenes of education; one of the titles given to the painting was *The Education of the Canary*. The scenario is the same: one person tries to make another do something, imitate something, more often than not. In this instance a lady turns the handle of the bird-song organ (an art requiring only regularity of motion) making the captive bird sing along. Putting aside the tradition of blinding canaries (males, as only the male sings)

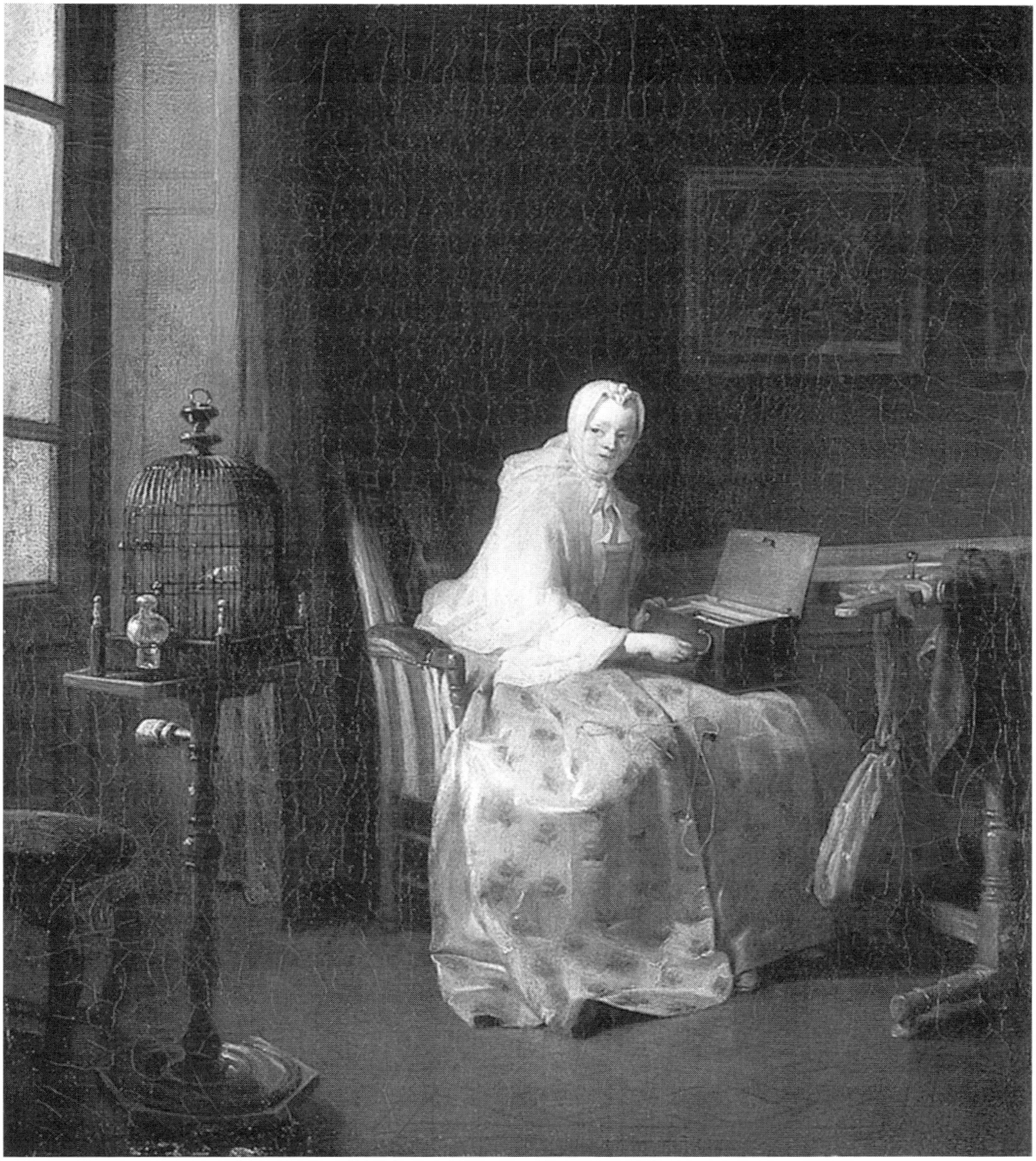

7.8 Jean-Siméon Chardin, *The Bird Organ*, 1751. Oil on canvas, 50 × 43.5 cm. Paris: Musée du Louvre. Photo: Réunion des musées nationaux.

and its inevitable connection to fantasies of castration, it is essential to note that darkness is a necessary condition of the bird's song. It is achieved with the aid of coverings or a screen (the mechanism by which this is attached is visible in the canvas). As in the mother–child dyad, there is a suffering subject here: the canary. The pastoral bird let the voice of nature be heard. To gain his love song, the lady here substitutes an artificial, instrumental music, which demands no personal participation on her part. In short, it is the organ, the machine, which imposes its law on the bird. As for the lady, she remains at a fair distance from the bird: in contrast to Mouhy, there is no question of contact, and her gaze, fixed on the cage, is of an exemplary coolness, a controlling gaze of a kind first discernible, perhaps, in *The Kitchen Maid* (plate 7.1). We are thus witnesses to a process of *dénaturization*. Education is certainly another example of this. When governesses and mothers inflict displeasure on a child it is at least without apparent pleasure, and seemingly for the child's own good, that is to say, in the name of social and moral imperatives of which the child is later supposed to reap a benefit. Here the lady is concerned only with her own pleasure. Before the suffering subject, another subject finds her pleasure in an exercise of ultimately cruel control. No more is this the happy collaboration of the *Morning Toilet*. In this game, the lady finds herself in the position of the playing children before their soap bubbles and their tops, the difference being that her object is a living creature, capable of suffering. In retrospect, does this not imply that the domestic space in which children are taught to sing along is also a kind of cage? The interior harbours an enterprise here which has the alienating structure of the adult project, isolated from the affective components which suffuse the educative project in earlier canvases. To make one last connection one could think of the 'torture' of which Diderot has Chardin speak in 1765; that of inflicting the copying of masters' drawings on the pupils of the Académie, thus prohibiting them from 'learning to look at nature'.[40] It is possible that Chardin theorized the content of his late genre scenes more than was his wont, without preventing the partisans of the familial values from finding in them what they were looking for.

ACTIONS AND PASSIONS

Contemporaries accorded Chardin the merit of having invented 'a new genre'. They were careful not to define it, and with good reason. The more perceptive of the critics realized the extent to which this invention threatened established categories. Others limited themselves to praise of 'truth', a 'magic touch', and with proclaiming the artist unique and inimitable (like Marivaux), praise that rendered his art safe.

To bring the low high involved a re-evaluation of the object. 'To care only to render it true, I have to forget everything that I have seen and even the manner those objects have been represented by others,' Cochin has Chardin say in front of his first hare.[41] Creative forgetting involved – and not only in the case of hares – separating the subject from the representational codes to which it was traditionally attached (the servant from dirt, the 'low' body from the crude proportions attributed to the vulgar, the child from laughter, etc). Yet this had to be done in such a way that the spectator could still identify the subject, something which required complex strategies. It involved making the spectator recognize the experience of emotion or pleasure (condemned or repressed) before objects that were apparently not worth the trouble, and which social prejudice discounted (the servant, the earthenware pot). It required representation to take up 'ideas', as Marivaux would say, for which there was as yet no language.

Chardin was concerned initially with a domestic space, a feminine space, envisaged at its 'lowest', at the level of the most everyday household tasks, and he depicted it without adding the supplement of the picturesque or the spice of a story or an anecdote. Diderot remarked in his *Entretiens sur le fils naturel* (1757) that the novel can take liberties in recording the weak and lifeless moments in a plot which theatre is obliged to exclude.[42] Chardin seems to have included none but these. They made possible the representation of the body outside the social sphere, at a distance from the worldly scene. Sensualist philosophy had revealed the place which these everyday, seemingly inconsequential moments – linked nevertheless to the survival of the species – had had in the elaboration of the individual, and had underlined the complexity of the operations which primitive gestures demanded. It was for the same reason that attention was brought to bear on childhood. In his scenes of servants, Chardin operated in the zone that Condillac later characterized as the province of 'habitual judgement' and 'practical knowledge' to demonstrate their survival in the civilized individual.[43] For Condillac, this regime preceded the invention of verbal language in the evolution of mankind. In Chardin's domestic universe few words are exchanged, except on occasions of recital by rote. What happens there is communicated by gesture, posture, the arrangement of bodies, below the level of language, in a silence in which, for all that, the individual does not cease to exist and to feel. And there again Chardin joins Marivaux, who tried, by means of language itself, to suggest that which escapes it.

Chardin's 'rare and particular genre' did not require, according to Baillet de Saint-Julien, the study of the passions; at the most it involved a command of character (which amounted to situating the artist, honourably, on the side of the theatre and with Molière). It was, however, the expression of the passions that in the theory of the abbé Du Bos, constituted the principal merit of painting because the spectator was moved in proportion to the passion exhibited by the figure depicted. This theoretical position which made of the body, following the theatrical model, the vector of the movements of the soul, guaranteed a 'heightened' enjoyment of and an elevated status to the stronger passions, those of tragedy or history painting. Willingly were confused – and Diderot is the best example of this – the affect produced on the spectator and the legibility of the depicted passion; transparency allowed it to be named. Hence Diderot's formulation: 'each movement of his (man's) soul paints itself across his face in clear, visible characters, about which we can never be mistaken. [. . .] The expression is weak or false if it leaves us in doubt about [the nature of] the feeling.'[44]

To all intents and purposes, Chardin eschewed this version of the expression of the passions which led Diderot and Greuze to import strong emotion into social milieux traditionally assigned to comedy: those of the bourgeoisie and the 'low'. Far from playing the inexpressive card, Chardin concerned himself with the imperceptible movements of the soul (the passions, in the Cartesian sense of the word), whose feeble intensity often prevents language from capturing them. In this he came close to Marivaux who, in one of his rare theoretical writings, discussed different means of articulating ideas that defied the perfect clarity of discourse and were linked to the discovery of new things.[45] The unexpected sidelong glance of the laundress, the raised eyes of the scullery maid, the 'horizontal' gaze of the turnip scraper in the paintings (plates 7.4 and 7.7) hold the viewer's attention, and prevent dismissal of the work by simple categorization: 'here is a servant at work.' The thoughts and feelings passing through the minds and hearts of children and those who govern the domestic world are irreducible to an index of passions such as those defined by Charles Le Brun's gallery of expressive heads. The effect produced by Chardin is due largely to the question addressed by the work to the viewer, and to the failure of verbal language to respond adequately to it. The mother's gesture in *The Morning Toilet* could arise just as easily from habit as from deep affection, or perhaps from the two at once. This is to say that the encounter with the depicted figure occurred under the sign of ambivalence and through a glass darkly, closer, no doubt, to what was actually and generally experienced in the confrontation with the 'other'. By treating the insignificant moment as if it were significant, Chardin engaged the viewer in a quest for meaning, a quest in which the latter must needs draw on his own experience, a non-verbalized experience. It is perhaps in this sense that the statement in the *Lettre à M. de Poiresson-Chamarande* of 1741 should be understood; it evokes the 'woman of the third estate', who comes *to recognize herself* in the painter's canvases, without need of the mediation that language provides.

In 1753 Baillet de Saint-Julien evoked the manner in which the eye of the spectator, in search of Chardin's secret, 'plunges into, looses itself' in the painter's touch; 'without ever being satisfied, it moves away, comes closer, and leaves only with a promise to return.'[46] Transferring this observation about technique to the realm of expression prompts a final reflection of Chardin's depiction of the passions, this time in terms of the *non-finito*. The human soul resembles here a rabbit's fur about the representation of which Cochin remarked that 'one should not think of counting the hairs or of rendering it in detail.'[47] Rather it required treatment as the whole, irreducible to analysis, a treatment that fascinated and secured the return of the spectator. Ultimately, it proffered an invitation to dream: for instance, about what might happen to the woman sealing her letter and her valet.

In this game the spectator's attention focuses on bodies, but leaves to one side erotic love, that which dominated historical as well as galant genres. The two small figures conversing in the background of *The Kitchen Maid* (plate 7.1), curiously overlooked by contemporary criticism, are the only ones that incite a narrative of love, and their restraint marks a threshold in Chardin not to be crossed. A stranger to all lewdness, he nevertheless depicted desiring beings, whether the object of that desire was a canary, or a soap bubble, or a book –

possibly a novel – or the vapour rising from a teacup. Moreover, the refinement of costume and posture, that is the eroticization of the dress worn by Chardin's adolescents and ladies of leisure, bespeaks desiring beings not only responsive to the desire of others but open, possibly, to a pleasure in their own beauty, even to the extent of confirmation by a look in the mirror in *The Morning Toilet*. The domestic sphere is a space where one can often take pleasure in one's own self.

Chardin did not take part in the moral idealization of the *familial* which flourished after 1750. He respects the ambiguity of domestic space: if there is love, it belongs to the painter and not to his figures. However, it is possible that he opened the door to moralization in, for example, *Saying Grace* and *The Diligent Mother*, a moralizing for which he took no responsibility. If *The Bird Organ* (plate 7.8) concludes Chardin's meditations on the domestic interior, it appears that his was ultimately a fairly sombre vision of that world. The gaze of the lady has found an object, but this gaze is without tenderness. She is the castrating rather than the nurturing mother; she stokes a fear of woman variously expressed during the century, included in the form of its denial in libertinage. Hers is the dark side of the domestic sphere, which Chardin explored as though it was a new world and one which, in the case of the music box and the caged canary, is disconnected with the order of nature.

Translated by Mia Jackson and Katie Scott

Notes

1 Jean-Bernard Le Blanc, *Lettre sur l'exposition des ouvrages de peinture et sculpture de l'année 1747 et èn général sur l'utilité de ces sortes d'exposition*, Paris, 1747, 95.

2 *Mercure de France*, November 1753, 193.

3 Marivaux, 'Histoire de l'inconnu', in *Journaux et oeuvres diverses*, eds F. Deloffre and M. Gilot, Paris, 1969, 238–65.

4 Marivaux, *Le Paysan parvenu*, ed. F. Deloffre, Paris, 1992, 46. These texts are contemporaneous with Chardin's genre paintings. It was from 1730 that Marivaux's plays moved in the direction of domestic space.

5 See A. Furetière, *Dictionnaire universel contenant généralement les mots françois tant vieux que modernes et les termes de toutes sciences et des arts …* , 3 vols, La Haye-Rotterdam, 1690, reissued Paris, 1978: 'Famille, se prend plus particulièrement pour un ménage composé d'un chef et de ses doméstiques, soit femmes, enfants ou serviteurs.'

6 Marivaux, *Pharsamon*, in *Œuvres de jeunesse*, ed. F. Deloffre, Paris, 1972, 605.

7 See Th. Laffichard, *Caprices romanesques*, Paris, 1745, 63.

8 Denis Diderot, *Essais sur la peinture* (1766), eds J. Chouillet and G. May, Paris, 1984, 88.

9 Diderot, *Salon de 1765*, eds E.M. Bukdahl and A. Lorenceau, Paris, 1984, 121.

10 René Démoris, *Chardin, la chair et l'objet*, Paris, 1991, chaps 3 and 4.

11 La Font de Saint-Yenne, *Réflexions sur quelques causes de l'état present de la peinture en France avec un examen des principaux ouvrages exposés au Louvre le mois d'août 1746*, Paris, 1747, 109.

12 *Mercure de France*, June 1735, 1386.

13 Etienne Bonnot de Condillac, *Essai sur l'origine des connaissances humaines*, Amsterdam, 1746. See also Réné Démoris, 'Condillac et la peinture', *Condillac et les problèmes du language*, Geneva, 1982.

14 Diderot, *Salon de 1765*, Paris, 1984, 111.

15 *Mercure de France*, May 1738, 1142.

16 The print is by Étienne Fessard, published in 1738.

17 One is reminded of Marivaux's erotic novel *Le Paysan parvenu* in which the plot centres round a young servant Jacob and a pious woman, a letter to be written and a pen that does not work. Equally, there is a scene in his *Fausses confidences*

(1737), where a lady makes her steward, a disguised lover, write a letter for her.

18 *Réponse aux vers de M.Gresset*, 1737, 11.

19 Engraving by F. B. Lépicié, 1743; see Pierre Rosenberg, *Chardin 1699–1779*, Paris, 1979, 232.

20 Engraving by F. B. Lépicié, 1740; *Mercure de France*, October 1740, 2282, Rosenberg, 228.

21 Engraving by F. B. Lépicié; undated; Rosenberg, 234.

22 *Mercure de France*, December 1740, 2710.

23 *Mercure de France*, December 1740, 2710.

24 *Mercure de France*, January 1743, 148–9.

25 Diderot, *Salon de 1769*, eds E.M. Bukdahl, M. Delon and A. Lorenceau, Paris 1984, 45. Neufville de Brunaubois-Montador, *Description raisonnée des tableaux exposés au Salon du Louvre*, 1739, p.9.

26 *Mercure de France*, September 1739, 2217.

27 *Mercure de France*, December 1740, 2710.

28 Jean-Bernard Le Blanc, *Observations sur les ouvrages de MM. de l'Académie de peinture et de sculpture, exposés au Salon du Louvre en l'année 1753 et sur quelques escrits qui ont rapport à la peinture, à M le president de B∗∗∗*, Paris, 1753, 23.

29 Engraving by Lépicié, 1740; *Mercure de France*, October 1740, 2282; Rosenberg 234.

30 Marivaux, *La Vie de Marianne* (1731–34), ed. F. Deloffre, Paris, 1957, 44–63.

31 *Lettre à M. de Poiresson-Chamarande* (1741), in René Démoris, *La peinture en procès: la naissance de la critique d'art au siècle des lumières*, Paris, 2001, 51. See also the review in the *Mercure de France*, October 1741, 2290.

32 Démoris, *La peinture*, 50.

33 *Mercure de France*, December 1741, 2699.

34 Pierre Rosenberg has identified the engraving after Coypel on the wall in *The Bird Organ*, see his *Chardin 1699–1779*, 289.

35 La Font de Saint-Yenne, *Réflexions*, 1747, 111.

36 Charles Léoffron de Saint-Yves, *Observations sur les arts et sur quelques morceaux de peinture et de sculpture exposés au Louvre en 1748; où il est parlé de l'utilité des embellisements dans les villes*, Leiden . . . , 1748, 90.

37 'Sur la mort d'un serin', *Mercure de France*, April 1747, 69.

38 Hervieux de Chanteloup, *Nouveau traité*, Paris, 1745, 102–103.

39 *Mercure de France*, November 1753, 160.

40 See the discourse of Chardin reported by Diderot in the *Salon de 1765*, Paris, 1984, 23–5.

41 C. N. Cochin, *Essai sur la vie de Chardin*, in Charles de Robillard de Beaurepaire, *Précis analytique des travaux de l'Académie des sciences, belles lettres et arts de Rouen*, Rouen, 1875–76, vol. 28, 421.

42 Diderot, *Entretiens sur le fils naturel* (1757), *Œuvres esthétiques*, ed. P. Vernière, Paris, 1965, 81.

43 Condillac, *Essai sur l'origine des connaissances humaines*.

44 Diderot, *Essais sur la peinture*, Paris, 1984, 45.

45 Marivaux, 'Pensées sur la clarté du discourse', *Journaux et oeuvres diverses*, 52–5.

46 Baillet de Saint-Julien, *La Peinture, ode de milord Telliab*, London, 1753, 5.

47 C.N. Cochin, *Essai sur la vie de Chardin*, 421.

NOTES ON CONTRIBUTORS

Mary Sheriff *is Daniel W. Patterson Distinguished Professor and Department Chair in the Department of Art at the University of North Carolina at Chapel Hill. Her most recent book is* Moved by Love, Inspired Artists and Deviant Women in Eighteenth-Century France *(Chicago, 2003).*

Elisabeth Lavezzi *is Maître de Conférances at the Univerisity of Paris* III *Sorbonne-Nouvelle. She has published a number of articles on seventeenth- and eighteenth-century art terminology and art theory, especially with regard to painting. Pertinent here is her 'La drame de la matière ou "L'art de peindre sur émail"', in* La Matière et l'homme dans l'Encyclopédie *(Paris, 1998).*

Lesley Ellis Miller *works at the University of Southampton in the Centre for the History of Textiles and Dress. She is currently co-editor of* Textile History. *She is in the process of completing a book,* Portraits in Silk: Seven Designers and Manufacturers in Eighteenth-Century France *(forthcoming Ashgate, 2007). Her other publications include a monograph on the twentieth-century Spanish fashion designer* Cristobal Balenciaga *(Batsford, 1993), and a number of articles on the nature of education, work and the culture of appearances in eighteenth-century Lyons.*

Leora Auslander *is a professor of Modern European Social History at the University of Chicago. She is the author of* Taste and Power: Furnishing Modern France *(University of California Press, 1996). She is currently working on a book-length project (from which this essay is drawn) entitled* Revolutionary Taste: Everyday Life and Politics in England, Colonial America, and France.

Katie Scott *is Reader in the History of Art at the Courtauld Institute of Art. Since the publication of* The Rococo Interior: Decoration and Social Spaces in Eighteenth-century Paris *(Yale University Press, 1996) she has written essays on Watteau, Chardin, Boucher and Bouchardon.*

René Jean Démoris *has been Professor at the University of Lille III and at the Sorbonne-Nouvelle-Paris III. He has published widely on French seventeenth and eighteenth-century fiction and painting theory. His most well known works include,* Chardin, la chair et l'object *(1991/1999),* La peinture en procès: la naissance de la critique d'art au siècle des Lumières *(2001).*

The editor of Art History wishes to thank Sarah Sears and at Blackwell Publishing Jenny Phillips and Jacqueline Scott for their support and commitment in the making of this book.

Index